The Other Elephant in the (Class)room

The Other Elephant in the (Class)room

White Liberalism and the Persistence of Racism in Education

Edited by Cheryl E. Matias and Paul C. Gorski

TEACHERS COLLEGE PRESS

TEACHERS COLLEGE | COLUMBIA UNIVERSITY
NEW YORK AND LONDON

Published by Teachers College Press,® 1234 Amsterdam Avenue, New York, NY 10027

Library of Congress Cataloging-in-Publication Data

Names: Matias, Cheryl E., editor. | Gorski, Paul, editor.
Title: The other elephant in the (class)room : white liberalism and the persistence
   of racism in education / edited by Cheryl Matias and Paul C. Gorski.
Description: New York : Teachers College Press, [2023] | Includes bibliographical
   references and index. | Summary: "To help educators adopt more authentically
   justice-oriented approaches to antiracism, this volume exposes the racism upheld
   by schools and districts that claim an antiracist commitment"—Provided by
   publisher.
Identifiers: LCCN 2023006764 (print) | LCCN 2023006765 (ebook) |
   ISBN 9780807768822 (paper : acid-free paper) | ISBN 9780807768839
   (hardcover: acid-free paper) | ISBN 9780807781968 (ebook)
Subjects: LCSH: Liberalism—United States. | White people—
   United States—Psychology. | Racism in education—United States. |
   United States—Race relations—Psychological aspects.
Classification: LCC JC574.2.U6 O8 2023 (print) | LCC JC574.2.U6 (ebook) |
   DDC 320.510973—dc23/eng/20230321
LC record available at https://lccn.loc.gov/2023006764
LC ebook record available at https://lccn.loc.gov/2023006765

ISBN 978-0-8077-6882-2 (paper)
ISBN 978-0-8077-6883-9 (hardcover)
ISBN 978-0-8077-8196-8 (ebook)

Printed on acid-free paper
Manufactured in the United States of America

For Charles Mills. Your scholarship on the racial contract and the fight for racial justice lives on.

For Christine Sleeter. Thank you for modeling for us and countless others how to evolve as a scholar and artist.

Contents

PART IV: WHITE LIBERALISM IN POPULAR PROGRAMS AND INITIATIVES

Contents

Introduction

Cheryl E. Matias and Paul C. Gorski

Despite the glittering displays of BLM[1] signs, the enthusiastic book clubs, and the safety pins suggesting liberal white allyship, racism and white supremacy persist. The question is, "Why?" Why is it that, despite all the liberal do-gooder efforts in the guises of book clubs, diversity and inclusion training, No Place for Hate programming, and BLM marches, racism continues to manifest? What are we overlooking?

That word, *liberal*, in the white *liberal* racism we name in the title of this book is important. A truism often discussed among those of us who study racism in education and who act for racial justice is that in many cases the schools and districts where we have the toughest time finding antiracist traction are not those with the biggest populations of explicitly racist people—the ones who will own their racism publicly. Instead, we often have the hardest time finding traction in schools with large numbers of liberal-ish white educators: the ones who are enthusiastic about celebrating diversity and learning about cultures, but squeamish when it comes to more significant efforts to redistribute access and opportunity.

We use *liberal* here the way McLaren (1997) described *liberal* multiculturalism. The important distinction is not one of party politics—liberal versus conservative—but rather one of social movement, between *liberal* and *critical*. Whereas *liberal* approaches to "racial equity" might include neat student programming like a diversity club or workshops on cross-cultural communication, *critical* approaches go right to the heart of the matter, uncovering systems of advantage and disadvantage, privilege and oppression. The trouble isn't necessarily the presence of the liberal approaches. Cross-cultural communication is a useful skill. Rather, the trouble is the absence of the critical approaches. In that absence, the liberal stuff creates the illusion of antiracist movement, the optics of racial inclusion, but not actual racial justice. We can't Multicultural Arts Fair our way to racial justice.

In *The Other Elephant in the (Class)room*, contributing authors explore the hidden dynamics of "liberal" programming, curricula, initiatives, and teacher training that purport to thwart racist practices in P–12 schools but that, in the end, fall short of that goal. We challenged them to uncover how, exactly, white liberalism operates—how it individualizes racism and obscures systemic oppression, how it undermines genuine antiracism efforts, and how ultimately it poses no serious threat to racial injustice in or out of schools.

It's an interesting time to explore this issue. Many scholars already have described how "in the time of COVID-19" there have been incalculable racial injustices: the murders of George Floyd[2] (see Dreyer et al., 2020) and Breonna Taylor[3] (see Martin, 2021; McCormack, 2021), anti-Asian racism[4] (see Bohr, 2021; Kurashige, 2016), mass shootings,[5] and the disproportionate death toll on communities of Color who on average have enjoyed less access than white people to quality health care. These racial injustices are tied to racio-politics; that is, they cannot be divorced from how people experience race, how popular discourses about race inform or misinform educators and everybody else, how we're socialized to understand what it will take to eliminate racism.

We would be foolish not to acknowledge how politics racially fuel, bait, scapegoat, and terrorize us all, especially today, given increasing radicalization across a two-party political system where struggles for the soul of education and everything else appear to be fought from opposite poles on ideas of progress, ideology, and, sadly, even humanity. It can be easy for those of us who philosophically embrace a more progressive view on issues like racial justice to assume we have it right and that everybody on the other side of the donkey and elephant show have it wrong, conflating party politics with racial politics. The problem is, we don't all have it right. And when people who see themselves as having it right don't have it right, the result is potentially more dangerous because of the illusion of rightness. In schools today, a lot of damage is being done by "racial equity" programs and initiatives championed by educators who embrace a liberal racial ideology. If racism is the elephant in the room, this sort of liberal racism is the other elephant. We charged authors with demystifying it, and also with charting a different, more critical, more transformative antiracist path forward.

In 2020, CUNY Brooklyn distinguished professor Jeanne Theoharis (2020) drew from Martin Luther King Jr.'s words from 1965 to write the following passage for the *Washington Post*:

> "As the nation, Negro and white, trembled with outrage at police brutality in the South, police misconduct in the North was rationalized, tolerated, and usually denied," [King] wrote. Leaders in Northern and Western states "welcomed me to their cities, and showered praise on the heroism of Southern Negroes. Yet when the issues were joined concerning local conditions, only the language was polite; the rejection was firm and unequivocal."

It is shameful that the 1960s conditions Dr. King described survive today. The worst aspect of hope is one that is deferred (see Duncan-Andrade, 2009);

although white liberal folks, including educators, may be excited to see change via BLM rallies and occasional challenges to racist conditions, indications are they still are not doing enough to incite change in white polity (see Lipsitz, 2006). As Lipsitz (2006) suggested years ago, there is a possessive investment to whiteness that creates a societal condition of hope deferred. In other words, despite the outward appearance of engaging in racial justice, white people's voting patterns have historically served, and continue to serve, white interests (Allen, 2009; Jones-Rogers, 2019; Roediger, 2005). The same might be said of the neoliberal school reform movement. Or, as Derrick Bell (1980) so cogently argues in his analysis of the consequences of *Brown v. Board of Education*, the hope for change only seems to manifest if the interest of change converges with the interests of white people. Hope for racial justice becomes faint when one is more interested in showboating support than actually engaging in the transformative action needed to undo white supremacy.

To explain further, we draw from Dr. King. He wrote, "The white liberal must see that the Negro needs not only love but also justice. It is not enough to say, 'We love Negroes, we have many Negro friends.' They must demand justice for Negroes" (King, 1957/2000). Simply stated, a love that does not seek justice is not an unconditional love, so we must stop pretending it is. We don't mean to sound flippant; we say this with urgency because the backyard-sipping-wine-book-circles by themselves pose no real threat to the racism currently pounding Black and Brown students and staff in schools, much less the killing of Black and Brown people.

We say, pun intended, that do-good antiracist liberalism is the other elephant, perhaps the more insidious elephant, because it assumes that surface-level outward displays of racial justice are enough to end white supremacy. We must recognize that this outward appearance is nothing but the narcissism of white supremacy (see Matias, 2016; Miller & Josephs, 2009); that is, if one seeks a "good white people's medal" (see Hayes & Juárez, 2009) for simply doing what is humanly right, then the effort is all for naught. Racial justice is not about who gets recognized; it's about how we liberate us all. The focus needs to shift.

Harkening back to Dr. King's (1957/2000) words, a shift away from liberal antiracism requires that white people stop conflating their friendship with or love for Black people with social media posts seeking antiracist validation, especially if their "slacktivism" (see Cabrera et al., 2017) does nothing to make Black lives truly matter. Furthermore, any type of love that is transfixed on outward appearance alone is shallow and utterly incapable of handling the depth of justice so needed for Black, Indigenous, and People of Color (BIPOC) both in and out of schools. These actions are only slightly different from those of political liberals who quickly point the finger at conservatives, claiming "those people are racists and we're not" by virtue of party politics alone. Racism persists in both the donkey and the elephant shows, so finger-pointing is just more optics; it does nothing to lessen any-one's culpability. Again, the focus must shift.

OWNING UP TO WHITENESS

As much as we critique the other elephant in the (class)room, we also acknowl-edge that many white educators *do* commit to antiracist work (e.g., Sleeter, 2018). This commitment is noteworthy because the work is not easy; if it were, racism would no longer be an issue. Despite the daunting task of antiracism, the work of which is frequently met with ostracism, isolation, vitriol, skepticism, claims of racial traitorism (see Ignatiev & Garvey, 1996), and temporary loss of white racial privileges, there are those, like many critically minded educators, who endure simply because it is the just thing to do. That we, as educators, are committed to racial equity, culturally responsive teaching, and educational justice for all is not what is contested. What is contested are the approaches by which we engage in them. If the hope for racial justice is ever to be enacted, honored, or even entertained, the struggle toward it should never be perceived as a process for *them* more so than for *us*. The unintended tragedy of fixating on helping, saving, or supporting *them* moves us farther away from recog-nizing the humanity of us all. As W. E. B. Du Bois argued (1903/2005), the problem of the color line is not a Black problem. Building on Du Bois asking Black Americans about how it feels to be framed as "the problem," white-ness studies asked white people whether they realize *they are the problem* (Leonardo, 2013). This interrogation of whiteness is what often is missing in efforts to engage in racial justice. The problem was never melanation for people of Color more so than white people creating laws that targeted mela-nin (see "Virginia Codes" in Thandeka, 2007).

A lack of understanding of how racism and whiteness operate together has caused many unintentional consequences in U.S. history. Take, for ex-ample, the 1954 *Brown v. Board of Education* verdict. Though it repealed the *Plessy v. Ferguson* "separate but equal" clause—noting that separate was not inherently equal, especially with respect to Black-populated versus white-populated schools—it also left many Black teachers out of their teach-ing jobs (Tillman, 2004). If we fail to acknowledge this historical fact, we overlook the societal and legal preconditions that lead us to today's almost 80% white teaching force (see National Council of Educational Statistics, 2018): white supremacy continues to be historically cultivated.

Further, Tillman (2004) explores how then-attorney Thurgood Marshall realized after trying the case that the question was not about how to make Black and white schools more equal. It was about why white-populated schools were so over-resourced compared to their counterparts. That is, the real issue is not only the racism leveled against Black students in under-resourced schools, but how white supremacy allows the conditions for which white schools are disproportionately resourced. That problem hasn't changed.

These sorts of court cases, educational policies, and other efforts at racial equity were, and oftentimes still are, too narrowly focused on remedying the symptom (racial inequity) while ignoring the insidiousness of white supremacy. What we're interested in in this book is how that disease is perpetuated, not just by rabid racists, but also by institutions and individuals posing as, and even seeing themselves as, antiracist.

Take for instance the social structure of patriarchy whereby boys are heralded for their gregariousness, initiative, leadership, and presumed proclivity for science, technology, engineering, and mathematics (STEM); the same characteristics are held *against* girls. Educational programs that attempt to attract more girls into STEM fields with afterschool programming, scholarships, and even hiring more women STEM teachers can go only so far in thwarting the sexist practices that sustain male privilege. Though positive in some ways, these Band-Aid programs do not get at the crux of the problem.

That said, we are sensitive to the benefits these types of programs and support systems have for nondominant groups. Indeed, representation matters. In fact, Cheryl admits to having considered academia only upon seeing a Filipino education professor, Zeus Leonardo, with her own Pinay eyes. We do not argue that these programs are useless. To be clear, much like the responses to address the verdict after *Brown v. Board of Education*, such as bussing or school integration, these Band-Aids were never enough to address the underlying problem. And, with no writ large understanding of how white supremacy truly, systemically, institutionally, and even individually operates, education will continue to focus on finding temporary fixes to address the symptoms without ever understanding their root causes.

The trope in liberal ideology is acknowledging that racism and institutional white supremacy (beyond equating white supremacy to white supremacist groups like neo-Nazis or the Ku Klux Klan) indeed exist. But if we conceptualize white supremacy only in macro-institutional ways, individuals are left with abstract understandings of larger social structures. What's often missing is a nuanced understanding of the relationship between individual behaviors, speech, and actions and larger, more systemic understandings of white supremacy. Indeed, white supremacy is in some ways an individualistic belief system; individuals can act (or not act) based on their personal beliefs. Those beliefs become institutionalized when individuals exercise their power by, for example, performing a commitment to racial justice by supporting educational policies and programs that create the illusion of antiracism—anti-bullying programs, for example—while balking at the idea of more transformative action. Individual prejudice can coalesce into larger discriminatory practices.

Further, when the connection between individual actions and larger institutionalization is not recognized, individuals can dodge culpability; if we fixate solely on larger issues of institutional white supremacy via court systems, state law enforcement, federal immigration policies, governmental sanctions, and executive orders, or even federal education policy, it can be easy to overlook how individual micro-actions, ideologies, and rhetoric help to uphold those systems. When white people, and particularly white people who are invested in seeing themselves as well-intentioned when it comes to racial equity, overlook their individual responsibility in systemic white supremacy, it can be easy to feel absolved of guilt, despite the benefits they derive from other people's oppression. Similarly, when white people recognize racism and white supremacy solely as individual attitudes and actions, they can feel absolved of responsibility for the conditions that advantage them even if they aren't actively, purposefully perpetuating them. So we must embrace a more complex understanding of white supremacy and the role of individuals in upholding it. We challenged the contributors to this book to address the role white liberal ideologies play in keeping this relationship in motion.

THE ENTANGLEMENT: RACE, RACISM, WHITENESS, AND WHITE SUPREMACY

In *Feeling White*, Cheryl (Matias, 2016) explores this interconnection, claiming that the overarching system of race is not racism but white supremacy. She shows how white supremacy, like all -isms that force group binaries, impacts both people of Color and white people, albeit in very different ways. Though many scholars have defined racism in a variety of ways, from individual prejudice to systemic power, all of which are important, there are varied expressions of racism: racial microaggressions, racial stereotypes, policing and surveillance, internalized racism, nativist and xenophobic racism. These "dynamics of racism" are all used to subjugate, control, surveil, and manipulate people of Color into a system of white supremacy (Matias, 2016).

However, when whiteness is not understood, people often overlook how white supremacy impacts white people. To aver that white supremacy merely privileges white people understates the vast dynamics in which white people participate to maintain that power. In fact, white people maintain their elevated position in white supremacy by asserting various elements of whiteness, including anti-Blackness, white emotionality, investment of whiteness, white privilege, nativism, white racial identity, whiteness as property, coloniality, colorblindness/evasiveness, white gaze, false victimization, and Eurocentrism, among others.

Simply understanding that white supremacy bequeaths white privilege upon white people is insufficient for fully understanding and transformatively responding to the complex dynamics of how individuals who enact these elements of whiteness can still uphold a larger system of white supremacy. We need to understand the interconnectivity between white supremacy, racism, and whiteness. If we overlook any these dimensions, we strip ourselves of the ability to bind our racial liberations together. This leads some white people to disingenuous and patronizing efforts to help/save *them* when the change that is needed starts with the self. In fact, how does one pretend to lead Black and Brown students toward racial liberation when they themselves have not been through the challenges of racial identity discovery (Helms, 1990)? White educators, however "diversity-minded," can start by owning up to their own whiteness before attempting to enact racial equity as a way to "help" others.

WHITE RACIAL RECKONING

We would describe the field of teaching and education in general as one of love, care, passion, and morality. Noddings (2013) conceptualizes moral education as one that *must* be caring. Palmer (2017) argues that teachers must have passion, heart, and courage. Grandmother of multicultural education Sonia Nieto (2003) even proclaims that teaching is an act of love. All these emotions are often invoked when we ask people why they became teachers. In fact, in both Paul's and Cheryl's experiences teaching predominately white preservice and in-service teachers, many claim they wanted to or currently do teach because they "love children" or want to "give back" to communities, especially economically marginalized communities of Color, who have not had the opportunities they had growing up. On the surface, we may not see the need to question these orientations so often associated with a passion to teach. In fact, within liberal discourse, expressions of love and giving back, especially in a field like teaching, may be perceived as socially just. How can anyone deny the altruism in "serving" people who are "less fortunate"?

The trouble is, this common liberal-ish orientation is tied up in several presumptions. For example, it presumes that the giving and receiving of love and care are universally expressed with no social influence. But Matias (2016) clearly details how this presumption is troublesome precisely because emotions like love and care are influenced by socialization. The care of white supremacy often looks like a savior mentality; it's racist care. Second, it presumes that naming your love and care aloud is enough for anyone to be considered a loving and caring person. According to Matias and Zembylas (2013), false proclamations of love and care can be sentimentalized to mask deeper racial disgust. For example, as Zembylas (2008) argued, sentimental-ization can actually be violent and dangerous. Finally, if educators self-label as loving and caring, it disregards how others witness or experience their supposed love and care. Without caution, this practice of defining oneself as loving or caring, irrespective of whether the love and care being provided is what others need or ask for, reflects a sort of narcissism. In fact, Miller and Josephs (2009) argue that whiteness is imbued with narcissistic tenden-cies such that race relationships often mirror the experiences victims face in narcissistic abuse.

In examining the nature of love, care, and empathy in K–12 teaching, we should consider the many scholars of Color who adamantly demand *real* love (Johnson et al., 2019; Love, 2019), *authentic* care (Valenzuela, 1999/2005), *critical hope* instead of "hokey hope" (Duncan-Andrade, 2009), and true empathy instead of *false* empathy (Duncan, 2002). Repeated over and over again in these scholars' analyses is this theme that, too often, who white educators presume to be may not be who they truly are.

Our argument here is not that white educators are meeting in teachers' lounges plotting how to harm students. In a way, our concern is more seri-ous than that. It may be even more concerning when white educators do racial harm through good intentions, by embracing a vision for racial equity that protects their privilege, their emotionalities, their advantage and oppor-tunity even while seeing themselves as do-gooders who celebrate diversity and enjoy learning about culture. This may be of graver concern than pur-poseful, explicit racism because it is damage done through power attained at least in part by constructing a narrative of benevolence, altruism, and saviorism. These are the same ideals so often recycled in Hollywood films about "heroic" white teachers (see Vera & Gordon, 2003) who, when we dig a little deeper, actually embrace the same ideological blockages as more explicit racists but hide them behind presumptions of good intentions. This is white liberalism in action.

When educators, and especially white educators who self-identify as equity-minded, own up to whiteness, this simplistic rendering of the benevo-lent, altruistic educator is made more complex. For example, if we reflect the notion of "loving" students as a litmus for being a good teacher, the ques-tion might become, What makes a person's love so special that they believe it's what makes them a good teacher? How has that love been investigated to consider its utility for Black and Brown children? What does it mean for a white teacher to "love" Black and Brown students when they may have few relationships with Black or Brown people? What kind of twisted love isn't rooted in antiracism, anyway?

The liberal presumptions of altruism and love are made more com-plex when considering the role white women played in chattel slavery.

Per Jones-Rogers's (2019) historical analysis on white women as enslavers, which counters most characterizations of white women as chaste, innocent, and all-loving, "Slave-owning [white] women not only witnessed the most brutal features of slavery, they took part in them, profited from them, and defended them" (p. ix). Knowing that the field of teaching and education is dominated by white women, we must look with scrutiny when they refuse to reflect on, identify, or even consider their participation in white supremacy. Matias's (2020) *Surviving Beckys* addresses this gendered and raced dynamic: that white women are subjected to male privilege, rape culture, and sexism in a patriarchal system is not contested, but when complicated with Crenshaw's (2017) intersectionality, white women, unlike Black or other women of Color, enjoy white privilege in a system of white supremacy. hooks (1994/2014) described this paradigm in her analysis of white feminism that continued to position Black women as servants and white women as needing to be served by them. Claiming love is clearly not enough to manifest a loving condition in schools or anywhere else.

Beyond love, the commonplace liberal discourse of "giving back" is typically received as well-intended social justice. In fact, the narrative of "growing up in a middle class community," rich with resources, which compels some white people to want to "give back" by becoming educators in under-resourced communities is common within liberal "diversity and inclusion" circles. On the surface, this is the do-gooder liberal thing to do. However, deeper issues must be ferreted out before we call this claim antiracist. For instance, Matias and Allen (2013) describe how sadomasochism operates in whiteness:

> Whites willingly and knowingly engage in the surveillance of a racialized social structure that sadistically inflicts harm onto people of color. However, they are largely unconscious to what motivates them to do so. They are disconnected from what Lacan calls "the subject of their unconscious" (as cited in Roseboro, 2008), namely, how they masochistically deny themselves the opportunity to experience humanizing love in the name of white superiority. Rather than dealing with this condition positively by undoing the racist social structure, whites instead repress their racial knowledge, creating psychological defense mechanisms that allow them to continue reaping benefits (DiAngelo & Sensoy, 2012; Du Bois, 1903/2005; Fanon, 1967; Leonardo, 2009). As white group members ensure this repression continues Loving Whiteness to Death 299 via social operations of surveillance (see Foucault, 1995), whites are instilled with the sense that if they become traitors to whiteness, they will be alone, isolated, and, thus, without love (Thandeka, 1999). Fearing loneliness, whites masochistically cling to the white polity, expecting to find some wholeness and love there. (pp. 298–299)

If we consider the idea that white people adhere to whiteness in ways that curtail *their own humanity* while harming the humanity of others, we have a more nuanced picture of the conditions that require rectifying actions like racial justice. Essentially, they force us to ask, Why? Why give back to a community you don't know? Why do you assume that the community will benefit from what you have to give?

This entanglement is made more complex by Ahmed's (2004/2013) theorization of racial interpellations: The point of interaction is not void of social conditions, even if those conditions are just human emotions. Take, for instance, the feeling of *giving back*. Per Ahmed (2004/2013), individuals who "give back" often are trying to feel better. But simply feeling better does not create justice; it does not redistribute access or opportunity. Instead, the feeling better that should be of concern is among "victims of injustice" who must engage in "speaking about the past" to "expose the wounds" (Ahmed, 2004/2013, p. 201). If white educators who care about equity focus too much on giving back as a form of morality, as their contribution to antiracism, then the justice they seek may not be for those for whom they claim it to be. It can look like a clearing of conscience. In our view, this is what so many programs adopted in the name of racial justice, despite having little or nothing to do with racial justice, begin to look like, including trauma-informed practices, social emotional learning, some forms of restorative justice, and others explored in chapters in this book.

We might ask, what have you *taken* such that you feel so compelled to give back? Is it acknowledging that white wealth was built at the expense of Black wealth (see Oliver & Shapiro, 1997/2013), that many of the resources provided to middle-class white communities were unjustly funded (see Lewis & Manno, 2011), and that today's socioeconomic structure has created school systems that are more racially segregated than in the past (Orfield, 2001)? Is it that generations of racial covenants, redlining, and fictitious school "choice" policies (that tend to create more choice for families that already have the most choice) have taken a significant toll on communities of Color? Or that centuries of white affirmative action programs like access to GI bills, homestead property, spoils of war post-Japanese internment, FHA loans, grandfather clauses, and labor unions contributed to the racial inequities we still see today? Perhaps this giving back rhetoric attempts to assuage the conscience of knowing the accumulative advantage all these endeavors created for white people. Perhaps it's about wanting to hold on to that advantage while gently mitigating its impact. Of course, celebrating diversity or performing some other mitigative inclusion act does not absolve, or *should not* absolve, that conscience. A more serious racial reckoning compels us all to explore more deeply why we are drawn to teaching and what it means to "give back." It sounds kind. But kindness is not antiracism.

FUTURITY OF THE ANTIRACIST, LONGEVITY
FOR RACIAL JUSTICE

All is not lost. Though we can offer many critiques about liberal manifestations of racism that do not consider a nuanced understanding of white supremacy, we also see reasons for hope. If we remain mired only in the critiques—or the hopes, for that matter—we might lose sight of our movement toward racial justice. As the late great critical race theorist Derrick Bell (1992) points out, fixating too narrowly on the search for racial utopia has us overlooking the "Afrolantica Awakening, a liberation—not of place, but of mind" (p. 46). We don't want to fixate too eagerly on a future that is not here when the present heart, and the ongoing struggle, are what constitute humanity. Fighting racism is not an either/or situation; as mentioned above, white supremacy and similar oppressive social structures encourage us to think in simple binaries. We can reject those binaries. Instead of relying on them, we can expand our racial justice vision from either/or to both/and. In a time when COVID-19 has caused a tremendous worldwide death toll and unprecedented attacks on anything resembling antiracist efforts in schools, we also saw messages of #BLM continuing to spread globally, and the United States swearing its first Black and Asian woman into the Executive Branch.

Why must we hope for an unknown future when the present day is a wake-up call? We can do better. We will do better.

A FEW CLARIFICATIONS

As a way to contextualize this book a little further, we wanted to share our vision for this book and our general approach to the topic of white liberalism. As mentioned earlier, the distinction we're making is not between liberal and conservative or Democrat and Republican, but rather between fluffy approaches to "diversity" that fail to attend adequately to injustice and more serious, transformative commitments to racial justice. This is key to understanding this book and how chapters were chosen for it. Authors were tasked with discussing how white liberalism—an approach to antiracism that revolves around those fluffy approaches like celebrating diversity, learning about cultures, making small, mitigative changes within big, oppressive systems while never getting around to addressing the oppression—operates in some aspect or facet of education. We were especially interested in programs, organizations, or contexts often held up as equity-supporting, often embraced by liberal-leaning educators, from teacher unions to restorative practices to Montessori schools.

We challenged contributors to focus on how white liberalism operates *institutionally* to sustain racism and white supremacy while creating the optics of racial justice. In other words, we didn't want authors' primary focus to be on white educators who might think of themselves as liberal, although it's difficult to write about these concerns without delving somewhat into those educators' mindsets and commitments, as we discussed earlier in this introduction. We were less interested in, for example, how individual white educators might use Positive Behavior Intervention and Supports (PBIS) to do or sustain damage to students of Color, but rather what makes PBIS and other programs so alluring that schools will grab on to them, imagining they will solve problems they can't possibly solve.

Our point here is that this book is not an attack on white teachers or white educators who see themselves as "liberal." Quite the opposite. It's a book that challenges all of us to ensure that the efforts we put into racial justice have an actual shot at cultivating racial justice. It's a challenge to embrace something more than the illusion of progress. It is, as much as anything, an exploration of tendencies on which even we, the coeditors, as people who have constructed our professional lives around racial justice, must check ourselves. And it's an attack on racism perpetuated under the guise of diversity, equity, inclusion, belonging, or whatever word is embraced in the moment.

SUMMARY OF CHAPTERS

In *The Other Elephant in the (Class)room*, racial justice educators, scholars, and activists begin with the action of *naming* injustice, explicating the shortcomings and dangers of white liberalism in P–12 schools. Contributors examine liberal doctrines guiding much of the "racial equity" work in schools under language like *diversity* and *inclusion* and *belonging* and show how they fall short on antiracism in the present day. Perhaps more importantly, they detail better ways, more transformative ways, to enact racial justice that prioritize change over the feelings, emotions, and comfort of white educators.

We have divided the book into four parts. Part I, "white Liberalism and the Illusion of Transformative Intent," contains chapters that explore how educational institutions, including schools, districts, and unions, skillfully cultivate the optics of racial equity while failing to adequately address racism and white supremacy. In Chapter 1, "'Peel It Like an Onion': A Proactive Challenge to White Liberalism Inside a Progressive Teachers Union," Theresa Montaño and Betty Forrester describe how women of Color organized against efforts to undermine antiracism efforts within a famously "progressive" teachers union. They draw on interviews with some of the women who fought to support those efforts. In Chapter 2, "The End of Altruism: Moving from White Hero Discourse to Racial Justice Praxis," JPB Gerald critically analyzes the idea of altruism often found in liberal approaches to antiracism. He describes how practices of altruism so prevalent in white liberal ideology fall short of racial justice. Instead of focusing on hero-making, Gerald invites white educators to "take the time to unpack your own racial history and reframe your work accordingly." In Chapter 3, "Exposing the Other Elephant: White Liberal Discourses and the (Re)Production of Racism in K–12 Education," Lindsay Lyons and Cherie Bridges Patrick reveal how punitive measures and disciplinary actions that are disproportionately aimed at Black, Brown, and Indigenous students (despite the rhetoric of saving or helping students) are antithetical to antiracism. They recommend a stronger, more transformative antiracist approach. In Chapter 4, "How Toxic Positivity Prevents Equity for ESOL Students: Getting Uncomfortable for the Sake of Equity," Elisabeth Chan, Lavette Coney, and Heidi Faust explore the nature of toxic positivity and how it might show up in English to Speakers of Other Languages (ESOL) programs. They offer three scenarios to illuminate how toxic positivity operates, inviting readers to practice recognizing its impact; they then provide an action plan on how to take a more meaningful antiracist stand.

Part II, "White Liberalism in Diversity, Equity, Inclusiveness, and Belonging Efforts," includes three chapters that unpack what happens when attempts at institutional racial justice are inhibited by white liberal approaches. In Chapter 5, "Colorblindness, White Paternalism, and the Limits of School Desegregation and Diversity Reform," Anna Kushner examines how white paternalism informs colorblind racism in educational reforms like school desegregation and diversity. Claiming that student diversity is not enough to claim success, Kushner argues that staff, faculty, administrators, and all stakeholders must engage in race-conscious reporting and strive for a deeper antiracist approach. In Chapter 6, "Deploying White Liberal Antiracism to Avoid Accountability: Racial Appropriation in Educational Leadership," Tracey A. Benson shares how district leaders created the optics of an antiracist commitment by engaging in professional learning and other activities while dodging personal responsibility and hampering real antiracist efforts. He then lays out an approach for more transformative antiracist leadership.

In Chapter 7, "'We Aren't Going There Today!': Unpacking and Challenging White Liberalism, Racial Silence, and What Kids Are 'Ready' for in the Early Childhood Classroom," Andréa C. Minkoff and Katherine Wood challenge the idea that early childhood students are not "ready" to discuss race and racism. In fact, they argue that racial silence makes racism worse and they challenge early childhood teachers to explore racialized emotions and decenter whiteness so that racial discourse can ensue.

Part III, "White Liberalism in Curriculum and Instruction," consists of chapters that analyze the impact of white liberalism on curriculum and instruction. In Chapter 8, "White Teachers' Black Historical Consciousness: Can We Teach Black History?," Brianne Pitts, Daniel Tulino, and Greg Simmons ask whether white teachers can teach Black history. Then, offering Black historical consciousness as a pedagogical strategy for more genuinely engaging with Black History teaching, they answer their own inquiry. In Chapter 9, "Overpromising and Underdelivering: White Liberal

Narratives in Arts Education," Alina Campana and Amelia M. Kraehe examine ways white liberalism operates in arts education, especially through
sometimes-unspoken assumptions that the arts are, by nature, progressive.
In Chapter 10, "White Liberalism in the U.S. History Curriculum: Issues of
Diversity and Accountability," Chris Seeger and Maria Gabriela Paz take
U.S. history curriculum to task, focusing specifically—and compellingly—
on history standards in three "liberal" states. Beyond performative racial justice teaching, whereby teachers may include a snippet here and there about
people of Color, Seeger and Paz argue for the abolition of standards that
cater to white supremacy.

Chapters in Part IV, "White Liberalism in Popular Programs and
Initiatives," explore how white liberalism operates through popular programs that often are adopted in the name of antiracism despite not having
been created to support antiracism. In their analysis of Montessori schools in
Chapter 11, "Liberalism to Liberation: Reimagining Montessori Education,"
Daisy Han and Katie Kitchens explore how to move from white liberalism
to racial liberation. They provide a racial analysis of Dr. Montessori's history and the pedagogical approaches behind Montessori schooling, showing
how, despite claims of freedom, Montessori concepts are imbued with racism. The rise of restorative justice education (RJE) has made its way across the
United States. How might it still embody white liberalism? In Chapter 12,
"White Liberalism, Racism, and Restorative Justice in Schools," Crystena
Parker-Shandal claims that although RJE should be rooted in antiracism,
few teachers have the motivation or confidence to integrate antiracism prop-
erly and thus may exacerbate racism. Parker-Shandal provides advice to
white allies who claim to want to engage in racial justice more deeply. In
Chapter 13, "Seeing Systems: The Case for Systemically Trauma-Informed
Practice Instead of White Saviorism," Debi Khasnabis, Simona Goldin,
and Addison Duane interrogate the white saviorism so often found in
trauma-informed practices (TIP). They explain how TIP can be weaponized to delete the existence of structural racism, ultimately pathologizing
students of Color, their home lives, and the communities from which they
hail. They end by outlining a TIP approach that is systemic and antiracist.
In Chapter 14, "Interrupting the White Liberalism of Social Emotional
Learning," Jennifer C. Dauphinais and Jenna Kamrass Morvay argue that the
growing acceptance of social emotional learning (SEL) without critical understandings of white saviorism, colorblind racism, and racial marginalization can recycle white do-gooder liberalism, which has no impact on racism.
They provide direction on how white teachers should investigate their emotionalities before thinking they are prepared to support the social emotional
learning of students of Color. Finally, in Chapter 15, "White Liberalism,
Positive Behavior Supports, and Black, Indigenous Students of Color: 'We're
Teaching Them to Do School,'" Jeanne Connelly interrogates how white
liberalism operates in Positive Behavior Intervention and Supports (PBIS)

despite claims that PBIS supports BIPOC students. Arguing for DisCrit and further exploration of discomforting white emotions, Connelly offers ways to better support BIPOC students.

EXPOSING THE OTHER ELEPHANT

From arts-based education to PBIS, contributors to *The Other Elephant in the (Class)room* explore how white liberalism, despite its presumptions of good intentions, has negative impacts on the hope for antiracism in education. They expose how overlooking this showboating of do-gooder-white-liberal approaches to racial equity can mask the harsh realities it creates for communities of Color.

Although some may argue that it is out of line to critique the well-intentioned actions of others, we see it, instead, as an act of love and justice. It is necessary if we are to achieve a better, more racially harmonious, society. If we truly believe in racial justice, we should not be afraid to critically examine the actions, policies, and practices into which we invest resources and energy that work against racial justice in the name of racial justice.

Put simply, as antiracist and racially just educators, we must do better. Part of doing better means looking more critically in the mirror so we can more deeply reflect on how our intentions match our impact. We hope this book will help readers do just that.

SPECIAL NOTE

For the many teachers, educators, and administrators who believe, act, and fight for racial justice every day, we respect you and thank you. May you continue the fight and lead us toward a better humanity.

REFERENCES

Ahmed, S. (2004/2013). *The cultural politics of emotion*. Routledge.

Allen, R. L. (2009). "What about poor white people?" In W. Ayers, T. Quinn, & D. Stoval (Eds.), *Handbook of social justice in education* (p. 209–230). Routledge.

Bell, D. (1992). *Faces at the bottom of the well: The permanence of racism*. Basic Books.

Bell, Jr., D. A. (1980). *Brown v. Board of Education* and the interest-convergence dilemma. *Harvard Law Review*, 93(3), 518–533.

Bohr, SJ, A. (2021). Homiletic reflection on anti-Asian racism. *New Horizons*, 5(2), Article 7.

Cabrera, N. L., Matias, C. E., & Montoya, R. (2017). Activism or slacktivism? The potential and pitfalls of social media in contemporary student activism. *Journal of Diversity in Higher Education*, 10(4), 400–415.

Crenshaw, K. W. (2017). *On intersectionality: Essential writings*. The New Press.

DiAngelo, R., & Sensoy, Ö. (2012). Getting slammed: White depictions of race discussions as arenas of violence. *Race Ethnicity and Education, 17*(1), 103–128.

Dreyer, B. P., Trent, M., Anderson, A. T., Askew, G. L., Boyd, R., Coker, T. R., Coyne-Beasley, T., Fuentes-Afflick, E., Johnson, T., Mendoza, F., Montoya-Williams, D., Oyeku, S. O., Poitevien, P., Spinks-Franklin, A. A. I., Thomas, O. W., Walker-Harding, L., Willis, E., Wright, J. L, & Stein, F. (2020). The death of George Floyd: Bending the arc of history toward justice for generations of children. *Pediatrics, 146*(3).

Du Bois, W.E.B. (1903/2005). *The souls of Black folks*. Bantam Books.

Duncan, G. A. (2002). Critical race theory and method: Rendering race in urban ethnographic research. *Qualitative Inquiry, 8*(1), 85–104.

Duncan-Andrade, J. (2009). Note to educators: Hope required when growing roses in concrete. *Harvard Educational Review, 79*(2), 181–194.

Fanon, F. (1967). *Black skin, white masks*. Grove Press.

Foucault, M. (1995). *Discipline and punish: The birth of the prison*. Random House.

Hayes, C., & Juárez, B. G. (2009). You showed your whiteness: You don't get a "good" white people's medal. *International Journal of Qualitative Studies in Education, 22*(6), 729–744.

Helms, J. E. (1990). *Black and White racial identity: Theory, research, and practice*. Greenwood Press.

hooks, b. (1994/2014). *Teaching to transgress*. Routledge.

Ignatiev, N., & Garvey, J. (1996). *Race traitor*. Routledge.

Johnson, L. L., Bryan, N., & Boutte, G. (2019). Show us the love: Revolutionary teaching in (un)critical times. *The Urban Review, 51*(1), 46–64.

Jones-Rogers, S. E. (2019). *They were her property*. Yale University Press.

King, Jr., M. L. (1957/2000). Non-violence and racial justice [article submitted to *Christian Century*]. In C. Carson, S. Carson, C. Clay, V. Shadron, & K. Taylor (Eds.), *The Papers of Martin Luther King, Jr. Volume IV: Symbol of the Movement, January 1957–December 1958*. The University of California Press at Berkeley and Los Angeles. https://kinginstitute.stanford.edu/king-papers/documents/nonviolence-and-racial-justice

Kurashige, L. (2016). *Two faces of exclusion: The untold history of anti-Asian racism in the United States*. UNC Press Books.

Leonardo, Z. (2009). *Race, whiteness, and education*. Routledge.

Leonardo, Z. (2013). *Race frameworks: A multidimensional theory of racism and education*. Teachers College Press.

Lewis, A. E., & Manno, M. J. (2011). The best education for some: Race and schooling in the United States today. In M. Jung, J. H. Costa Varga, & E. Bonilla-Silva (Eds.), *State of white supremacy* (pp. 93–109). Stanford University Press.

Lipsitz, G. (2006). *The possessive investment in whiteness: How white people profit from identity politics*. Temple University Press.

Love, B. (2019). Dear white teachers: You can't love your Black students if you don't know them. *Education Week, 38*(26), 512–523.

Martin, J. (2021). Breonna Taylor: Transforming a hashtag into defunding the police. *Journal of Criminal Law & Criminology, 111*, 995–1030.

Matias, C. E. (2016). *Feeling white: Whiteness, emotionality, and education*. Brill.

Matias, C. E. (2020). *Surviving Beckys: Pedagogies for deconstructing whiteness and gender*. Lexington Books.

Matias, C. E., & Allen, R. L. (2013). Loving whiteness to death: Sadomasochism, emotionality, and the possibility of humanizing love. *Berkeley Review of Education, 4*(2).

Matias, C. E., & Zembylas, M. (2013). "When saying you care is not really caring": Emotions of disgust, whiteness ideology, and teacher education. *Critical Studies in Education, 55*(3), 319–337.

McCormack, M. B. (2021). "Breonna Taylor could have been me": Bearing witness to faith in Black (feminist) futurity at the Speed Art Museum's "Promise, Witness, Remembrance" exhibit. *Religions, 12*(11), 980.

McLaren, P. (1997). *Revolutionary multiculturalism: Pedagogies of dissent for the new millennium*. Routledge.

Miller, A. E., & Josephs, L. (2009). Whiteness as pathological narcissism. *Contemporary Psychoanalysis, 45*(1), 93–119.

National Council of Educational Statistics. (2018). https://nces.ed.gov/programs/coe/indicator/clr

Nieto, S. (2003). *What keeps teachers going?* Teachers College Press.

Noddings, N. (2013). *Caring: A relational approach to ethics and moral education*. University of California Press.

Oliver, M., & Shapiro, T. (1997/2013). *Black wealth/White wealth: A new perspective on racial inequality*. Routledge.

Orfield, G. (2001). *Schools more separate: Consequences of a decade of resegregation*. The Civil Rights Project, Harvard University. https://civilrightsproject.ucla.edu/research/k-12-education/integration-and-diversity/schools-more-separate-consequences-of-a-decade-of-resegregation/?searchterm=resegregation

Palmer, P. J. (2017). *The courage to teach: Exploring the inner landscape of a teacher's life*. John Wiley & Sons.

Roediger, D. (2005). *Working toward whiteness: How America's immigrants became white*. Perseus Books.

Roseboro, D. (2008). *Jacques Lacan and education: A critical introduction*. Sense Publishers.

Sleeter, C. (2018). *The inheritance: A novel*. CreateSpace Independent Publishing Platform.

Thandeka. (1999). *Learning to be white: Money, race, and God in America*. Continuum.

Thandeka. (2007). *Learning to be white*. Continuum.

Theoharis, J. (2020). Martin Luther King and the "polite" racism of white liberals. *Washington Post*. www.washingtonpost.com/nation/2020/01/17/martin-luther-king-polite-racism-White-liberals

Tillman, L. C. (2004). (Un)intended consequences? The impact of the *Brown v. Board of Education* decision on the employment status of Black educators. *Education and Urban Society, 36*(3), 280–303.

Valenzuela, A. (1999/2005). Subtractive schooling, caring relations, and social capital in the schooling of U.S.-Mexican youth. In L. Weis and M. Fine (Eds.), *Beyond Silenced Voices: Class, Race, and Gender in United States Schools* (pp. 83–94). SUNY Press.

Vera, H., & Gordon, A. M. (2003). *Screen saviors: Hollywood fictions of whiteness.* Rowman & Littlefield Publishers.

Zembylas, M. (2008). Trauma, justice, and the politics of emotion: The violence of sentimentality in education. *Discourse: Studies in the Cultural Politics of Education, 29*(1), 1–17.

WHITE LIBERALISM AND THE ILLUSION OF TRANSFORMATIVE INTENT

Part I

WHITE LIBERALISM
AND THE ILLUSION OF
TRANSFORMATIVE INTENT

CHAPTER 1

"Peel It Like an Onion"

A Proactive Challenge to White Liberalism Inside a Progressive Teachers Union

Theresa Montaño and Betty Forrester

INTRODUCTION

"It won't be easy," President Myart-Cruz said about taking office. Referring to the layers of white liberalism in her new position, she said, "We will have to peel it like an onion."

On July 1, 2020, Cecily Myart-Cruz became the first Womxn of Color (WOC) elected to lead the 50-year-old United Teachers Los Angeles (UTLA), the second largest teachers' union in the United States, with a 72.5% female membership composed mostly of teachers of Color. This biracial, Black Latina womxn president believes that an explicit racial justice lens must be embraced to continue the advancement of UTLA's progressive anti-privatization agenda, which included Black Lives Matter, Immigrant Rights, Restorative Justice, and Ethnic Studies.

The moment was not just a change of leadership. It was a leadership changer. One activist claimed that "having a black female leader speaking as a teacher voice makes a difference."

Cecily Myart-Cruz's educational trajectory led her right to the UTLA presidency. Cecily's father instilled a thirst for racial justice. Her first solidarity act was jumping the fence and standing with her teachers in UTLA's 1989 strike. Teaching positions in Compton and Los Angeles motivated her not only to excel at instruction but to always stand with students. It was "justice fighting" that led her to the union and to become a passionate school-based advocate. Cecily's move into citywide union leadership came with a slate of other progressive activists intent on creating a union more devoted to social justice.

Myart-Cruz's challenges with white liberalism are personified by leadership "style" criticisms for being "too loud," although white activists are seldom criticized for their booming voices or "large presence."

"I am OK with being the 'Angry Black Womxn'; there is a lot to be angry about. But I also understand the urgency the students of Color face." In this respect, she is not alone.

In this chapter, we share stories of elected and rank-and-file womxn of Color (WOC) union activists personally and systemically challenging white liberalism inside one of the most powerful unions in the nation; these are WOC who are explicit in their pursuit of a greater racial justice agenda. The UTLA WOC describe manifestations of white liberalism inside the union and discuss how these manifestations contradict the "social justice" lens used by white progressives to represent activist work within the union. We use their narratives, specific to UTLA, to expose the physical and emotional toll that racial microaggression, a manifestation of white liberalism and implicit bias, has on the lives of union activists in other places.

The womxn have allowed us to share their experiences with white union leaders, believing that while it is critical to identify those manifestations, it is even more important to provide a proactive, productive process for countering those pitfalls within an organization. We share a few of the coping strategies identified by the WOC educators as groundwork for centering racial justice initiatives and projects for change in democratic unions, where we believe the power of collective action can lead to positive change for students, schools, and communities.

WHITE LIBERALISM: INSIDE THE ONION

Women responding to racism means women responding to anger, Anger of exclusion, of unquestioned privilege, of racial distortions, of silence, ill-use, stereotyping, defensiveness, misnaming, betrayal, and co-optation.

—Audre Lorde, 1981

White men continue in key positions in governance and staff and as the public voice of many teachers' unions. A transition to womxn of Color in leadership positions wasn't easy even in a city with predominantly students of Color. Challenges to spokespeople or internal campaigns were minimized because many of the womxn we interviewed agreed with the social justice agenda, even though it didn't go far enough on racial justice issues. Maintaining union unity was a high priority for them. As one of our activists confessed, "We maintained our silence for the greater good of the union of educators. We held everything in because we are team players." Conversely, while the WOC we highlight expressed that they did "feel safer" verbalizing their critiques with more womxn of Color in the most powerful positions in the union now, they are also conscious that in open discussions of race at all levels in the union they have been met with resistant responses, including boredom, defensiveness, ridicule, and anger.

The UTLA WOC share a common critique. These womxn are proactive and hopeful and, without exception, remain willing to work with their white social justice allies. They have deliberately selected the union as their site of activism. Their goal is to create a network of union activists who can provide sustenance, solidarity, and support for those engaged in racial justice movements. Their narratives demonstrate the impact that racial microaggressions (RM) and racial battle fatigue (RBF) can have on WOC union activists and possible ways to address them. These WOC educators have already laid the groundwork for centering racial justice initiatives and projects within teachers unions.

In the remainder of this essay we describe two specific manifestations of white liberalism described by WOC union activists:

(1) Not centering racial justice projects while claiming to support a racial justice agenda, and
(2) Limiting the leadership experience, cultural or experiential knowledge, and organizing skills of WOC.

"IT CAN'T JUST BE ABOUT RACIAL JUSTICE"

For more than a decade, activists in UTLA struggled to merge social justice and union organizing. President Jinny Sims visited LA after her British Columbia Teachers Federation 2004 union strike, when the "a teacher's working conditions are a student's learning conditions" campaign used an explicit social justice lens for educational organizing. In 2008, the idea of a social justice union became a unifying factor for an internal Womxn's Progressive Caucus, which also began a campaign for UTLA's first African American womxn president. The majority womxn slate was defeated, and another white male was elected as president. He returned the union focus to "bread and butter" issues. Nevertheless, progressive rank-and-file activists continued to organize around social justice issues such as collaboration with parents and students and a rejection of standardized testing.

Progressive officers and members organized together under a broader coalition called Union Power (UP) to support the "Schools LA Students Deserve," campaign, inspired by the Chicago Teachers Union model. In 2014, all UP officer candidates were elected and moved to a social justice union, building stronger connections internally and externally, eventually leading to a powerful 2019 strike with educational, "common good," and racial justice demands like increased student resources (nurses, librarians, counselors, lower class sizes), ethnic studies, community schools, and limits to charter school growth. Although the bargaining chair of UTLA was a WOC, the president and a majority of leaders were white.

WHITE LIBERALISM, RACIAL MICROAGGRESSIONS, AND RACIAL BATTLE FATIGUE

Sleeter (2001) argues that white liberalism interferes with racial justice agendas even when white leaders see themselves as progressive social justice advocates. In this union, white liberals had unconsciously engaged in practices that diminished racial justice organizing agendas, thereby suppressing or decentering antiracist organizing in the union. Issues like defunding the police, supporting ethnic studies, and advocating immigrant rights are part of the union's political agenda, but moving such an agenda forward and putting people of Color into leadership positions remains a problem.

Racial justice initiatives had been stifled through inaction. For example, when one of the WOC union leaders tried to center BLM (Black Lives Matter) work and organization in the union, she was told by some elected leaders that UTLA "can't just be about racial justice." This response, while marginalizing the womxn, serves as a stark reminder that white liberalism can articulate a social justice agenda, thereby giving the illusion of working for racial justice while, by not prioritizing a response to the actual violence of racism, failing to do just that. Lalik and Hinchman (2001) explain:

> Race is not the only factor governing these things and people of goodwill everywhere struggle to overcome the prejudices and barriers of race, but is never not a factor, never not in play. (p. 1)

Leaders who assume that dealing primarily with racial justice issues might alienate other unionists who are not people of Color capitulate to white discomfort, white emotion, or white fragility (Takahashi & Jefferson, 2021). This judgment preserves a racist hierarchy and the othering of complex multiple subject positions.

PUTTING RACE AT THE CENTER

The womxn's primary critique was the union's unwillingness to put "race" at the center of the union's social justice organizing agenda. Cecily resolutely clarified that the issues of racial justice for her members and students would be *her* priority and that it would require "all hands on deck." Shortly after her election, COVID-19 further exposed the vulnerabilities of the Black and

Brown communities where most LA students reside by surfacing inequities in internet access, healthcare access, poverty, and rates of housing insecurity. President Myart-Cruz has said, "there is no playbook for during a pandemic"; for her transition into the presidency she quickly responded with weekly Facebook Live broadcasts to members and racial equity training to the UTLA Board of Directors.

She stood beside members, students, and parents taking it to the streets at racial equity and social justice marches, rallies, and demonstrations. She pointed out that

> it is the Black and Brown communities that suffer most and we should just say it! It is our Black youth who are targeted by racial profiling. It is our Brown youth who experience the pain of racial nativism. You can't do social justice work without calling out racism in our schools, communities and yes, in our union.

Myart-Cruz understood that the internal struggle against white liberalism is essential to building a unified and powerful union. She said, "It is my intent to peel back white liberalism inside the union and to center racial justice work." The WOC activists we interviewed expressed unanimous optimism in Cecily's leadership, describing her as a "storyteller," "role model," "coach/mentor," and "truth speaker." The WOC felt seen and heard: "I know she sees me and supports me, and it seems like she is talking right to me." Another activist exhaled, "Now I can step up and tell *our* truths." The strongest expression of solidarity and hope came from the many WOC who now believe that we are "on this journey together."

RACIAL JUSTICE IS SOCIAL JUSTICE WORK

A veteran activist and elected union leader we talked to, Erika Jones, explained,

> Racial justice work should be centered in communities [bringing the organizations into the union to set the union's political agenda and lead the work]. When the union embeds the racial justice issues into their existing social justice agenda, it moves it away from community leadership and the communities' goals. It's an individualistic move, based on a white liberal social justice agenda. Furthermore, it does not create authentic change. If there is a win, it will never be a real win for BIPOC [Black, Indigenous and People of Color] communities.

> White liberalism feels like the only way to address a racial justice issue is by placing it into other "broader issues," like testing, privatization, etc. It can never just be about racial justice. As BIPOC, we see racial justice as a core to all of these issues, it is the thread to all we do.

When racial justice issues are embedded into a social justice agenda, union members avoid personal involvement in the issue and still present the façade that their union actively combats racism.

White liberalism nullifies the importance of racial injustice or anti-Blackness by focusing on the "broader issues," which fails to recognize how "racial justice" work ultimately benefits everyone. It moves the conversation away from the question of "race," an absurdity in a city like Los Angeles, into a sort of colorblind approach to organizing. Without addressing racism as a central problem in other issues, and by relegating womxn of Color to do the racial justice without accepting leadership and by not incorporating the will of their communities the institutional and structural patterns of inequality continue. It also represents a significant racial microaggression (Bonilla-Silva, 2006; Franklin, 2015; Pérez Huber & Solórzano, 2020) that refuses to acknowledge communities' lived experiences and expertise on matters such as police injustice or racism.

In the case of UTLA, Black womxn led the BLM work. Cecily, Erika, and other womxn in UTLA's Racial Justice Taskforce attended BLM-LA meetings, mobilized members for rallies and demonstrations, and developed the "Black Lives Matter" curriculum presented nationally. UTLA leadership, as a whole, did not create strong relationships with BLM before Myart-Cruz's presidency. These womxn felt the union's inability to engage with BLM community leaders, develop a reciprocal relationship with BLM, or allow community leaders to lead the BLM-LA work inside of the union were reflections of the limitations of white liberalism.

Lupe Carrasco Cardona, a respected Chicanx community and educational justice educator, is the daughter of a well-known New Mexican Chicano activist. Lupe, relatively new to union involvement, reflected, "I was always pro-union and pro-labor," but when it came to union work, she always felt "out of the loop, not so much at UTLA but when I taught in other districts where white members are often not liberal at all." It was the important role unions played in California's ethnic studies movement that compelled Lupe to connect her activist work to them. She also partially credits Cecily's election for that decision.

In reflecting on the union's racial justice work, however, she doesn't hesitate to say that "white allies need to quit doing most of the speaking." Echoing Erika's concerns that white liberals often want to speak on behalf of WOC, basically silencing people of Color and squashing their leadership authority, Lupe finds that the dominance of white voices on every issue is problematic. While "White liberals acknowledge and articulate, they do not move the work far enough and do not allow the affected community to determine the agenda or strategy for the racial justice work."

Lupe is also quick to point out that when the struggle gets tough, white liberals often take a back seat by thrusting people of Color into the forefront to face any pushback from other white liberals or racists. As a recognized leader in the struggle to secure ethnic studies as a graduation requirement, she has been party to racist pushback by anti-ethnic studies zealots. In defending ethnic studies, she has had to remind well-meaning white liberal politicians who promote ideas like calling for "multiple perspectives" on the country's racist history, that ethnic studies centers the stories of people of Color. As ethnic studies activists remind white liberals over and over, self-determination and solidarity are fundamental elements in Chicanx, Black, Asian American, and Native American Studies and that "sometimes it's not about you!"

YOU DON'T SEE ME: WOMXN OF COLOR ARE UNION LEADERS!

Lupe pointed to the very few Chicanx activists in the union: "White union members either don't see our people's suffering or negate it, even though we are the majority."

She further commented:

> White liberals compartmentalize and pit BIPOC communities against one another. Racial Justice issues are still "black and white" for them. Not for the BIPOC folks, who always connect issues like BLM to broader issues of racial injustice, but for some reason white liberals think they can only promote certain issues at a time. Listen, I am in complete solidarity with my Black and Asian comrades, so I often remain quiet, but I am tired of white liberals erasing Brown voices.

She doesn't feel this angst in her ethnic studies efforts, where womxn of Color are respected and often co-lead work. For Lupe, this coalition work is also where the impact of racism and oppression of all POC communities is understood. Antiracism struggle is not without conflict, but "this is where I really experience solidarity."

Though the struggle to move antiracist work led by womxn of Color inside the union is difficult, the UTLA WOC believe it is still essential to do. For example, Erika, with a father who is a leader and executive director of state-wide NEA locals, never questioned whether the union would be her site for racial justice work. As an African American womxn teaching in the San Fernando Valley of Los Angeles, she confronted white liberalism in her first organizing projects around reduction in force (teacher layoffs) and privatization. She often heard the words "let me explain things" or "I'll show you how to do it" from her white colleagues, perpetuating the idea that "womxn of Color can't organize on bread and butter issues without the guidance of white men."

Elected UTLA officer Arlene Inouye understands as WOC members say that "invisibility," "feeling unheard," and "being excluded from decision making" is a regular experience for them. Arlene further illustrates the treatment of womxn of Color, saying, "I think it comes down to, womxn are not being seen as equals. We are put down, patronized and compartmentalized. We are not given the respect for who we are."

Although individually WOC have always been actively leading in narrow parts of UTLA, the treatment of womxn and the everyday examples of white liberalism, racial microaggressions, and racial battle fatigue persist, often unacknowledged by white union activists, leaving WOC feeling undervalued and dejected, and forcing them to periodically drop out of union work.

Arlene, an Asian-American womxn, described feeling "sometimes invisible." She believes that the persistent stereotypes others have of Asian womxn is a significant factor. "I think the 'model minority' stereotype is ingrained and I had to work through to reject the feeling that I wasn't as oppressed as other womxn of Color." Even in her elected positions, she has experienced the condescending attitudes associated with white liberalism. She explains:

> I sometimes feel that I am not taken seriously or listened to. For example, when I have suggested that our approach to organizing includes listening sessions to build relationships with members, this approach was rejected as counter to an aggressive timeline of actions, which is a white liberal trait.

Other womxn describe lack of focus on leadership training, specifically ignoring how WOC approach activism, so that their feelings of imposter syndrome inhibited them from taking on more roles and responsibilities within the union.

According to Erika, while white liberals rebuff leadership from WOC unionists on "bread and butter" issues, their liberalism individually drives them to Black womxn for advice on racial justice issues. As a "union baby," Erika believes she also possesses the qualities of union leadership around organizing, mobilizing, negotiating, and other issues considered "union" skills and explains how this demonstrates the pigeonholing or compartmentalization of WOC into areas associated only with racial justice issues. She explains:

> On issues of racial justice, white men come to me for direction or advice. Not only am I constantly teaching white men about Black lives, but I am also uplifting Black women who must deal with white men. I feel like I am the "codeswitcher."

According to Erika, "I need white liberals or folks who think they are progressive to understand all of the extra labor they put on us. They don't reflect or seek to understand our perspective. In fact, they think they know more than we do, because they read a book."

An antiracist professional development is not the same as antiracist work. Antiracism requires white liberals to engage in racial justice work, not simply seek advice.

Many educators demand social justice in education, but UTLA WOC activists are clear there is no social justice unless it centers racial justice and actively insists on change. Racialized students and communities must be the focus of social justice work. Marcela Chagoya, a Chicana special education instructor, explains:

> A social justice agenda is not only about the whole child but about the whole family. Racial equality for all, not just zip codes. No child should be taken advantage of due to their skin color, health or state of mind. We need healthy children, families, and communities.

Responding to the history of white voices speaking on their behalf, Cecily argues that "POC voices need to articulate those demands, not white progressives. It is our experience, and these are our babies."

In our experience, the union misses the point of social justice when strong POC voices feel silenced, but these womxn maintain that they have been silenced in the past and refuse to be silent in the future.

SUSTAINING OUR SPIRITS WITH ACTION FROM WHITE LIBERALISM TO RACIAL JUSTICE

There is zero understanding of the emotional labor that goes into the full process of explaining, codeswitching, checking my feelings, checking their feelings and, then, maybe getting to action.

—Erika Jones

These WOC average 10–15 hours per week on union work beyond their teaching and prep hours. If they are community activists, add more hours. Implementing a racial justice agenda comes at a concrete cost. All of them confirmed the daily toll racial battle fatigue has on their bodies, hearts, and souls. Lupe explains that since "I have to work with white liberals inside the union and white trumpites outside," the work is exhausting, isolating, and demoralizing. As WOC choose to take on the racial justice fight inside the social justice work, we asked where they look for solace and support.

Mirroring the voices of *all* the UTLA WOC, the essential coping strategy is meeting with other womxn of Color. Lupe explains: "We must create a support system for ourselves, be visible and encourage one another, allow the time and space to be our most authentic selves."

Maya Suzuki Daniels, a biracial Asian and white womxn, initiated a possible alternative space. Maya's "Womxn in Organizing" series, supported by UTLA's Racial and Justice Task Force, was groundbreaking. The goals of the 50 participants in 3 days were to

(1) create a space where womxn's voices do not need to compete or argue with those of men,

(2) work on strategies for reflection, and,

(3) connect with "badass womxn."

Maya explained, "We gave one another a seed of hope for another year of healing through the struggle."

UTLA WOC advocate for teachers of Color mentorship programs, establishing a "culture of care" and increased mental health support for students. While they do not agree on every issue, they agree on the need for POC voices and issues in union work. They are committed to the collective need to push back on white liberalism, including countering the overtly racist emails, texts, and social media posts sent to their WOC President.

The womxn are concerned that Cecily is "taking the brunt of white fragility." One activist expresses that concern, saying, "I worry about Cecily and Erika because I see what people say. I realized they are strong women, but words hurt and I worry about how bad things can get. I worry about any attempt to silence them." Collectively circling President Myart-Cruz is also circling their own power to make change.

The ultimate goal of the womxn is to promote a racial justice agenda inside the union—in word and in action. They want a union climate that honors their experiences and helps them to challenge white liberalism productively. White liberalism protects the interests of white people, and until that chain of disrespect is broken, until racist behavior is challenged, and until union activists of Color are centered, change is not possible.

It is not enough to be progressive.

This collection of personal stories naming the racial microaggressions, racial battle fatigue, and white liberalism faced by 20 WOC union activists will hopefully contribute to productive changes in the union, allowing it to fully access the strengths of all its members. The UTLA WOC hope to construct specific spaces for women of Color in leadership positions, to create programs that will support leadership development projects for future activists of Color who are womxn, but most of all to build strong alliances between communities of Color and the nation's most progressive union for the sake of racial equity in public education for all children.

REFERENCES

Aanerud, R. J. (1998). *Maintaining comfort, sustaining power: Narratives of white liberalism*. University of Washington Press.

Bonilla-Silva, E. (2006). *Racism without racists: Color-Blind racism and the persistence of racial inequality in the United States*. Rowman & Littlefield Publishers.

Franklin, J. D. (2015). Racial battle fatigue and coping in a "postracial" era for African American and Mexican American students: Implications for higher education institutions and students. Unpublished dissertation. University of Utah, Salt Lake City, Utah.

Gorski, P. (2019). Fighting racism, battling burnout: Causes of activist burnout in US racial justice activists. *Ethnic and Racial Studies*, *42*(5), 667–687.

Lalik, R., & Hinchman, K. A. (2001). Critical issues: Examining constructions of race in literacy research: Beyond silence and other oppressions of white liberalism. *Journal of Literacy Research*, *33*(3), 529–561.

Pérez Huber, L., & Solórzano, D. G. (2020). Racial microaggressions as a tool for critical race research. *Race Ethnicity and Education*, *18*(3), 297–320. https://doi.org/10.1080/13613324.2014.994173

Sleeter, C. E. (2001). Preparing teachers for culturally diverse schools. *Journal of Teacher Education*, *52*(2), 94–106. https://doi.org/10.1177/0022487101052002002

Takahashi, K., & Jefferson, H. (2021). When the powerful feel voiceless: White identity and feelings of racial voicelessness. https://psyarxiv.com/ry97q

CHAPTER 2

The End of Altruism

Moving from White Hero Discourse to Racial Justice Praxis

J.P.B. Gerald

INTRODUCTION

Several months ago, as the 2020 Black Lives Matter uprising began, I was in front of my apartment building with my dog and baby boy, Ezel. Another dog owner approached with her energetic pet. Based on her shirt, it was clear she was an employee of a well-known charter school network.

I told her I was in education and asked what she did for a living. She said she taught high school, and then offered, "But now, I walk the streets." Looking directly at Ezel, she added, *"for you."*

It is rather difficult to deliver an eyeroll from behind a mask, so I nodded. This moment, while singular in its specifics, reminds me of many others I have experienced in my years as a student, educator, and scholar. There was something about the way that she felt compelled to brag about her racial bona fides that compelled me to include this vignette as I consider the ways a performative altruism borne directly of white liberalism has become an intractable impediment in the battle for racial justice in education.

Along similar lines, I once attended a conference presentation on the topic of language learners and dis/ability labels. With permission, I took a picture of one slide containing a racist quote from a teacher and shared it on social media with a critical comment. A friend's wife, also a teacher, pushed back by saying, in part, "Teachers work hard." What teachers' level of effort had to do with racism was unclear to me at the time, but her odd comment, part of a much longer rant, helped me form a fuller understanding of the damage that these paeans to sacrifice can do when racial justice is sought in education. Simply put, this adherence to individualistic heroism and the performative declarations thereof are at odds with the solidarity required to dismantle the racism undergirding our system of education, and white liberalism is deeply and destructively enamored with this ideology.

At its core, white liberalism is an ideology structured around a narrative of risk-free social progress, the arc of history somehow bending itself toward justice without making anyone uncomfortable. Within white liberalism, exceptional racialized individuals will continue to be handed power by altruistic white people and celebrated for it without any fundamental disruption to the status quo, a pattern with which I am personally familiar. I have spent most of my life as a Black, neurodivergent student labeled as "smart"—which often has meant *skilled at performing aspects of whiteness and ability* (Leonardo & Broderick, 2011)—in institutions proud of their altruistic white liberalism. Often the only Black face in these white spaces, I was praised when I upheld their values and scorned rather than supported when my isolation led to visible expressions of discomfort. Their heroic sacrifice went far enough to give me a seat in the classroom, but not far enough to give me a seat at the table.

I write this chapter with the intent to disabuse any white educators who might be reading of the notion that this sort of altruism is a productive way to achieve racial justice. In these pages, I explain the connection between altruism and white liberalism, and provide guidance for how white teachers can move beyond attempts at supposed heroism and into genuine racial justice. But first I think it is important that I detail exactly what I mean when I refer to "altruism," and how that can be problematic in education.

ALTRUISM AND CONCEPTUALIZATIONS OF WHITE HEROISM

White liberalism promotes what it considers to be prosocial behavior, or behavior that is seen as benefitting others (Eisenberg, 1982). Building off Veblen's (1899) influential sociological concept of *conspicuous consumption*, in which citizens compete to display their worth through their visible acquisition of material possessions, white liberals can be said to practice what I call *conspicuous altruism*, which is visible, if superficial, sacrifice to maintain public image. In the United States in particular, one of the ways public image can be maintained within white liberal circles is by creating visible distance from the popular conceptions of racism, which is seen primarily as the province of individual acts of cruelty committed by people who are decidedly bad (DiAngelo, 2010). Accordingly, avoiding explicit interpersonal antipathy helps to create a stark binary between altruistic white heroes and the racist white villains, all of whom might as well be wearing white hoods.

The more conservative version of white heroism revolves around "men in uniform" such as police, firefighters, and soldiers (Connor, 2012), whereas white liberal heroism tends to focus on helping professions such as social work and education. Particularly after the events of 2020, it is tricky to offer criticism of these groups that are perceived as altruistic, but the rhetoric around sacrifice poses potential problems. As Connor (2012) explains, "the discourse of heroic sacrifice denies the all too real sacrifices of welfare, property, and life made by poor American communities of color" (p. 101). Connor was writing about a previous series of tragedies, but the analysis maps easily onto current calamities, and so the amount of effort teachers put into their work combined with their status as nominally good means that there is little cause to question their commitment to racial justice.

If we consider, briefly, Helms's (1990) stages of white racial identity development—Contact, Disintegration, Reintegration, Pseudo-Independent, Immersion/Emersion, and Autonomy—white educators may often find themselves stuck in "Reintegration," which is characterized by discomfort and bitterness after initial attempts at evolution are proven to be insufficient—in other words, getting fed up that their level of effort is not, itself, enough. I suspect this is what leads to the common refrain I have heard, that "teachers work hard," and the understandable frustration that can follow a lifetime of being told this was an inherently good profession, even a heroic one.

Crowley (2016) categorizes white individuals who challenge racial hegemony as being in possession of *transgressive white racial knowledge*, and I tend to agree, though I suspect some steps are being skipped by white liberal educators, who assume that challenging the most egregious forms of racism—or, perhaps, voting for Democrats—is transgressive in itself. Ultimately, I believe it comes down to *interest convergence* (Bell, 1980; Milner, 2008), or a lack thereof. The concept holds that racial justice is possible only when it is truly in the interests of white people, regardless of their political leanings, and when your professional identity has been constructed such that you internalize the idea of heroic sacrifice and conspicuous altruism, then it is necessarily a challenge to question one's actions. Any acceptable changes will only reinforce the racial status quo, no matter how much visible sacrifice is made. Accordingly, the type of altruism employed by white liberal educators is a stubborn impediment to racial justice.

ALTRUISM AS OBSTACLE TO RACIAL JUSTICE

Many of the white educators I know joined race discussion groups in the summer of 2020, with books on the topic dominating the best-seller list for a time (Andrew, 2020), and we will see how much of that energy is sustained, although the summer 2020 discourse around "pandemic pods," which I wrote about elsewhere (Gerald & Debs, 2020), did not leave me much optimism. Unfortunately, reading a book by itself will not cure anyone of what scholars call *color-evasiveness* (Annamma et al., 2016), a more accurate, and less ableist, way of referring to what many once called being "colorblind," as it is a conscious choice to avoid the reality of racism and one's potential complicity within it. In other words, and this is just one example, you cannot actually help Black students if you cannot bring yourself to say the word "Black," and although more white liberals are saying that they believe Black lives matter, it remains to be seen how much their actions match their temporary willingness to, say, walk the streets for my son.

Any substantive attempt at racial justice will endeavor to transfer power from whiteness to students, educators, and families of Color, and too much of white liberalism depends upon a sort of warm dishonesty, peddling the untruth that defeating the individual bad people will resolve a centuries-old, foundational issue. Accordingly, white liberalism is truly no different from what Zamudio and Rios (2006) refer to as *liberal racism*, in which nice white people create distance between themselves and the bad racists to which they are superior, while they, at the same time, "deny the existence of the structural disadvantage of people of color" (p. 488). This may yet be changing to some extent, as many of my peers were quick to refer to "systemic racism" as a more nuanced talking point in 2020, but few went so far as to question the narratives sold by the country itself and its institutions. White liberalism ultimately does not question the system that created it, continuing to insist that racism—even if it has now learned to add "systemic" as a modifier—is a temporary malady that can be excised from an otherwise healthy body. In truth, white liberalism falls short in its attempt at racial justice because it sees the system as broken instead of the reality that it is functioning exactly how it was designed.

With this mindset, the altruistic white liberal educator is firmly ensconced within the nobility of hero discourse, and can create villains to defeat on their path to a diluted facsimile of racial justice. White liberalism tends toward what van Kessel and Crowley (2017) refer to as *villainification* because it makes complex concepts easier to digest, and acknowledging one's role in oppression certainly qualifies as an admittedly understandable challenge. So, instead of grappling with these issues honestly, white liberalism tells us the story that certain jobs are inherently good for society, and as such, to criticize education, social work, nonprofits, and other such professions as not just vulnerable to the infiltration of racist bad apples but rather grown and cultivated from rotten soil is essentially blasphemous. Elsewhere, I have referred to the tendency for white educators to use their profession itself as a defense against potential complicity in white supremacy as the *altruistic shield* (Gerald, 2020), and I believe this idea demonstrates how, as nice as the heroic sacrifices of teachers might seem at first glance, this approach to the work actually serves to prevent racial justice from occurring.

FROM ALTRUISM TO RACIAL JUSTICE PRAXIS

For the reasons outlined above, I am often skeptical of white educators when it comes to racial justice. Nevertheless, over time, I have built trusting relationships with a handful who have moved away from these patterns of conspicuous altruism and into what I would say is a genuine path toward helping foster racial justice. I spoke to a few of them in crafting this chapter, with the hope that hearing from examples of such white educators might be productive for readers who are interested in making such a change.

I asked these colleagues how they saw the difference between the altruism of white liberalism and authentic racial justice. One expressed the opinion that white liberal altruism is satisfied with never actually achieving racial justice, depending instead upon *not* accomplishing racial justice for self-sustenance, and to, so to speak, keep the lights on. Considering that the diversity, equity, and inclusion field, no matter the acronyms it chooses to employ, exists, in my view, not to redistribute power but to comfort the powerful, then it follows that this failure to achieve racial justice is itself a core tenet of white liberal behavior. In my colleague's estimation, actual racial justice requires collective action as well as a genuine desire to right wrongs, instead of the individualized inability to reach the finish line that white liberalism represents.

Another colleague analyzed the discrepancy between altruism and racial justice through the lens of her identity as a white woman, and as a former teacher. According to her, this self-sacrifice has become part and parcel of the white female teacher identity, with enough benevolent individuals extending their helping hands to somehow counteract systemic issues. Accordingly, this leads said individuals, thus imbued with tremendous power, to focus on themselves and their own choices instead of the larger systems in need of dismantling. This focus on the individual is tied directly to the image of the teacher as hero, and the focus on the self rather than broader systemic oppression is a key feature, and failing, of white liberalism. My colleague explained to me that feeling insulted when someone suggests possible complicity in a system that harms racialized groups is to be expected, since it flies in the face of their self-image as saviors reaching down from on high. As my other colleague noted, the shift from individual benevolence to collective reformation is necessary for white liberal educators.

As I hope I have made clear by now, the point is not that helping others is bad, but that the way that white liberalism conceives of "help" leaves us mired in a model of maternalistic martyrdom while allowing oppressive systems to go unchallenged. Matias (2016) wrote of the process of *racial re-humanization* for white educators, or an attempt to break away from the inhumanity and oppression inherent to whiteness through a narcissistic attachment to racialized students. The ideology of white liberalism demands that educators express affection for the marginalized while at the same time preventing the solidarity required to deliver the justice of which they often speak.

Nevertheless, from some teachers and mentors I have come to trust, the colleagues featured in the discussions above, and in interviews I have conducted, it is clear that some white educators have found a way to evade the trappings of white liberalism. Accordingly, I will now offer a framework for how to begin this necessary evolution. For any white educators reading, there are no quick fixes to be found among my suggestions, and your efforts will necessarily be imprecise. Take the following advice with the understanding that you might well have to stop and start several times, and that that is not only okay but indeed beneficial in your attempts to free yourself from the trappings of white liberal altruism.

From Enthusiasm to Interrogation

We all remember the teacher who came into the classroom full of energy more fondly than we do the dry lecturer, but without a deep questioning of one's own history and epistemology, racial justice will remain elusive. Many of the discussions about how to approach antiracism in education have been led by eager teachers without expertise on such issues, and as such, whenever that flame flickers, the efforts will cease. Accordingly, instead of hoping that enthusiasm for racial justice will provide the necessary ballast for substantive change, white educators need to begin with deep interrogation of themselves and their pedagogy, from the ground up.

White teachers: Start by writing a racial autobiography (Ullucci, 2012), asking yourself how whiteness has shaped your life, from the people around whom you were raised, to the unmentioned beliefs you brought into your career as a teacher. Were you raised in an area that was designed as white, from which people of Color were largely excluded? What impact did that have on your vantage point, and how might that have changed the way you approached teaching students of Color? In the whiteness courses I teach to educators, I often ask when the participants learned they were categorized into their race. The handful of racialized educators in my courses can usually pinpoint a moment from childhood, whereas the white educators often struggle to remember beyond a foggy recognition of the fact that some classmates looked different. Start from this point, then trace your story to the present day to begin to unpack the lived experience you are bringing to any discussion of racial justice.

From Sympathy to Solidarity

Part of the issue with white liberal feints toward racial justice is that the ideology is designed to elicit sympathy for the marginalized, descending from a feeling of superiority and even pity. One of the reasons this sort of altruism retains its salience is the implication that teaching racialized students is desirable only because of the dire circumstances in which the students live, from which the heroic educator can help provide a long-term escape. The self-sacrifice of working in poor neighborhoods was a central selling point of the profession when it was pitched to me and my classmates as undergraduates at an exclusive school, an alternative to the supposedly less virtuous jobs in financial services and management consulting. I ultimately went to teach in South Korea instead, though the language teaching field is rife with its own brand of hero discourse, so I was unable to escape these same patterns.

Pity helps no one. It is little but a manifestation of a deficit mindset, and racial justice cannot be achieved by anyone who believes their students are inherently lacking. White educators, it is imperative that you find a way to achieve genuine solidarity with racialized students, though I know this task is easier described than accomplished. Use the interrogation recommended above to find genuine common ground, and then work toward goals that are built alongside your students, rather than imposing upon them.

During some interviews I conducted last spring with white educators, it quickly became clear that growing up with a relative who was a person of Color had helped them learn early on how important this solidarity was. For everyone else who might not have relatives of Color, you'll have to find a way for your own interests to converge with that of your students, and this is only possible by moving away from the sympathetic mindset espoused by white liberalism.

From Passion to Patience

This work takes a long time. The cosmetic changes are quick, which is why they are so often sought. Removing a white novel from your curriculum and replacing it with a Black or Indigenous author is nice, but without the necessary groundwork to provide a useful pedagogy around this new selection, these sorts of changes do little more than flatter. All the book clubs and discussion groups that arose in the past several years are a good way to try to capitalize on a collective sense of urgency, but I sure do hope people are ready to keep working long after the initial passion subsides.

I certainly will not say that passion is a problem when it comes to racial justice, merely that it is not sufficient. The interviewees I mentioned above have been working toward these goals for years, even long before they were educators, and they know that, even if they win a small battle, they can only pause briefly before moving on to the next. It is dispiriting to consider the possible harm that transpires while waiting for the wheels of progress to slowly turn, and, as mentioned above, seeing one's initial efforts rebuffed can lead to a regression in one's commitment to racial justice. This is why I believe that planning for a very long struggle is the only way to avoid falling for the alluring nature of altruism, for the quick-fix heroics that would be wonderful if they were real. So, white teachers, it's up to you to begin to write down each step you plan to take in your fight for racial justice, and to extend this agenda across months or even years. Find people to build with, and expect to fail repeatedly before you succeed. And then keep going.

CONCLUSION

For educators who have been told that a combination of color-evasiveness and the choice to become a teacher is enough to exempt oneself from racism, hearing anything that might contradict one's identity as "not racist" is uncomfortable. To unlearn their closely held beliefs about themselves is a challenge, and one with little guarantee of success or professional benefit, especially if their career is comfortable thus far. In other words, white liberalism's interest does not converge with a shift in power away from the teachers who uphold it, and underneath the tossed-off retorts about effort is, I suspect, an understanding that they are, in fact, working hard to preserve their place in the current system. In truth, I do not believe that teachers who claim racial justice is too much work are ignorant so much as that they are well aware that their identity and pedagogy are not compatible with the changes that would follow; they simply do not want things to change. But if you are reading this, you do want substantive changes, and it is for people who want to move away from these aspects of white liberalism that I wrote this chapter.

Centering the virtues of white liberal teachers rather than the lived experiences of the racialized cannot bring one closer to justice. Actively participating in and prolonging systems of oppression cannot be virtuous even—or especially—if done with a smile. In addition to walking the streets for my son, examine the power structures in your classroom, school, district, and state, and seek out others who are willing to help you dismantle them. Take the time to unpack your own racial history and reframe your work accordingly. And do not demand any labor from racialized colleagues unless you are prepared to compensate us as the experts we are.

Teachers are not automatically heroes or villains—it all depends on how they choose to approach the work. Some will continue to choose the comfort provided by altruism, and some will make the choice to turn toward racial justice. I truly believe racial justice can be achieved in education, but only if we make the choice to put an end to altruism. Accomplishing this task will not be fast, and it will not be easy, but that is no reason not to put forth the effort—after all, teachers work hard.

REFERENCES

Andrew, S. (2020, June 3). *Amazon's best sellers list is dominated almost entirely by books on race right now.* CNN. www.cnn.com/2020/06/03/us/amazon-best-sellers-books-race-trnd/index.html

Annamma, S., Jackson, D., & Morrison, M. (2016). Conceptualizing color-evasiveness: Using dis/ability critical race theory to expand a color-blind racial ideology in education and society. *Race Ethnicity and Education, 20*(2), 147–162.

Bell, D. (1980). *Brown v. Board of Education* and the interest-convergence dilemma. *Harvard Law Review*, 93(3), 518–533.

Connor, M. (2012). Real American heroes: Attacking multiculturalism through the discourse. In D. Rubin &. J. Verheul (Eds.), *American Multiculturalism after 9/11* (pp. 93–104). Amsterdam University Press.

Crowley, R. (2016). Transgressive and negotiated white racial knowledge. *International Journal of Qualitative Studies in Education, 29*, 1016–1029.

DiAngelo, R. (2010). Why can't we all just be individuals?: Countering the discourse of individualism in antiracist education. *InterActions: UCLA Journal of Education and Information Studies, 6*(1).

Eisenberg, N. (1982). *The development of prosocial behavior.* Academic Press.

Gerald, J. (2020). Combatting the altruistic shield in English language teaching. *NYS TESOL Journal, 7*(1), 22–25.

Gerald, J., & Debs, M. (2020, July 22). Answer Sheet: The huge problem with "pandemic pods" suddenly popping up. *The Washington Post.* www.washingtonpost.com/education/2020/07/22/huge-problem-with-education-pandemic-pods-suddenly-popping-up

Helms, J. (1990). *Black and white racial identity: Theory, research and practice.* Greenwood Press.

Leonardo, Z., & Broderick, A. (2011). Smartness as property: A critical exploration of intersections between whiteness and disability studies. *Teachers College Record, 113*(10), 2206–2232.

Matias, C. (2016). White skin, Black friend: A Fanonian application to theorize racial fetish in teacher education. *Educational Philosophy, 48*(3), 221–236.

Milner, H. (2008). Critical Race Theory and interest convergence as analytic tools in teacher education policies and practices. *Journal of Teacher Education, 59*(4), 332–346.

Ullucci, K. (2012). Knowing we are white: Narrative as critical praxis. *Teaching Education, 23*(1), 89–107.

van Kessel, C., & Crowley, R. (2017). Villainification and evil in social studies education. *Theory and Research in Social Education, 45*(4), 1–29.

Veblen, T. (1899). *The theory of the leisure class: An economic study of institutions.* Unwin Books.

Zamudio, M., & Rios, F. (2006). From traditional to liberal racism: Living racism in the everyday. *Sociological Perspectives, 49*(4), 483–501.

CHAPTER 3

Exposing the Other Elephant

White Liberal Discourses and the (Re)Production of Racism in K–12 Education

Lindsay Lyons and Cherie Bridges Patrick

INTRODUCTION

Educators have been talking about the system-wide "discipline problem" for over a decade. Teacher-prep programs address the need to close the achievement gap, and more schools have been talking about the need to interrupt the school-to-prison pipeline. We propose that discourse—the ways we talk about what we talk about—is directly involved in the creation, maintenance, and (re)production of racial injustice, and specifically as it relates to our topic, punitive discipline. We also argue that discourse shapes equity, justice, and transformation efforts. We know that school discipline policies often mirror those in jails and prisons—Meiners (2007) calls this the "school-prison nexus"—and that punitive discipline is disproportionately and discursively applied to Black, Brown, and Indigenous students. We also know that these realities have negative consequences for students' mental health (American Institutes for Research, 2016).

The intentional or blatant engagement of racist discourse is not required for its reproduction; rather, institutional routines and arrangements "marginalize or exclude minorities" (van Dijk, 2011, p. 47). Racial equity efforts intended to address the long-term consequences of disproportionate discipline in education are often accompanied by discourses that subtly perpetuate racial marginalization. Counterfeit racial justice is masked by discourses of white liberalism that undergird and cultivate practices of everyday racism. Rooted within the reproduction, maintenance, and injury of racism is denial. Antiracism scholar Ibram X. Kendi (2019) notes that "the heartbeat of racism is denial," adding that "it always has been . . . I think we have to recognize just how deep-seated the denial is."

School discipline cannot be viewed in isolation. Any disparity ultimately contributes to overall student and school performance. Using the term "achievement gap" exemplifies how discourse blames students by subtly individualizing performance and shifting the problem of systemic deficits onto marginalized students. On the other hand, the phrase "opportunity gap" highlights the reality that school performance indicators such as academic achievement are predicted by the opportunities schools provide for students to learn, not just students' individual capabilities. Discipline practices that remove students from the classroom limit students' opportunities to learn. So, it is no surprise that disciplinary action is associated with "course failure, academic disengagement," and ultimately students leaving school (Losen et al., 2014, p. 5).

In attempting to fix the problem, we often contribute to it. The research is clear. In K–12 schools, the race of a student is the primary culprit in their suspension, expulsion, or other type of punishment (U.S. Department of Education's Office for Civil Rights, 2014). Recently, the gaze has turned to the intersection of student identities. Attention to punitive discipline makes clear the impact on Black male students, who are 3.5 times as likely to be suspended as white boys. Black girls are 5.5 times more likely and Native American girls are 3 times more likely to be suspended from school than white girls (Onyeka-Crawford et al., 2017), with the most frequent infractions being for dress or behavior that violates ideas of (white) femininity. Further, students with dis/abilities are suspended at twice the rate of students without IEPs (Carter et al., 2014), and girls with same-sex attraction are approximately twice as likely to be disciplined than heterosexual girls (Mittleman, 2018).

In this chapter we aim to expose the "other elephant" that perpetuates harm in the name of just and equitable discipline practices. We first define white liberalism and then take an adaptive approach to identify, diagnose, and discuss the challenges. We then pivot to offer ways to move toward more authentic efforts for racial justice.

FROM DEFICIT NARRATIVES TO SYSTEMIC CHANGE

A common practice in education is to label students "at risk," but a deeper dive tells us it is really the schools that are at risk of failing the students. Attention is more recently being given to "cultures (of schools, administrators, communities, policies) that systematically produce inequalities and then punish those who typically receive the short end of the achievement opportunities" (Carter et al., 2014, p. 1). It's not just individual schools.

Entangled social and economic systems make it difficult to change education's approach to discipline. Systemic external obstacles such as time and financial constraints, increased numbers of "transient teachers/long-term substitutes," and school police and security presence have turned discipline into management strategies to try to meet accountability mandates (Carter et al., 2014, p. 1), often absent racial justice accountability metrics.

When we talk about racial equity in disproportionate discipline, we too often use language that upholds hegemonic policies, practices, and structures. Notions of racial justice masqueraded through white liberal discourses skillfully blame the victim—the students themselves. By digging into how schools talk about and identify the root causes of disparities in school discipline, we draw attention to the ways discourses of white liberalism, and how they operate in policies and institutions, perpetuating and simultaneously denying racism while espousing justice.

HOW WE INTERPRET WHITE LIBERALISM

We broadly approach white liberalism as a particular amalgam of mentalities, actions, and discourses sanctioned by white people (educators in this case) that consistently present external individual and collective images of racial justice while reproducing and maintaining various forms of racial dominance. The denial of racism is an organic element of white liberalism; an "appearance" of justice conceals racial dominance. Denials also permit truth to be subjugated, promote fairy tales of liberty, perpetuate hegemonic structures, and permit equity-focused policies that result in racialized winners and losers. It is important to acknowledge the ubiquity of white liberalism and, despite the "white" in its name, to understand that no one escapes the harm of structural racial dominance. People who are not white can and do engage in practices of white liberalism, often as part of white-dominated systems and institutions.

We explore three characteristics of white liberalism and dissect discourses that claim to apply equity to the phenomena of disproportionate discipline in schools: (1) a desire for innocence that denies complicity in racism; (2) an unexamined commitment to a creed of embodied, specialized knowledge of racism and racial justice; and (3) access to all psychological, cultural, and linguistic spaces. In our discussion, we take an adaptive approach to examining racism and justice. White liberalism is not restricted to these elements or individual actors, constrained by professional, industry, or system boundaries, nor is its presence or impact limited to any practice, policy, or process.

The desire for innocence refers to processes by which (primarily) white women maintain non-implication in systems of oppression and domination (Heron, 1999). Constructions of helping, in the case of teaching, white, middle-class values, knowledge, and ways of doing things are presented as preferable and right, thus centering white people while erasing the Other. Notions of innocence are underpinned by "a view of self as superior to Others" bestowed with a "moral imperative and entitlement to intervene in/'improve' the lives of those very Others" (Heron, 2007, p. 126).

The second characteristic is *an unexamined commitment to a creed of embodied, specialized knowledge of racism and racial justice.* In a vague commitment to help all children achieve literacy, the race of those being helped is identified without acknowledgment of the larger social history and dominant prescriptions of race.

The third characteristic relates to *access to all psychological, cultural, and linguistic spaces.* White actors unconsciously and habitually assume that any and all spaces are "available to and open for white people to enter whenever they like" (Sullivan, 2014, p. 20). This sanctioned practice offers unfettered access that permits white people to occupy spaces of Black, Brown, and Indigenous bodies in the "well-intentioned name of promoting diversity" for the cause of eradicating white domination (p. 20).

Adaptive solutions require changes to people's values, beliefs, and habits. Modification creates an opening to examine an array of system operations such as cultural norms and forces, structural implications, and underlying values that drive behavior. A mindset shift supported by Heifetz, Grashow, and Linsky's (2009) work on adaptive leadership challenges the assumption that organizations or social systems need to be changed because they are broken and draws us to the "illusion of the broken system" (p. 17). Examination through this lens requires consideration that "any social system is the way it is because the people in that system (at least those individuals and factions with the most leverage) want it that way" (p. 16). This perspective allows us to examine the system of white supremacy as a social system that is functioning exactly as it has been designed and to see that one's engagement contributes to its functioning, whether intentional or not. As active, living parts of the system, our responsibilities include examination of ourselves, how we contribute to its maintenance, and how it functions to maintain and reproduce the status quo. Actors can begin to understand its durability as they engage in efforts to create equity. We start with an example that captures white liberal discourses of leadership within a school.

WHITE LIBERALISM IN ACTION

To highlight how characteristics of white liberalism show up in professional educator conversations, we present a brief scenario and then examine how white liberalism operated in that real-life example. The following conversation took place among members of a school leadership team who were performing a root cause analysis as part of a mandated School Improvement Plan, which they were required to submit to the state after the school was categorized as needing "Comprehensive Support or Improvement":

A school leadership team, consisting of the principal and about 10 teachers—predominantly white women—broke into two small groups to conduct a root cause analysis of the challenges their school was facing. The root cause analysis is a method that schools can use to identify underlying reasons for problems, in this case, disproportionate discipline. The school leadership team used the "5 Whys," a protocol commonly used during root cause analyses, in which participants name what they believe to be the cause of the challenge, and then ask "Why is the cause we just named happening?" Participants ask "Why?" going deeper until five whys have been named. The final why is supposed to be the root cause and assumes that if that root cause was addressed, the challenge would no longer exist.

One group's discussion started with: the challenge we are facing is that our school is failing because we have a discipline problem. When prompted to consider "why is that happening?" the white leadership team determined that students are not following the rules that prohibit hoodies, hats, or earbuds, specifically in the hallways. Why is that? Students don't understand it's disrespectful, they said. The group spent a lot of time considering what might be the cause of this third why. They decided students don't understand that wearing hoodies, hats, or earbuds is disrespectful because teachers don't explain that to them. Then, the group determined this explanation doesn't happen because teachers don't see hallway dress code policing as part of their jobs.

DISPROPORTIONATE DISCIPLINE AND SCHOOL LEADERSHIP

In the root cause analysis conversation, the leadership team's claim that dress code violations were at the core of the school's discipline problem reflect a desire for innocence. Notions of respectability were the pretext for discipline problems to be immediately ascribed to students not following the dress code and thus responsible for school failure. As the group went further down the chain of "Whys," they reached a moment when things could have gone differently. They grappled with the third why. At this point, Lindsay, a facilitator, interjected and asked members to think about the quote from adaptive leadership theory she had shared with the group earlier in the day. She was referring to Heifetz, Grashow, and Linsky's (2009) insistence that "adaptive challenges can only be addressed through changes in people's priorities, beliefs, habits, and loyalties" (p. 19). She asked them to consider the underlying belief(s) that might be present in this example. In reaching the conclusion that teachers were failing to enforce the rules, the group did reach an underlying belief, but avoided digging into issues of dominance.

That the group identified they were not reinforcing the rules is not benign; that determination lacked a critical examination of larger system dynamics that thrust Black and Brown students to the perimeter of academic opportunity and that create barriers to opportunity. They were equipped with authority in their positions as leaders, but hegemonic structures encouraged them to enforce policies without consideration of their impact. This also permitted the initial gaze to be on "problematic students" and away from the possibility that the conflation of dress code policy and disrespect warranted interrogation.

The process of engaging in the work of school turnaround with only white educators at the table, particularly when the school's student population was mostly Black and Brown, "innocently" devalued the expertise or authority of people of Color. Students and their families were excluded from weekly turnaround planning meetings and were not asked prior to the meeting to share their thoughts on why the school was failing. (Or, if they were asked, that information did not make it into the root cause analysis.)

Returning to *what* was discussed in this example, the team's decision to double-down on enforcing a dress code created without student input was a demonstration of "specialized knowledge" that further silenced students' voices as they were attempting to use nonviolent civil disobedience to express their disagreement with the rules through what they wore. This highlights the hypocrisy of white liberalism, considering its tendency to celebrate people like Dr. Martin Luther King Jr. for employing the same activist strategy: nonviolent civil disobedience.

Also contributing to the outcome were desires for comfort and avoidance. There were long pauses as the group grappled with their third why, which suggests the deployment of an avoidance strategy, likely to preserve participants' comfort. (It would have been disruptive to examine or throw out the dress code!) The participants were not the only ones who prioritized their own comfort over the difficult introspective work. As a facilitator, Lindsay thought about pushing the group to further interrogate the value of the dress code itself, but she didn't, prioritizing her job stability and the comfort of participants over racial justice.

We move next to consider broader systems that support education to further examine white liberal discourses.

DISPROPORTIONATE DISCIPLINE BEYOND SCHOOLS

Efforts to claim a commitment to racial justice are supported by research and training that have been institutionalized within educational systems to justify initiatives that do not have an impact on racism. For example, we can identify research that claims that the root cause of disciplinary issues is students' lack of Social Emotional Learning (SEL) skills (American Institutes for Research, 2016). In response, large investments may be made to train teachers on how to help students cope with stress and self-regulate their behavior while ignoring institutional racism.

Deficit constructions of Black, Brown, and Indigenous students paint them as academically inadequate and often as lacking mental and emotional stability and parental engagement. These supposed inadequacies are often linked to race-based disparities that such students are unprepared for academic success and thus "at risk," setting them on a path for failure. White liberalism posits an answer, but one that protects racial advantage.

We wish to highlight liberal discourses that express expert knowledge of racism and racial justice as they "innocently" meander mental, cultural, and linguistic spaces with impunity. To do this, we use a partial excerpt of a video published by the American Institutes for Research (AIR), titled "Long Story Short: How Can Schools Reduce Disparities in Disciplinary Action and Promote Student Mental Health?" featuring principal researcher Ken Martinez. AIR is a nonprofit, nonpartisan behavioral and social science research, evaluation, and technical assistance organization. This language is typical of an SEL approach to address disproportionate discipline:

> Schools can do many things to reduce racial and ethnic disparities [in discipline]. They can focus on helping teachers learn tools that are going to address some of the disruptive behaviors that they confront by employing mental health promotion and universal prevention programs. They can also provide behavioral health consultation in preschool in order to mitigate the trajectory of children who may engage in some of that disruptive behavior that leads to longer term negative effects . . . [Data] helps us focus on addressing the root causes of those disparities and disproportionalities so that we can do something about them. And by working with teachers that can help students in positive growth producing ways we're going to see better outcomes and we're going to see success in schools that eventually is going to reduce the achievement gap and the school-to-prison pipeline.

The mission of AIR is to contribute to a better, more equitable world. Yet, we still see a displacement of responsibility from the school structures onto the students and their families in this explanation. Conflating racial and ethnic disparities with disruptive behaviors pathologizes Black students while shifting attention away from layers of discriminatory practices embedded within the educational structure and other systems. Now marking students as "disruptive" and in need of specialized treatment that helps them with their problems can be attributed to supposedly race-based behavior while the actual causes of discipline disparities are ignored. While the recommendation is an adjustment to teacher practice, there is no attempt to challenge institutional or ideological causes. There is no definition for or questioning of the term "disruptive behaviors." Does this refer to violence or merely standing up while the teacher is talking? Research tells us that discipline disparities are most evident when the "disruptive behavior" is a nonviolent, subjective offense (Carter et al., 2014).

Also present in this explanation are deficit narratives about students and their families. By using the word "mitigate," we presume schools are innocent, that they do not contribute to a student's "trajectory" toward "longer term negative effects." Instead, it is assumed that blame falls on students' families and other factors outside of the school. Martinez names the importance of identifying the root causes of student behavior and working with teachers to support students, but does not question the system's role in perpetuating racism. This can be seen in the use of the term "achievement gap," which puts the failure on students' shoulders, rather than a term like "opportunity gap," which calls attention to the larger systems that are failing students. There's no acknowledgment of a school-to-prison nexus, no analysis of common practices that many schools and prisons have in common, no consideration of how the system or educators in it view people of Color as innately dangerous and thus in need of constant monitoring.

While it is helpful for all students to have the capacity to manage stress, the introspective work required to identify and dismantle systemic practices and policies that contribute to students' stress is unaddressed. Teaching SEL skills (or performing a root cause analysis) to address discipline disparities without addressing the harmful role of the school system is white liberalism in action. Or, to use the words of Dena Simmons (2021), "white supremacy with a hug" (p. 30).

There is a tendency for white liberals to rush to action without critically examining the underlying conditions even when utilizing the root cause analysis. In performing this type of analysis without interrogating how white supremacy shows up not only in educators' ways of thinking but throughout the educational system, the practice becomes a tool of white supremacy, a superficial desire for racial justice without doing the meaningful work that would include the voices of racially marginalized stakeholders.

For example, Vorley and Tickle (2002) define root cause analysis as "An objective, thorough, and disciplined methodology employed to determine the most probable underlying causes of problems and undesired events within an organization with the aim of formulating and agreeing on corrective actions to at least mitigate if not eliminate those causes and to produce significant long term performance improvement." But the claim that a root cause analysis is objective is problematic. Without intentionally strengthening participants' abilities to interrogate white supremacy and white liberalism during the root cause analysis and ensuring representation of all stakeholder groups on the team performing the root cause analysis, there's no chance of objectivity.

MOVING TOWARD RACIAL JUSTICE

We now pivot to offer ways to move toward more authentic racial justice. Equipped with an understanding of white liberalism that manifests as a desire for innocence that denies complicity in racism; an unexamined commitment to racial justice; and denial of access to all spaces, how do we first diagnose and then dismantle white liberalism in our schools? Returning to our school-based example of the leadership team's root cause analysis, let's consider how an adaptive racial justice approach might have changed the conversation.

From the moment the leadership team was created to address the school's challenges, a racially just approach would ask, Who has access to this space? Recognizing the default response in situations like this is to invite only teachers and administrators, an educator could ensure students and their families were included in the strategic planning, either in the meetings themselves or through channels for stakeholders to communicate their ideas.

In the conversation about root causes, when the initial root cause was named as student discipline, questions such as, *What deficit narratives underlie this selection?* and *How are we as schools and individuals contributing to the problem?* would shift the focus from individual students to systemic policies, practices, and assumptions.

Finally, in a moment of pause, any one of the educators or the facilitator could have named the pause and asked, *What are we avoiding? Which of our beliefs and loyalties could we challenge right now?* If the intent is to avoid discomfort, white supremacist beliefs and loyalties will remain intact. This is not comfortable work, but a commitment to engaging in uncomfortable discourse and exploring how white supremacy operates within each of us is critical for advancing racial justice and achieving real liberation for all students, staff, and families.

REFERENCES

American Institutes for Research. (2016, March). *Long story short: How can schools reduce disparities in disciplinary action and promote student mental health?* [Video]. www.air.org/resource/long-story-short-how-can-schools-reduce-disparities -disciplinary-action-and-promote-student

Carter, P., Fine, M., & Russell, S. (2014). Discipline disparities series: Overview. *Discipline Disparities Collaborative*, 1–5. https://indrc.indiana.edu/tools-resources /school-discipline-dsparities-behavior-management.html

Heifetz, R., Grashow, A. & Linsky, M. (2009). *The practice of adaptive leadership: Tools and tactics for changing your organization and the world*. Harvard Business Press.

Heron, B. A. (1999). Desire for development, the education of white women as development workers (Doctoral dissertation, National Library of Canada [Bibliothèque nationale du Canada]).

Heron, B. A. (2007). *Desire for development: whiteness, gender, and the helping imperative*. Wilfred Laurier Press.

Kendi, I. 2019. "The heartbeat of racism is denial:" Author Ibram Kendi talks with Mayor Nikuyah Walker. www.c-ville.com/the-heartbeat-of-racism-is-denial -author-ibram-kendi-talks-with-mayor-nikuyah-walker

Losen, D. Hewitt, D., & Toldson, I. (2014) *Eliminating excessive and unfair exclusionary discipline in schools policy recommendations for reducing disparities.* The Equity Project at Indiana University Center for Evaluation and Education Policy.

Meiners, E. R. (2007) *Right to Be Hostile: Schools, Prisons, and the Making of Public Enemies.* Routledge.

Mittleman, J. (2018). Sexual orientation and school discipline: New evidence from a population-based sample. *Educational Researcher, 47*(3), 181–190. https://doi. org/10.3102/0013189X17753123

Onyeka-Crawford, A., Patrick, K., & Chaudhry, N. (2017). *Let her learn: Stopping school pushout for girls of color.* National Women's Law Center. https://nwlc .org/resources/stopping-school-pushout-for girls of color

Simmons, D. (2021). Why SEL alone isn't enough. *Educational Leadership, 78*(6), 30–34.

Sullivan, S. (2014). *Good white people: The problem with middle-class white anti-racism.* SUNY Press.

U.S. Department of Education. (2014). Guiding principles: A resource guide for improving school climate and discipline. http://www2.ed.gov/policy/gen/guid /school-discipline/guiding-principles.pdf

van Dijk, T. A. (2011). Discourse analysis of racism. In J. H. Stanfield II (Ed.), *Rethinking race and ethnicity in research methods* (pp. 43–66). Left Coast.

Vorley, G., & Tickle, F. (2002). *Quality management: Tools and techniques.* Quality Management and Training Publications.

CHAPTER 4

How Toxic Positivity Prevents Equity for ESOL Students

Getting Uncomfortable for the Sake of Equity

Elisabeth Chan, Lavette Coney, and Heidi Faust

INTRODUCTION

Out of politeness, many of us seek the positive to avoid discomfort. "Look on the bright side!" or "It is what it is!" Such banal comments can deflect from conversations on issues such as oppression or "race." We learn not to talk about "race," that doing so is impolite or even racist, and that it doesn't belong in school. Sometimes we view oppression through rose-colored glasses: "Things are better than they were. We've come a long way." These are examples of how toxic positivity operates through white liberalism.

In this chapter, we liken white liberalism to what Dr. Martin Luther King Jr. (2010) called "the [W]hite moderate, who is more devoted to 'order' than to justice; who prefers a negative peace which is the absence of tension to a positive peace which is the presence of justice . . ." As an ideology, white liberalism is a form of colorblind racism (Bonilla-Silva, 2017). It ostensibly values equality and antiracism, but in practice it maintains the inequitable status quo. White liberalism promotes toxic positivity as a rationalization for actions that maintain inequitable systems as nonracist. We replace "race" with more palatable ways of discriminating, such as *culture* or *language*. We prioritize comfort by controlling situations and remaining silent on issues of racism, allowing what Brown (2015) called "polite *w*hite supremacy" to persist. Often this tendency is called *toxic positivity.*

Toxic positivity has consequences for us as human beings and educators, and especially for our students. Its impact on English learners (ELs) and BIPOC (Black, Indigenous, and People of Color) students often goes overlooked. In this chapter, we challenge readers, and ourselves, to reflect on our reliance on toxic positivity and its harms, and to consider how we might refocus on justice.

LANGUAGE, RACE, AND ESOL

The United States has a large EL population. Though not all K–12 teachers are ESOL (English to Speakers of Other Languages) teachers, many are now teachers *of* ESOL students. Thus, a short history lesson may be useful before delving into how toxic positivity as a form of white liberalism creates inequitable learning environments.

ESOL has roots in white British imperialism and colonialism. The English language was imposed upon the Indigenous peoples and those colonized with lasting and overwhelmingly negative effects. Two effects educators should understand are that

(1) the English language is linked to whiteness, and
(2) whiteness carries more power and privilege, which means English does, too.

For example, Asian Americans are often told "Your English is so good!" despite speaking English from birth because non-whiteness equates to presumptions of "non-English-speaking." Further, language is often used as a proxy for the more controversial "race," which contributes to toxic positivity. Power and privilege are exerted through presumptions of English as prerequisites for success, like the reduction of ELs' accents to sound "native," or the attitude that if ELs could just learn English, they would catch up with their peers academically. However, Kanno and Cromley (2013) found that under-preparation from inequitable schooling and the lack of schools' efforts to meaningfully engage immigrant families are what hold ELs back, not language. If we rely on messages like, "But education is the great equalizer. We're doing our best with what we've got" to avoid hard discussions, we maintain white supremacy and white liberal ideologies.

UNDERSTANDING TOXIC POSITIVITY AND ELS

We believe equity means giving people what they need—not giving everyone the same thing. Justice means removing structural barriers that prevent equity. *Toxic positivity* refers to "the excessive and ineffective overgeneralization of a happy, optimistic state across all situations" (Quintero & Long, 2019). We expand this definition by equating toxic positivity as a pillar of white liberalism to Brown's (2015) explanation of polite white supremacy, which serves three goals: avoiding tension, maintaining comfort, and controlling negativity.

Acts of toxic positivity when it comes to racism and other oppressions serve several goals, all protecting white privilege, such as avoiding tension and maintaining comfort. We also maintain *toxic positive environments,* such as when well-intended white educators say things like "It's not a big deal!" to avoid difficult discussions about racism. Inequity's roots must be addressed through real dialogue about oppression in ourselves and our ways of thinking, between people, and in the education system.

In the following example of a common way toxic positivity might operate, consider that many ELs in U.S. schools are U.S.-born U.S. citizens, but many are viewed as immigrants because they aren't white. Being "American" is linked to whiteness; it's also linked to speaking English even though the United States has no official national language.

In efforts to celebrate diversity, ELs are frequently assigned reports on their "home country," or the country of their parents or ancestors. One student says she doesn't know what to write because she doesn't know much about that country, and the teacher responds, "It's okay. You can do it! Just try your best." To please the teacher, the student complies.

While this exercise might appear to be an attempt to encourage ELs to share their knowledge in class, it also is based on harmful presumptions. Some never lived in the country their teacher is imagining they ought to write about. Some might have experienced trauma in that country. The underlying assumption is they aren't *really* "American," regardless of where they were born. This may alienate ELs of Color, in particular, by marking them not only as language outsiders but also as racial and cultural outsiders.

Let's consider another example related to assessment.

Ms. Smith is a compassionate high school teacher but doesn't adapt lessons or assessments so that her ELs, including Lourdes, will understand them. Lourdes memorized her notes but still failed her exams. She feels badly about herself and stares at her exam with teary eyes. Ms. Smith says, "It's okay, Lourdes. You'll get an A for effort. Keep working hard. You'll do better next time." Lourdes nods quietly.

Ms. Smith's encouragement and grade inflation may create the illusion that the issue is resolved, but Lourdes still cannot access the learning and loses ground academically. English learners should never receive failing grades because they cannot understand the curriculum. But passing them without teaching them is a form of violence. Schools and teachers should provide adaptations so students learn and advance academically.

In both scenarios, teachers are well-meaning, but their toxic positivity maintains the harmful illusion that everything is okay. As we mentioned earlier, Dr. Martin Luther King Jr. (2010) cautions that what's more harmful than an overt racist is "the white moderate, who is more devoted to 'order' than to justice; *who prefers a negative peace which is the absence of tension to a positive peace which is the presence of justice.*" Toxic positivity is an example of negative peace because it's a tool that sustains order and avoids tension. To achieve equity, we must address the issues that cause harm.

SCENARIOS

In the following scenarios, inspired by real situations impacting multiple ELs, you'll read about situations commonly impacting ELs or their families. You'll be asked to answer questions and reflect on how toxic positivity is operating.

They obviously aren't meant to stereotype ELs. No single scenario applies to all ELs or all the impacts of toxic positivity. Also, while ELs may or may not be part of the BIPOC community, the scenarios help us understand some of the intersectional inequities BIPOC ELs may face.

Scenario 1: "Don't Open That Can of Worms"

Sue is an ELL coordinator. A colleague told her about an Individualized Education Program (IEP) meeting with parents who understood some English but didn't know what it meant when they were told their child was possibly on the Autism Spectrum. Staff tried to explain, even draw it, and apologized awkwardly when they couldn't help the parents understand. "It's okay," the parents said, politely, perhaps grateful for support services they didn't have in India.

Knowing that, legally, parents were entitled to an interpreter at IEP meetings, Sue told her supervisor about this situation. Her supervisor responded, "Let's not open that can of worms. Besides, no one is complaining."

There was no budget for or knowledge of where to locate multilingual interpreters even though Sue knew interpreters were regularly provided for deaf parents, most of whom were white. Unfortunately, interpreters hadn't been provided for parents who are masters of languages other than English at any IEP meetings. Understanding the constraints, Sue obediently followed her supervisor's guidance. Later, she mentioned it to another school leader, who responded, "It's okay. You're a teacher, not an advocate."

1. Where do you see toxic positivity in the story?
2. Who benefits and how? What is the goal of the positivity?
3. What harm does it cause?
4. What would a focus on racial equity and justice look like?

Scenario 2: Toxic Positivity Over Mental Well-Being

Dong-Sun came to the United States as a 5th-grade EL to attend a predominantly white boarding school. He was always smiling, but was extremely sad.

Teachers and residential faculty complained that he did not complete his assignments, did not make connections with his peers, and failed to keep a tidy dorm room, so he was referred to the school counselor. The adults at the school attributed these issues only to his age and limited English proficiency.

He didn't have the language or maturity to express his feelings of aban-donment because his parents sent him away; and their physical absence made it difficult to explain the cultural differences he was experiencing and negotiating on his own, despite their deep involvement. He also couldn't contradict his parents' celebrations of the benefits of sending him to an American English-speaking school. He knew being sent away to this school was supposed to be positive, but he didn't feel he belonged in this new en-vironment where his Asian background stood out and was often exoticized. He felt pressure to conform to the "model-minority" myth.

He often cringed when well-meaning teachers asked how to pro-nounce his "real name," highlighting his difference in front of the class, which made him more eager to use an "American" name just to be ordinary.

Everything familiar was absent. The adults didn't know enough about his life and culture in Korea or the inner conflict he experienced observing the freedom his peers had to make their own decisions, in contrast with the cultural expectations of his own family. When he expressed his deep sad-ness, his parents told him to push through it and be patient. School coun-selors told him to be happy. Others said, "You are lucky to be here," and "Cheer up. It will get better," so he pretended to be happy. When classmates made fun of his eyes, he laughed it off, trying to remain positive.

While he was grateful for the teachers who tried to be supportive, he recalls one who just thought he was a bad student when he didn't do well in class. It didn't get better until his final year in high school when he got sup-port to manage his feelings around missing home. He developed resilience through these painful experiences, but refers to this time as "surviving, but not thriving" (Love, 2019).

1. Where do you see toxic positivity in this story?
2. Who benefits in this scenario and how? What is the goal of the positivity?
3. What harm does it cause?
4. What would a focus on racial equity and justice look like?

Scenario 3: What's in a Name? Comfort and Invalidation

Example 1: Jenniflore is a Haitian student whose name is blended to honor her grandmothers, women who were revered in their families and communi-ties. As a talented student from a predominantly Black community and city public school, she was selected to attend the advanced magnet school.

The principal, a white male, called her "Jennifer" for 2 solid years, em-barrassing her in front of her peers who knew it wasn't her name, so she avoided him. Even after her advisor corrected him privately, he continued using the wrong name. He even made light of his consistent mistake, saying "Don't be so sensitive."

Example 2: When Khampha Konekhamsompnou was a student teacher, her mentor instructed her to have students call her Mrs. K. because they'd never remember Konekhamsompnou. To please her supervisor, she agreed, although this made her uncomfortable. Twenty years into her career, she is still known to students and faculty as "Mrs. K.," a daily reminder of the way she mutes her cultural and linguistic diversity to be acceptable in her school community.

1. Where do you see toxic positivity in these stories?
2. Who benefits and how? What is the goal of the toxic positivity?
3. What harm does it cause?
4. What would a focus on racial equity and justice look like?

CONCLUSION

"If you are silent about your pain, they'll kill you and say you enjoyed it."

—*Zora Neale Hurston*

In this chapter, we explored examples of how toxic positivity affects both teachers and students. To push back against its effects, we must name and address all inequities rather than avoiding them to "keep the peace." Keep in mind what is culturally, historically, and socially appropriate for you and your students as you consider some final reflections.

Where do you see toxic positivity in your school?
When have you participated in toxic positivity? When have you relied on false positivity instead of prioritizing justice?
How will you intervene?

Where and When

Did you consider colleagues who were conditioned socially to maintain order, who then conditioned others? Maybe you recalled a time you avoided a tough conversation after someone called out an inequity. Often we are quick to quiet them or chastise their negativity, but discomfort is part of the cost of equity work. Instead, we can learn to view this act of *calling us in* as a gift.

How to Intervene

Intrapersonally. Before and after interactions, think about others' points of view and how your messages may be perceived despite your intentions. Predict the impact of your words and actions from different angles and leave the door open for others to build upon and challenge your points of view. Use reflexive strategies focused on justice to, in Bolton's (2010) words, routinely "question our own attitudes, thought processes, values, assumptions, prejudices and habitual actions, to strive to understand our complex roles in relation to others." Uncomfortable questions might include: "When have I acknowledged or challenged toxic positivity?" or "Can I make amends?"

Institutionally. Matias (2019) points out that institutional policies like mission statements often proclaim they value socially just work but in practice lack humanizing elements that would cultivate equitable spaces and appropriate support for faculty, especially women faculty of Color, to engage in such social justice work. We can leverage the fact that the institution has in writing a commitment to social justice to justify changes that would lead to more equitable spaces where difficult but constructive work can be done rather than shelved out of "politeness" or the fear of discomfort.

Ideologically. We should co-create a shared vision for liberatory education, which means we must embrace dissension. In fact, research shows that increasing cognitive diversity improves problem-solving efficiency (Reynolds & Lewis, 2017).

Toxic positivity promotes fake equity and justice. It's like diversity and inclusion value statements that lack accountability measures. In an effort to make things comfortable for white people, toxic positivity sustains white supremacy (Brown, 2015). Despite the discomfort we as white people might feel when we talk about racism, it helps us develop our critical consciousness as educators (Chan & Coney, 2020). We must allow ourselves to be uncomfortable for the sake of equity. We can do this in part by recognizing how we contribute to toxic positivity, examining the systems at play, questioning how harm may be done to EL students and other students through our actions or inactions, and prioritizing justice.

REFERENCES

Bolton, J. (2010). *Reflective practice: Writing and professional development* (3rd ed.). Sage.

Bonilla-Silva, E. (2017). *Racism without racists: Color-blind racism and the persistence of racial inequality in the United States* (5th ed.). Rowman & Littlefield.

Brown, Y. (2015, August 14). The subtle linguistics of polite white supremacy. https://medium.com/@YawoBrown/the-subtle-linguistics-of-polite-white-supremacy-3f83c907ffff

Chan, E. L., & Coney, L. (2020). Moving TESOL forward: Increasing educators' critical consciousness through a racial lens. *TESOL Journal, 11*(4). https://doi.org/10.1002/tesj.550

Cooper, A. (2020). *And justice for ELs: A leader's guide to creating and sustaining equitable schools.* Corwin.

Kanno, Y., & Cromley, J. G. (2013). English language learners' access to and attainment in postsecondary education. *TESOL Quarterly, 47*(1), 89–121. https://doi.org/10.1002/tesq.49

King, Jr., M. L. (2010). *Why we can't wait.* Beacon Press: Boston.

Love, B. (2019). *We want to do more than survive: Abolitionist teaching and the pursuit of educational freedom.* Beacon Press.

Matias, C. E. (2019). Beyond white: The emotional complexion of critical research on race. In K. K. Strunk & L. A. Locke (Eds.), *Research methods for social justice and equity in education* (pp. 263–274). Palgrave Macmillan.

Quintero, S., & Long, J. (2019). *Toxic positivity: The dark side of positive vibes.* https://thepsychologygroup.com/toxic-positivity

Reynolds, A., & Lewis, D. (2017). Teams solve problems faster when they're more cognitively diverse. *Harvard Business Review.* https://hbr.org/2017/03/teams-solve-problems-faster-when-theyre-more-cognitively-diverse

Ross, L. J. (2019 Spring). *Speaking up without tearing down. Learning for Justice.* www.learningforjustice.org/magazine/spring-2019/speaking-up-without-tearing-down

Santa Clara Office of Education. (2016). *The my name, my identity campaign: A declaration of self.* www.mynamemyidentity.org

Valenzuela, A. (2010). *Subtractive schooling: US-Mexican youth and the politics of caring.* SUNY Press.

Yook, Eunkyong Lee. (2013). *Culture shock for Asians in U.S. academia: Breaking the model minority myth.* Lexington Books.

WHITE LIBERALISM IN DIVERSITY, EQUITY, INCLUSIVENESS, AND BELONGING EFFORTS

Part II

WHITE LIBERALISM IN
DIVERSITY, EQUITY,
INCLUSIVENESS, AND
BELONGING EFFORTS

Colorblindness, White Paternalism, and the Limits of School Desegregation and Diversity Reform

Anna Kushner

What do you imagine when you hear the word "desegregation"? Many may think of the infamous "Little Rock scream picture," the monochrome photo featuring Elizabeth Eckford, one of the nine Black students recruited to attend the newly integrated Little Rock Central High School in 1957, solemnly walking toward the building entrance while surrounded by angry white people. Observers often are drawn to the center of the photo, unable to look away from a screaming white, teenage girl, teeth bared, filled with hatred toward Eckford. It's an iconic and haunting image from the American Civil Rights movement, taken just 3 years after the Supreme Court ruled that state-mandated segregation in schools was unconstitutional.

Brown v. Board of Education (1954) is seen as a major milestone in the Civil Rights movement in the United States because it overturned the separate but equal precedent established by *Plessy v. Ferguson* in 1896. However, some critical race theorists remain skeptical about the potential for this ruling to eradicate racial inequality (e.g., Bell, 1980). In the majority opinion, Chief Justice Earl Warren challenged the *separate* component of *separate but equal*, overturning legal segregation not due to the different material conditions Black and white students experienced in segregated schools (e.g., access to books, school supplies, well-maintained school buildings), but because of the impact du jure segregation had on Black students' self-esteem. The courts located the harm done by racial segregation in the psyches of individual black students, not in the unequal conditions or power dynamics created by white racism and reenforced by segregation. This meant that segregation harmed individual people instead of creating systemic political, economic, and social inequality. The emphasis on individual harm rather than systemic injustice remains relevant nearly 70 years later.

The grainy quality of the image described above makes integration feel like ancient history, but school segregation remains a key concern for education policymakers decades after *Brown v. Board of Education*. Schools in the United States were more segregated in 2009 than they were in the 1960s (Orfield, 2009), and many major metropolitan areas are implementing education policies to make their schools more diverse and representative of their areas' demographics.

The way white people in the United States talk about desegregation has changed too. It's hard to picture someone reacting as violently as the teen shown in the Little Rock scream image. Instead, progressive white students and their families are more likely to express support for integration efforts and value school diversity (Roda & Wells, 2013).

In fact, desegregation is an increasingly popular reform topic. Many school leaders and policymakers are creating schools that are diverse by design, and some districts are even advocating for changing school selection mechanisms to achieve more diversity and less racial and socioeconomic isolation. In theory, this sounds better than desegregation efforts in the 1950s. However, liberal approaches to systemic problems can promote solutions that *feel good* and *seem* progressive but allow institutional and structural inequities to go unaddressed, resulting in more *diverse* schools that do not necessarily challenge unequal power structures or unevenly distributed resources. In this chapter, I show how contemporary school desegregation efforts and diversity initiatives can be part of a white liberal policy agenda that creates an illusion of racial justice while protecting the interests of white students and their families.

Desegregation, at its most basic, is the right for people of Color to occupy the same places and spaces as white people (Parham, 2015). The word "desegregation" is often used interchangeably with its counterpart, "diversity," or the presence of people from a variety of marginalized or minoritized groups. Both desegregation and diversity are popular but often insufficient because neither guarantees *integration*. Integration is the notion that people from different backgrounds not only have access to institutions like good schools but also feel welcomed, represented, and included within the institutions (Parham, 2015).

Ironically, enthusiasm for contemporary desegregation efforts can be a barrier to integration. Specifically, two characteristics of white liberalism inhibit efforts to achieve racial equity through desegregation efforts: colorblindness and paternalism. In the sections that follow, I briefly define each term, provide examples of how white liberal desegregation policy can stand in the way of integration and equitable resource reallocation, and ask questions and offer recommendations for avoiding common pitfalls when enacting a school integration or diversity policy.

COLORBLINDNESS

When confronted with questions of racial equality, well-meaning white liberals might proclaim that they "don't see color" and therefore could not possibly be racist. According to cultural theorist Ruth Frankenberg (1993), the white liberal tendency toward colorblindness is "a mode of thinking about race organized around the effort to not 'see,' or at any rate not to acknowledge race difference" (p. 142). While some white liberals consider it progressive to "see people, not race," efforts not to acknowledge race can actually *perpetuate racism* by offering raceless explanations for race-related issues of inequality.

Colorblindness is deeply tied to what sociologist Eduardo Bonilla-Silva (2006) calls colorblind racism, or the "powerful explanations—which have ultimately become justifications—for contemporary racial inequality" (p. 2), allowing white people to "safeguard their interests without sounding racist" (2006, p. 4). Colorblind racism draws on the values of classical liberalism, including equal opportunity, choice, and individualism, to explain away inequality and minimize racism. A classic example of colorblind racism is a white person opposing affirmative action in higher education because "everyone should have an equal opportunity." This colorblind explanation ignores historical inequality and unequal access for people of Color and instead draws on liberal notions of individual work ethic, meritocracy, and fairness to uphold a system that ultimately benefits the dominant social group.

How can desegregation be colorblind? Somewhat surprisingly, contemporary law takes a colorblind stance (Gotanda, 1991), and desegregation is no exception. In 2007, the Supreme Court heard *Parents Involved in Community Schools v. Seattle School District No. 1* (PICS) and ruled that school districts cannot use the race or ethnicity of individual students in making school assignments (PICS, 2007). In the majority opinion, Chief Justice Roberts (2007) wrote that allowing racial balancing would effectively assure "that race will always be relevant in American life" (p. 40). Embodying colorblindness, Roberts famously said, "The way to stop discrimination on the basis of race is to stop discriminating on the basis of race" (p. 41). Essentially, he proposed that ignoring race would make race irrelevant.

While this ruling continued allowing for school districts to consider the racial demographics of students overall when deciding on attendance zones and where to build new schools, it made it difficult to address segregation that occurred within a single district. As a result, most contemporary desegregation efforts use proxies for race, like socioeconomic status, English Language Learner status, and even academic achievement. Race-neutral desegregation policies can perpetuate racism by ignoring the racist and exclusionist history that people of Color, especially Black and Indigenous peoples, experienced in the United States, which can promote assimilationist school curriculums while ignoring the inequitable allocation of resources.

At the district level, race-neutral desegregation policies can fall into the white liberal trap of colorblindness. Most contemporary desegregation efforts incorporate family choice in school assignment (Frankenberg & DeBray, 2011). Some experts even claim that school choice is the optimal way to achieve integration (e.g., Kahlenberg, 2016), but others have found that school choice policies can actually lead to increased racial segregation (e.g., Saporito & Sohoni, 2006). How can both be true?

Consider this example. A district realizes that its student assignment policy results in schools with student bodies that reflect the stark housing segregation in the region. To try to make schools more demographically representative of the community, the district abolishes its neighborhood school model and introduces a system of choice for all middle and high schools. Increasing school choice creates "equal opportunity" across a district. Suddenly, all students, regardless of race, have access to more schools.

If school segregation persists, a white liberal response may be to put on the colorblind glasses and blame families of Color for not sending students to different schools. This individualizes a phenomenon that is structural. As a mechanism for desegregation, school choice alone does not address structural issues that people of Color might face, including residential segregation, access to public transportation, and school admissions criteria that disproportionally block access for students of Color. Colorblind desegregation policy might not consider access to culturally affirming curriculum and educators who share a cultural identity with students, nor will it address hesitation to integrate into a potentially hostile environment. Instead, when viewed through a colorblind lens, desegregation via choice alone locates the problem in families who are unwilling to change rather than a school system that lacks the infrastructure to support minoritized students in all schools.

Colorblindness can also operate within desegregated, diverse schools and classrooms. While a teacher embracing white liberalism might "not see color" in their classroom, they still notice how different students are performing. For teachers and other adults advocating for educational equity, a colorblind attitude can inhibit the ability to recognize educational inequities as a systemic problem rather than an individual problem.

For example, imagine a district that has recently implemented a desegregation plan. As a result, a school that had been predominantly white now has a larger enrollment of students of Color. You notice that, while the school overall has become more diverse, the advanced courses and gifted and talented program remain predominantly white. When this is pointed out to school leaders, they respond, "It's not that we don't want our new students to take advanced courses. They have an equal opportunity to be selected for the courses, but they just don't have the background in the subject areas to keep up with the rigorous instruction. Maybe next year, more students of Color will qualify."

In one way, evidence shows clearly that the desegregation plan is working: The demographics of the school building have changed. However, colorblind leaders are misconstruing a systemic racial problem as a problem with individual students, meaning the individual new students are unable to keep up because they are unprepared for the rigorous instruction. This is an example of desegregation not necessarily addressing inequitable resource allocation; although a campus is becoming more diverse, not all students are granted access to the resources (e.g., advanced coursework) that would increase equity in the district.

Colorblindness allows educators to point to nonracial factors to explain away racial problems. Equal opportunity does not necessarily translate to equity, and colorblindness is a barrier to fully understanding the factors that drive segregation in the first place.

Critiquing the outcome of the *Brown* case, legal scholar Lani Guinier (2004) stated, "The tactic of desegregation became the ultimate goal, rather than the means to secure educational equity." In this way, desegregation actually stood in the way of "a fair and just distribution of resources" (p. 95). This remains true today: Desegregation is not redistributive by definition because attending diverse schools is seen as "good for everyone," and desegregation alone does not guarantee equal access to courses or enrichment programs in a diverse school.

Put another way, diversity alone does not address the historical exclusions that students of Color in the United States face. Although the *Parents Involved* ruling largely prevents leaders from writing race-conscious desegregation policies, efforts to diversify schools should be evaluated in a race-responsive way. When writing policy, leaders should avoid depending on colorblind equal opportunity, and instead consider whether resources are being redistributed with equity in mind. This could include districts that are desegregating and also working to detrack classrooms so that no schools within schools are formed. As part of any integration efforts, teachers and school leaders should take time to carefully examine and challenge their colorblind attitudes and beliefs so they are able to identify unequal patterns that emerge within their schools and classrooms. Most importantly, policymakers must listen to the school community. Families of Color should play a key role in designing education policies that exist to serve them.

WHITE PATERNALISM

According to philosopher Gerald Dworkin (1972), paternalism is "the interference with a person's liberty of action justified by reasons referring exclusively to the welfare, good, happiness, needs, interests, or values of the person being coerced" (p. 65). Often, paternalism resembles a desire to "help those less fortunate," and involves people with power "knowing what's best" for marginalized people. Within the framework of white liberalism, paternalism and colorblindness go hand in hand.

An underlying assumption uncritical leaders risk when they advocate for liberal diversity policies is the idea that if schools treat students of Color just like their white peers, then "all students will benefit." In the case of school desegregation, paternalism centers the role of white teachers, school leaders, and students in education reform intended to benefit students of Color. Paternalism was easy to spot in early desegregation efforts. When schools began integrating in the 1950s, Black schools would generally close, dispersing students to "integrated" schools on previously all-white campuses. Black teachers and school leaders were often left unemployed, and their expertise was not valued. In contemporary desegregation efforts, paternalism shows up in two main forms: in the language used to discuss desegregation efforts and in how students of Color are treated in desegregated schools.

Well-meaning liberal white leaders and policymakers must think critically about who has agency in making policy decisions. By involving a diversity of school leaders, community members, academic experts, and families in the policymaking process, leaders can be more certain that a progressive diversity policy is truly responsive to the needs and desires of the community instead of paternalistically pushing an agenda of "what's best" onto a community. For example, imagine a scenario in which a group of white parents noticed that middle schools varied greatly in quality and were racially and socioeconomically segregated. First, feeling outraged and inspired to improve access for students of Color, white parents pushed for a desegregation plan that would require all schools in the district to enroll students such that the demographics in each building represented that of the district (at least on the factors allowed following the *Parents Involved* ruling discussed above). These parents were certain they did something to promote equity until parents of Color complained, claiming they would lose access to bilingual education programs as well as the teachers of Color at their neighborhood schools who they felt were better prepared to deliver culturally responsive curriculum and pedagogy.

This group of white parent advocates fell into the trap of white paternalist thinking. They identified the wrong problem and attempted to fix it on their own, without input from those who would be most affected by the change. Upon receiving this feedback, they worked together with officials and fellow community members to revise their proposal, intentionally including people from as many backgrounds as possible in the process. They developed a desegregation plan that removed access barriers for the district's most highly sought-after schools and expanded access to bilingual education. They also added programming and funding to the more geographically isolated schools that enroll the highest proportion of students of Color. Most critically, they also mandated that all teachers undergo training to interrogate colorblind attitudes and unconscious racial bias. This reform, designed by the community, met the needs of more stakeholders.

It is common for school desegregation advocates to tout the benefits of attending diverse schools; advocates proclaim that students of Color who attend diverse schools have better academic outcomes (Cook, 2021; Dee & Penner, 2017). Oftentimes, the way advocates and researchers describe this phenomenon is by using the concept of peer effects, or the impact of classroom peers' abilities on individual student achievement. Advocates of diversity reforms must evaluate their beliefs and language carefully. For example, imagine an elementary school teacher working in a diverse school in the district described above. They are happy that all their students score well on an interim assessment, and note that, on average, the Latinx students are earning higher scores than on previous assessments. The teacher is pleased with the growth and credits the diverse-by-design table groups they assigned as the source; students are learning better academic skills by working together.

In this scenario, the teacher may be embodying a paternalistic viewpoint that the Latinx students in class are benefitting from the presence of their white classmates. While positive outcomes are visible and even quantifiable in such cases, this could reify the belief that students of Color are better off adopting the cultural norms or imagined work ethic of white students.

In a study on Black superintendents who attended segregated schools and eventually served as leaders in integrated schools, one leader reflected on desegregation, stating,

> For a lot of people [the *Brown* decision] was going to be the hope and the change—from unequal segregation and from unequal opportunities and resources . . . I think where people made their mistake is that people thought the Black folks were bringing the suit so they could sit by White kids. That wasn't it. It was to equalize the resources . . . But people had the notion that [Black] people were suing so they could sit by White folks, cause if they sat by White folks, they could learn. (Steele, cited in Horsford, 2010, p. 303)

Put another way, the push for desegregation was not about the right to have white classmates; rather, it was seen as the most efficient way to ensure that Black students had access to resources such as textbooks and modern school facilities. Someone with a white paternalistic perspective might assume that students of Color are thriving in integrated schools because of the "good influence" of their white peers, rather than how students might now have access to more resources and teachers with more experience.

To address white liberal paternalism in diversity policy, the best thing white educators and policymakers can do is collaborate with community members and education leaders of Color to develop equity-oriented school reforms. School diversity initiatives may play a role, but so will resource reallocation, like funding, access to advanced coursework and electives, recruitment of experienced educators, and so on. Additionally, it is important for teachers to reflect on their own racialized assumptions about school diversity. For example, if someone considers students of Color "lucky" to attend a high-achieving school, this could be rearticulating the ideological proposition that white students attending this school already deserve to be there. Even if the teacher is happy that their school is more diverse, this attitude perpetuates colorblind racism and paternalistic attitudes toward students of Color. By actively challenging those assumptions, teachers can work toward making their classrooms a more integrated and inclusive environment.

CONCLUSION

Although most white people in the United States react to integration with less vitriol than they did in the 1950s, school desegregation policy can still perpetuate racism in schools. Without careful, critical thought, well-intentioned white liberal advocates of school diversity can exhibit racism, particularly in the form of colorblindness and paternalism. Diversity can become a *happy sign* (Ahmed, 2007) that signals we have moved past racism while potentially masking how white privilege is maintained by the way resources are distributed in a district.

Diversity is affective; it *feels* good, especially for liberal white families and policymakers. In many ways, it should. Moving toward a more just society requires that the decision-making table becomes representative, and that resources be redistributed to be more equal. However, it is critical not to allow the warm feeling we get from seeing a diverse school to become a barrier to interrogating the racially troubling attitudes and assumptions made by educators and policymakers.

This chapter is not a call to abandon desegregation efforts; school integration can be an effective tool to promote equal access to resources for all students in a school or district. Rather, it is a reminder that policymakers, school leaders, and teachers should maintain a healthy skepticism when evaluating the merits of school desegregation or diversity as a mechanism for social justice. Diversity policies must be designed, implemented, and evaluated in partnership with communities, families, and leaders of Color. When possible, include young people in the design and evaluation of policies that affect them; they are experts at understanding how changes in their schools affect changes in their lives. Liberal white policymakers can avoid falling into the trap of liberal white paternalism through active listening and authentic collaboration with people of Color.

For a desegregation plan to be grounded in social justice, it must do more than change the demographics of students enrolled in schools. School leaders, teachers, policymakers, and policy analysts must *evaluate* the impact of desegregation plans in a race-conscious way. Instead of using colorblind notions of equal opportunity, examine whether classrooms themselves are becoming integrated. Stakeholders and policy analysts must also ask *what* resources are being reallocated, whether resources are equitable, and whether students of Color are being affirmed and represented in school curriculum and traditions. By examining the assumptions embedded in progressive-sounding policies and the policymaking process itself, educators are better able to understand the message that a policy sends. This analysis asks, "Who is school diversity reform for?" and "Who benefits in the long run?"

REFERENCES

Ahmed, S. (2007). "You end up doing the document rather than doing the doing": Diversity, race equality and the politics of documentation. *Ethnic and Racial Studies, 30*(4), 590–609. https://doi.org/10.1080/01419870701356015

Bell, D. A. (1980). *Brown v. Board of Education* and the interest-convergence dilemma. *Harvard Law Review, 93*(3), 518–533. https://doi.org/10.2307/1340546

Bonilla-Silva, E. (2006). *Racism without racists: Color-blind racism and the persistence of racial inequality in the United States.* Rowman & Littlefield.

Brown v. Board of Education, 347 U.S. 483 (1954).

Cook, J. (2021). Race-blind admissions, school segregation, and student outcomes: Evidence from race-blind magnet school lotteries. https://ssrn.com/abstract=3818304

Dee, T. S., & Penner, E. K. (2017). The causal effects of cultural relevance: Evidence from an ethnic studies curriculum. *American Educational Research Journal, 54*(1), 127–166. https://doi.org/10.3102/0002831216677002

Dworkin, G. (1972). Paternalism. *The Monist, 56*(1), 64–84. https://doi.org/10.5840/monist197256119

Frankenberg, E., & DeBray, E. (2011). Integration after parents involved: What does research suggest about available options? In E. Frankenberg (Ed.), *Integrating Schools in a Changing Society: New Policies and Legal Options for a Multiracial Generation.* University of North Carolina Press.

Frankenberg, R. (1993). *White women, race matters: The social construction of whiteness.* University of Minnesota Press.

Gotanda, N. (1991). A critique of "Our Constitution Is Color-Blind." *Stanford Law Review, 44*(1), 1–68. https://ssrn.com/abstract=2306297

Guinier, L. (2004). From racial liberalism to racial literacy: *Brown v. Board of Education* and the interest-divergence dilemma. *The Journal of American History, 91*(1), 92–118. https://doi.org/10.2307/3659616

Horsford, S. D. (2010). Mixed feelings about mixed schools: Superintendents on the complex legacy of school desegregation. *Educational Administration Quarterly, 46*(3), 287–321.

Kahlenberg, R. (2016). School integration in practice: Lessons from nine districts. The Century Foundation. https://tcf.org/content/report/school-integration-practice-lessons-nine-districts

Orfield, G. (2009). Reviving the goal of an integrated society: A 21st century challenge. The Civil Rights Project [Proyecto Derechos Civiles] at UCLA. https://civilrightsproject.ucla.edu/research/k-12-education/integration-and-diversity/reviving-the-goal-of-an-integrated-society-a-21st-century-challenge/orfield-reviving-the-goal-mlk-2009.pdf

Parham, T. (2015, Dec. 17). Desegregation not same as diversity and inclusion. *Diverse Issues in Higher Education.* https://diverseeducation.com/article/79610

Plessy v. Ferguson, 163 U.S. 537 (1896).

Roda, A., & Wells, A. S. (2013). School choice policies and racial segregation: Where white parents' good intentions, anxiety, and privilege collide. *American Journal of Education, 119*(2), 261–293.

Saporito, S., & Sohoni, D. (2006). Coloring outside the lines: Racial segregation in public schools and their attendance boundaries. *Sociology of Education, 79*(2), 81–105.

Seattle School District No. 1, 551 U.S. 701 (2007).

CHAPTER 6

Deploying White Liberal Antiracism to Avoid Accountability
Racial Appropriation in Educational Leadership

Tracey A. Benson

On Wednesday, August 7, 2019, in Littletown, Connecticut, a Black mother returning home from an early morning errand discovered human excrement near her front porch, smeared across her front door, and inserted into her air-conditioning unit. Local Black community activists labeled the incident a hate crime, but according to media outlets, local law enforcement officials were reluctant to do the same. When interviewing the victim of the hate crime, it was uncovered that this was not the first time she and her family had experienced racism in the small town of 12,000, where nearly 90% of residents are white and a little under 2% are Black. The Black mother detailed to the newspaper reporter how this incident, along with other past incidents when she was called racial slurs, led her and her family to feeling extremely unsafe and wanting to move out of the community.

In the days following the incident, the Littletown school district partnered with a community-based racial equity firm to take the "Not in Our Town" pledge. By taking this pledge, school district leaders affirmed their commitment to display a visible logo to express shared values, to not be silent in the face of intolerance or hate, and to employ a collaborative approach to address issues of hate and intolerance. While not publicized in the local media, the superintendent held a 1-day event where she and her administrative cabinet, school principals, teachers, and school community took the pledge in response to the community event.

Serendipitously, my book, *Unconscious Bias in Schools: A Developmental Approach to Exploring Race and Racism*, was due to be released August 13. I was in the beginning stages of launching my antiracism consulting firm in July 2019 and reaching out to previous contacts to offer my services. I wrote an email to the superintendent on July 30 relaying information about a book talk I was scheduled to give at a local bookstore in October and solicited her interest in scheduling a similar book talk for her district. Her email response conveyed interest:

> It is so great to hear from you and to hear about this important work that you have engaged in. This book of yours is absolutely on point to the work that I have been doing . . . around inclusion, diversity, and understanding the cultural disconnect between our schools and the lives of our students. We will definitely be looking into buying the book for the leadership team as a book study. What do you have in mind? How big an audience are you willing to work with? Would you be willing to do something as professional development and a community forum involving other community agencies?

After one additional correspondence to coordinate our calendars for an initial conversation, we settled on a virtual meeting date of Friday, August 9, 2019. In her email to schedule our meeting, she wrote:

> How about next Friday at 9:00 am EST? . . . I am planning to buy the book for my leadership team and we are planning to do equity walks at all four schools this fall. We are low incidence for EL students and minority subgroups but growing. There is a cultural disconnect between the experience of the staff and the changing demographic of the community. It is not a very welcoming community for students of color and we are working on changing that.

As fate would have it, between our email correspondence and our phone conversation, the racial incident took place, so a majority of our first call was dedicated to the superintendent detailing the event and her thoughts about how the school district should respond. During the phone call, the superintendent also conveyed how pleased she was with the convenience of our impending partnership, as she saw this as an opportunity to highlight the district's dedication to equity to the community. Following our phone conversation, I put together a comprehensive professional development proposal that included two in-person, 6-hour trainings for all administrators, one to kick off the work in October and one to circle back on the year's progress in June. The program also included seven monthly one-on-one virtual coaching sessions for every school and district leader. Upon agreeing to the terms of the contract and solidifying the dates of the first in-person training, the superintendent proceeded to purchase a copy of the assigned textbook for every school and district administrator in preparation for our first professional development session scheduled for the second to last week in October.

In this chapter I chronicle my 8-month consulting relationship with that school district, including the role key district leaders played in obstructing antiracist efforts by embodying the common tropes of white liberal racism: white fragility, white privilege, and white rage. I conclude by offering a new paradigm for antiracist education professional development that empowers leaders to make tangible and measurable changes in the lives of Black and Brown students and faculty.

THE INITIAL TRAINING: PLANTING THE SEEDS OF DISCOMFORT

All of my trainings are designed to introduce and sustain productive discomfort around the concept of racism. I aim to quickly engage participants in reflecting on their experiences with race to help them tether their personal experiences to how they are implicated in perpetuating racism and white supremacy in society. While I weave consciousness and awareness-building and intellectual learning activities throughout the training, the reflections and points of discussion are designed to address the socio-emotional components of antiracism to surface and prompt participants, especially white participants, to reconcile with feelings of guilt, shame, anger, and frustration that come along with usurping the expectation of white racial comfort.

On the first day of training in early October, I was allotted 6 hours, punctuated by a 1-hour lunch, to lead an adult learning session around the concepts in *Unconscious Bias in Schools*. Understanding from the superintendent that the school and district leaders had not previously engaged in any substantive professional learning related to racial equity, I suggested she recommend that her leaders read the book prior to the training so that the concepts would be moderately familiar to them. However, as is often the case with busy administrators, no one had read the book prior to attending the training. It was disappointing, but not unexpected or disruptive, as I'd developed the workshop with the expectation of little to no prior understanding of the dynamics of racism in schools.

In attendance at the initial training were the three elementary school principals, the assistant principal and principal of the middle-high school, the district literacy and grants coordinator, the community outreach coordinator, the assistant superintendent, and the superintendent. The town's mayor even stopped in for 30 minutes to listen in on the training at the invitation of the superintendent. And while the superintendent attended the training, she excused herself several times throughout the 6-hour training to attend to other matters.

After 30 minutes of community-building activities and setting the stage for the work, I introduced the day's agenda, which was organized into three categories:

(Morning 1) Familiarizing ourselves with *Unconscious Bias in Schools*
- Grappling with real-life scenarios
- Building background knowledge
- Applying new insights to your work

(Morning 2) Data dive into discipline data
- Identifying trends in the data
- Discussion of next steps
- Developing processes of accountability

(Afternoon) Introduction to constructive developmental antiracism
- Exploring links between antiracism and constructive developmentalism
- Developing strategies to overcome antiracism-phobia
- Scheduling antiracist leadership executive coaching sessions

The consciousness and awareness-raising and reflection activities were pocketed to the Morning 1 session, with the Morning 2 session reserved for developing concrete next steps for engaging in antiracism with each school. The afternoon session was a foray into the cognitive barriers that prevent leaders from engaging in antiracism with others (e.g., fear of being seen as racist, fear of saying the wrong thing, negative self-talk regarding preparedness to engage in the work).

I call this inability to reconcile with these intrinsic fears prevalent among even the most well-meaning white leaders "antiracism-phobia." The reason I use this term is that the negative self-talk of individuals afraid to engage in antiracism is usually based in an irrational fear akin to someone who suffers from phobias, such as acrophobia (the fear of heights) or agoraphobia (the fear of being alone). All phobias, including antiracism-phobia, present the self with an overblown sense of the possibility of bad things happening, such as an acrophobic falling from a high place, while in reality the probability the overblown fear will be realized is minimal. Therefore, the afternoon session was spent on helping each participant more fully realize and confront their antiracism-phobia and make a plan to begin to address it as they simultaneously engage in antiracist work.

The constructive developmental sessions to address antiracism-phobias are very intense and involve deep introspection into thought patterns most white people have never been pushed to explore. This session triggered intense feelings of guilt and shame among many participants—so much so, that one principal commented, "Yuck! This is making me feel really bad. Who in their right mind would want to overcome this deep of a phobia?"

For this reason, I build into my professional development model monthly antiracist executive leadership coaching sessions to hold participants accountable for addressing their antiracism-phobias while they are concurrently pursuing their measurable antiracist initiatives. Experience has taught me that if leaders do not attend to their cognitively constructed barriers, the antiracist initiative is doomed to fail. Although I ended the professional development session 20 minutes early and requested each school and district leader to schedule their first coaching session with me, none chose to do so, not even the superintendent.

COLLECTIVE DERAILMENT: THE CHARACTERS OF WHITE "LIBERAL" FRAGILITY

White fragility, according to Robin DiAngelo (2018), is the intense stress, and responses to that stress, that white people feel when discussing matters of race and racism. I have added the word "liberal" to explicate the self-identity of the four white district leaders I engaged with in the school district. All four white women self-described as open-minded, left-leaning, leaders for equity. Each leader, at one time or another, relayed to me that they cared about students of Color, did not interact with racists, and understood racism exists and was bad for communities of Color.

It is this self-image that proved to be the most intense barrier to gaining traction in the district, because not only did white fragility present itself, but the self-image as a nonracist liberal added an almost impenetrable layer to process. The dynamics of white fragility, which I employ to tell these stories and as defined by DiAngelo (2018), include the following:

- Racial arrogance: Most white people are woefully ignorant about the function and dynamics of racism. Regardless of this deep ignorance, whites generally feel entitled to dismiss the racial wisdom of people of Color and other informed perspectives and place more value on their own limited understandings.
- Entitlement to racial comfort: White people, in general, have a very low tolerance for racial discomfort. When they experience racial discomfort, they typically blame it on the person or event that triggered the discomfort.
- Psychic freedom: White people do not experience the negative social impacts of race. They can avoid or choose to opt out of discomforting conversations about race, thereby freeing their psychological energy to focus on other issues.
- Racial belonging: White people enjoy a deeply embedded sense of racial belonging among one another. To interrupt the racism of another white person, thereby interrupting this sense of belonging, can be destabilizing and intensely frightening to white people.

While each leader embodied several aspects of white fragility over the course of our working relationship, I've focused on the most salient aspect that proved to be the most powerful barrier to progress for each of them.

Racial Arrogance

Amy, a white woman in her late 50s who had spent a majority of her education leadership career in the northeast, was in her third year as superintendent of the Littletown school district. During four of the seven allotted antiracist leadership executive coaching sessions she chose to attend, she conveyed that she believed she thrives in struggling school districts and that diversity and equity are foundational to sustain our American way of life. She wanted diversity and inclusion no longer to be an intellectual exercise but an act of realizing humanity. While Amy used the words "diversity" and "equity" frequently during her 3 years as superintendent, she'd only engaged her leaders in professional development training on trauma-informed instruction, fostering resilient learners, and teaching students living in poverty. The partnership with me marked the first time she'd considered a race-based professional development offering for her district and school leaders.

As we progressed through our coaching sessions, her racial arrogance, previously unnoticed by me, began to slowly erode our relationship. As defined by Robin DiAngelo (2018), racial arrogance is when white people feel entitled to dismiss informed perspectives on race and racism rather than have the humility to acknowledge that they are unfamiliar or ignorant. Although Amy saw herself as a progressive white person, she consistently conveyed that she was uncomfortable and unwilling to "talk about the experiences of others she does not share a specific identity with." In her mind, as she conveyed to me, "people need to hear stories" in order to grow their racial literacy.

She consistently came back to a specific event she felt had immense impact on white educators in which an elderly Black woman came to a professional development session for teachers at the high school and shared stories of her Black granddaughter. She felt this type of storytelling from people of Color was the most powerful way to engage in racial equity. Therefore, when asked if she was reading the textbook—which focuses less on other people's stories and more on what individual leaders can do to lead antiracism—or prompting her school leaders to read it, she avoided the question and returned to the ways she envisioned antiracism: Black faces telling stories to white people.

Amy also frequently circled back to the statements dismissing the need for specific antiracist work in her district: "We are low-incidence for Black students" and "If we address poverty then we will also be helping most of the students of Color." I often prompted her to reflect on her use of "low-incidence" as a dismissal of the racism experienced by students of Color. I also had a discussion with her about the differences between poverty and racism. However, during each of these discussions she would disagree and insist that their current initiatives focusing on poverty were sufficient to solve any issues students of Color were facing in her district, even racism.

As Amy repeated these statements with an increasingly aggressive tone, despite my strong suggestions that she reconsider her perspective, I came to an epiphany about what she considered to be my role as a Black male consultant in her vision of antiracism. She wanted to use my blackness and my standing in the field as her action plan to resolve racism in the school district. It was the appearance of antiracism that was most important to her, not actually engaging in antiracist work. Her racial arrogance further disenfranchised her Black families by using me, at worst, as a cover for inaction, or, at best, as one of the Black storytellers that she believed sparked change.

Entitlement or Racial Comfort

Attending four of her allotted seven coaching sessions, Isabel refused to engage in discussions about racism in the Littletown school district. As Amy's handpicked assistant superintendent, Isabel had extensive leadership experience at the school, district, and state levels. She conveyed that she had worked in racially diverse school districts during her career and appreciated learning from other cultures. However, at the same time, over the course of her 30+ years in education, she had never engaged in professional development specifically about racial equity, nor did she have experience talking about the concepts of racism and white supremacy.

Instead of focusing on race, she elected to challenge teachers to think about academic gaps in achievement with relation to cultural sensitivity. Yet, even as Isabel recognized the benefits of introducing teachers to more culturally relevant classroom pedagogy, she also admitted that this was not a complete solution since many teachers in the district continued to view students experiencing poverty and students of Color from a deficit perspective.

Similar to Amy, Isabel had the textbook in her possession but did not read it; therefore the consciousness and awareness-raising portions of the program highlighted within the text failed to stick. During our coaching conversations, she admitted that talking about racism was tough for her and agreed to experiment with talking about race with her inner circle between coaching sessions, but she never followed through, providing excuses such as "I forgot" or "I simply didn't get the opportunity," or "It just wasn't the right time."

The paradox in her thinking was that she felt that she and her colleagues were ready to dive deep into issues of race because they had engaged with Brené Brown's book, *Dare To Lead*; however, when I pushed her to explore concepts of racism and to reflect on how racism manifested in the Littletown school district, she often relied on similar talking points pushed by Amy: "We are low incidence for Black students" and "The students of Color struggle more with the effect of poverty, not racism." In the end, I surmised that I failed to penetrate Isabel's resistance to seeing herself as a part of the problem; she simply could not bear the discomfort of admitting racism existed in her school district.

Psychic Freedoms

In her early 30s and with a preschool-aged son, Maggy frequently thought about our conversations about race with relation to the type of school building she wanted her son to attend. She often would go on tangents about how she didn't want her son exposed to the types of racism perpetrated in Littletown schools and how her actions needed to reflect her desires for change.

However, while Maggy espoused a desire to learn more about and address the racism in Littletown schools, she constantly struggled with her fear of not knowing enough to adequately advocate for racial equity. During our coaching sessions, she made commitments to deepening her racial literacy, but similar to Amy and Isabel, she did not read the textbook, despite having had a personal copy. Also, at the end of nearly all of our sessions, she would commit to seeking out an audiobook on the topic of race and listening to it in her car on the way to work in the morning, but she always arrived at the next coaching session with an excuse as to why that hadn't happened.

Maggy demonstrated her commitment to meeting with me by attending all seven allotted coaching sessions and engaging in deep conversation and reflection for the duration of our hour together. However, her will to engage with racial discomfort during our coaching sessions quickly dissipated after our hour together.

As the community outreach coordinator, Maggy had many opportunities to broach the topic of race at district- and state-level meetings and trainings, but she consistently conveyed that she did not want to sully the waters during productive conversations about strategies to address poverty by bringing up race. Near the end of our time together, while reflecting on her lack of progress aloud, Maggy stated that she felt racism was something she wished would go away, but she simply did not have the headspace to think about it in the everyday without feelings of guilt and shame "getting in the way of my work."

Racial Belonging

Growing up in Littletown, Connecticut, and attending high school in Littletown, Nancy was all too familiar with the racism in the schools and community. Even as a 40-year-old director of literacy and grants coordinator who had left the community for college and returned several years later to work in the district, she remembered several racist incidents she had witnessed during her time in the school system as if they happened yesterday.

During one of our coaching sessions, she recounted an incident when she was chastised by her white neighbors for inviting Black friends to her house. She also remembered times when her Black friends would be openly discriminated against in high school by being discouraged to enroll in honors classes or Advanced Placement classes. Although she remembered these events and was fairly certain vestiges of racism still existed in the school district, she felt she couldn't challenge the status quo because she was expected to "stay in her lane." Like her central office colleagues, she had not read the assigned textbook for our program.

Although she attended all seven of her allotted coaching sessions, she constantly found it difficult to overcome her feelings of fear and trepidation at the thought of confronting racism in the school district. During an early coaching session, Nancy recounted a story about when she witnessed a school nurse accost a Black student over wearing his hat indoors but did not treat white male students in the same manner. Following her story, we role-played how she could follow up with the nurse about the incident. At the end of that particular coaching session, she appeared to be confident and ready to follow through by talking to the nurse. However, when I asked her about the outcome of the conversation at our next meeting, she made up excuse after excuse for why she didn't get to it and how, since over 2 weeks had passed since the event, it was now too late to address the incident with the nurse.

This behavior was emblematic of Nancy's approach to antiracism: "I see it, but I am afraid and unwilling to rock the boat amongst my white colleagues."

TAKING RESPONSIBILITY: MY THREE FUNDAMENTAL OVERSIGHTS

In her book *Good White People: The Problem with Middle-Class White Anti-Racism* (2014), Shannon Sullivan identifies several key barriers to white liberals truly engaging in productive antiracism. Of the barriers she names, the three that resonate the most with my inability to spark productive growth among school leaders in Littletown are (1) for many white middle-class individuals, it is more important to be seen as a morally good person than to enact practices of antiracism, (2) the failure to acknowledge the role of white superiority even when white people are acting with good intentions, and (3) the espoused inability and unwillingness to talk openly about race, racism, and whiteness.

Being Seen as Good White People

The proximity of the contract to the racist incident in town may have played a role in shifting the ways white participants engaged with the training. It was evident through my conversations with all the leaders that they were very much in disbelief that such a racist incident could happen in their town and woefully unprepared to address the issue within the schoolhouse. They were left feeling guilty and ashamed that they did not have a more productive response immediately following the event.

However, willfully engaging in the 1-day antiracism training gave the impression to the community, as well as the mayor who attended the initial professional development session for 30 minutes, that the school district was being responsible and responsive. Also, throughout the duration of my contract with Littletown, despite the facts that members of the superintendent's cabinet were essentially doing nothing to define and meet their measurable antiracist initiatives, school leaders failed to read the assigned textbook, and they refused to schedule, or cancelled, the majority of their one-on-one coaching sessions with me, I received almost monthly invitations to co-present at conferences with Amy and Isabel about the "work" we were doing together. This speaks to the optics orientation of white liberalism.

In hindsight, the mayor's brief visit to the initial training and the invitations to co-present at conferences should have been signs that the district's image was more important to the superintendent and the other leaders than engaging in tangible antiracist initiatives, but I did not realize this until it was too late.

The Racial Arrogance of the Superintendent

It wasn't until my final meeting with Amy and Isabel on May 18 that it dawned on me that Amy truly did not understand the concept of racism, did not understand the importance of school leaders engaging in the monthly coaching sessions, and sincerely believed her good liberal whiteness was enough. Amy used key phrases throughout our relationship together. She consistently circled back to the fact that the school district was "low-incidence" with regard to Black students and often cited the state-mandated Limited English Proficiency training for teachers as the answer to the gaps in achievement they were experiencing with their Latinx populations. When I pressed Amy to understand that even though the Black population was relatively small in comparison to the white student population, she was still responsible for addressing racism in the school district, she would turn the conversation toward the initiative they were implementing for low-income students.

In line with her train of thought on initiatives for low-income students, I would ask her if, in her mind, being Black was synonymous with being low-income. To this question, she would reply in a huff, "Well most of our Black families are poor, so our initiatives benefit them too." Amy's deep racial arrogance and unwillingness to act as a leader for antiracism undercut my efforts in the district, bled heavily into my relationships with other members of her cabinet, and fueled the unwillingness of her principals to engage in the coaching protocol.

"I Don't Feel Comfortable Talking About the Experiences of Others"

Amy and Isabel constantly returned to this talking point whenever I pressed them to take tangible actions within the district. They both kept this impenetrable cocoon of inaction around themselves and their positions that absolved them from taking any antiracist action. Amy regarded the grandmother who visited her school district and told stories about her granddaughter's struggle with standards of beauty while going to school in a predominantly white environment as the gold standard of antiracist professional development. She sincerely believed sad stories presented by Black people to a white audience was the best way to prompt change. Her understanding, as she conveyed to me, was that if teachers knew how painful racism was to Black people, their behaviors would change.

However, Amy had no idea what she wanted to change as a result of these stories, nor did she have a way to measure change. She assumed these stories would grant her teachers greater levels of sympathy toward students of Color and thereby eliminate racism. With this enduring cognitive framing of antiracism between Amy and Isabel, two white women who didn't have "stories," it was difficult to get them to understand their vital role in leading for antiracism.

A BITTER END: WEAPONIZING WHITE FRAGILITY AND ENACTING WHITE RAGE

Carol Anderson (2016) coined the term "white rage" to describe the reaction or backlash from white people that almost always accompanies Black advancement. In the case of Littletown, Black advancement came in the form of intense community attention on a singular racist incident. Prior to the racist incident on August 7, 2019, the community, local media, and local government had paid little attention to these types of events. According to Nancy House, who had grown up in the area and attended school in Littletown, these types of incidents happened at least three to four times a year, maybe more, and while the community would hear about them via word of mouth, they rarely, if ever, made it into the local news media.

A slow crescendo of racial awareness had been sweeping across the country since the founding of the Black Lives Matter movement in 2014, following the murder of Michael Brown in Ferguson, Missouri. As both social media and the mainstream media covered more and more stories of police murder of unarmed Black people, institutions, including schools, felt pressured to publicly respond to such incidents. Therefore, in 2019, when the racist incident happened in Littletown and made its way into the community media, the local government and school system felt the need to respond.

Amy and Isabel were clear in their intentions for bringing me in as their response to the community event. And though I was hazy about our conflicting goals, in hindsight, I realize they were using me as cover for inaction. They did not engage with antiracism because they did not feel comfortable talking about the experiences of those with whom they did not share a specific identity. When pressed to reconsider their role in leading for antiracism, they continually rejected the notion that it was a problem to be addressed by white people, rather seeing antiracism as a responsibility of Black people to tell their stories to rooms full of white educators in hope of prompting change in the schooling experience for Black students and families.

With this as their framing, and a refusal to engage in a growth process around their racial identity development, it is no wonder our final meeting triggered intense white rage. I confronted their deliberate indifference to their role in antiracism.

Prior to our final meeting to discuss the content for the end-of-the-year workshop for school leaders in Littletown, I emailed Amy and Isabel prework (see Table 6.1), which consisted of a link to two YouTube clips, an excerpt from MLK's Letter from the Birmingham Jail, and guiding questions to consider as they engaged with these items.

Upon logging in to our final meeting, which was conducted virtually, Amy immediately stated that she did not have time to engage with the prework, while Isabel stared into the camera in silence. When I asked if we should reschedule so they would have time to do the prework, Amy responded, "No, we won't have time later, either . . . but, this meeting shouldn't take long."

The aberration in Amy's voice was apparently because Isabel had been offended by my pressing her during our previous coaching call on her inaction over the course of our time together. During that call, I asked Isabel over and over again what had changed for students of Color in her district as a result of our work together. When she could not locate an answer, I walked her through how her inaction was a key cause of the lack of change. I reminded her of the foundational work we did at the initial training in October and how everyone developed a measurable action plan and made a commitment to carry out that plan, but without the leadership from her and Amy, the plans never materialized.

Our meeting that "shouldn't take long" lasted nearly 90 minutes. It consisted of staunch deflection by Amy and Isabel in an attempt to place the blame for their collective inaction on me. When I asked them directly why they had purchased but did not read *Unconscious Bias in Schools*, they responded, "Your expectations were not clear that we should read the book" and "You did not walk us through the book as we expected." When asked

Table 6.1. Prework for May 8th Meeting

Source	Item	Guiding Question
Tim Wise	Being White, Not Knowing Any Better and Recognizing Privilege www.youtube.com/watch?v =QwStYOWB7sI	How has "not knowing any better" impeded the racial equity work in Littletown Public Schools?
	Passive Formulation of Racism, Patriarchy, and other Forms of Supremacy	According to Tim Wise, what is the definition of Passive Racism?
	https://youtu.be/QURlpIxb_wM	According to Tim Wise, why is it difficult for people to address racism?
	Train yourself to see it www.youtube.com/watch?v =s5GDoUg4jOU	What does it mean to "Train yourself to see it"?
MLK's Letter from Birmingham Jail (1963)	Quote: "Shallow understanding from people of goodwill is more frustrating than absolute misunderstanding from people of ill will. Lukewarm acceptance is much more bewildering than outright rejection."	How might this quote apply to the leadership in Littletown Public Schools?

why they did not require the principals from the school district to attend the coaching sessions the district paid for, they responded, "We weren't confident that the principals would feel comfortable meeting with you one on one."

After noting their many gripes about my lack of responsiveness and guidance, I posed one last question to them. I asked, "If my service was so sub-par leading to your school district being unable to effectively engage in antiracism, why did you invite me to co-present with you at several conferences?" To this question, they had no answer. Likely, the honest answer was about their true goal of our relationship: projecting an image of themselves as good white people.

Near the end of our conversation, in retaliation for holding them accountable for their passive racism, they cancelled the final professional development session along with my contract and proceeded to pro-rate my compensation. Their white rage was on full display during our final conversation. They truly did not want to be inconvenienced by an expectation to respond to the racist event in the community, nor did they desire to address the racism within their school district. However, due to community pressure, they grudgingly pursued an action they thought would project an image of good white people.

They expected me to play along and be grateful for our faux partnership. However, when I actually expected them to engage in antiracism, they dodged their responsibility at every turn. Moreover, when confronted about their passive racism, they chose to weaponize their white fragility by ending our relationship and withholding funds they owed me.

A WAY FORWARD: CHANGING THE PARADIGM

Far too many diversity, equity, and inclusion (DEI) professional development opportunities, especially in the realms of K–12 and higher education, lean heavily on the belief that if people know better, they will do better. Many DEI specialists subscribe to the belief that we can intellectualize our way out of racism without directly confronting the difficult cognitive, socio-emotional components such as white fragility (DiAngelo, 2018), white privilege (McIntosh, 2007), and especially white rage (Anderson, 2016). While some trainers and consultants may name and discuss these concepts, many avoid direct confrontation with aspects of these socio-emotional components during trainings.

Ron Heifetz and Marty Linsky (2017) describe this misguided approach as an attempt to solve an adaptive challenge with a technical solution. An adaptive challenge requires a change in mindset, while a technical problem requires a change in skillsets. Mindsets, not skillsets, is what drives the persistence of racism. Therefore, approaches that rely primarily on building historical knowledge of societal racism, developing a knowledge base about different forms of racism, or developing technical strategies to interrupt interpersonal or systemic racism often prove highly ineffective in achieving deep and lasting change.

True and lasting interpersonal, systemic, and structural change regarding antiracism comes from a combination of deepening one's racial literacy as well as constantly developing the capacity to navigate the internal and external cognitive, socio-emotional components that are inextricably tied to the work.

For example, my current work with leaders of all races is a combination of increasing racial literacy, developing deep understandings of internalized cognitive barriers to becoming an antiracist leader, and forming measurable antiracist action plans. In conjunction with a litany of readings, videos, and talks with which my clients are required to engage to deepen their racial literacy, they also are required to engage in a reflective cognitive coaching process to identify their intrinsic barriers to change.

For the white leaders I coach, a prominent cognitive barrier to change is the fear of saying something wrong or being called out for being unintentionally racist. Even as we work for weeks on the technical portion of antiracist action plans and racial literacy building, this fear of saying the wrong thing persists. Therefore, the greater half of our work together involves pushing my clients to engage in difficult interactions to challenge their belief systems and overcome their fears. Much as a person who is extremely afraid of heights will likely not willfully climb a ladder, even when they clearly know how, out of intense fear of falling, a white leader who is terrified of possibly saying something racist will likely avoid leading conversations about racism out of fear of being labeled a racist.

Therefore, regardless of the levels of racial literacy an individual builds, they will be only as effective as they are willing to confront and overcome their fear of engaging in antiracism. This is the key to leading for antiracism: building one's own racial literacy while simultaneously attending to the cognitive, socio-emotional components that holds us back from engaging in the difficult work of usurping the myriad ways racism shows up in the schoolhouse.

My approach to antiracism incorporates a laser focus on deepening the understandings of the many vestiges of racism, how it is essential for leaders to acknowledge and interrupt their complicity in white supremacy and builds each leaders' capacity to engage in antiracism beyond performative forays that do not substantially change the experience for students and faculty of Color. "Performative antiracism," a term I introduced elsewhere (Benson, 2020), is when a person, group of people, or organization intentionally performs an action to signal their desire to "be seen as" antiracist (e.g., publishing a BLM statement, forming an "antiracist reading group," convening racial affinity groups to talk about racism) with no connection to or accountability for how these actions will address the racial oppression of people of Color. While well-meaning school leaders may not enter into a diversity or equity initiative with the intent on performing, in my experience, many end up in the performative antiracism space because of deep racial illiteracy and a lack of a clear strategy from the outset.

Common performative practices include posting an antiracist statement on a website, adopting books by authors of Color, and hiring more Brown faces to teach in the building. These practices alone are not performative and can be a positive step in a well-thought-out plan. However, they become performative when they alone are supposed to be an act of antiracism. The answer to racism is antiracism, not merely putting out statements, reading books, or hiring people with Brown skin.

Avoiding the Performative Antiracism Trap

Two simple questions absolutely must be answered at the onset of any antiracist initiative: "What's in it for Black and Brown students and teachers?" and "How will we know?" For example, if the antiracist initiative involves diversifying anchor texts used in the English and social studies curriculum, we need to be sure the faculty understand how to implement the curriculum with care. Just inserting a Black author into a curriculum does nothing in terms of changing the educational experience for students unless the teacher has the depth of knowledge to create a valuable learning experience.

There are far too many examples of good-intentioned, racially illiterate teachers traumatizing students of Color by teaching about topics such as colonialism or slavery in highly insensitive ways. Moreover, without answering the two questions above, even if the teacher has the wherewithal to teacher the new curriculum with care and sensitivity, we will have failed to develop measures of success to evaluate the positive impact this change has for students of Color as well as for white students.

T.A.M.E.ing Antiracism

In order to implement a tightly coupled antiracist initiative, I created a framework for leaders to use during the planning process—the T.A.M.E. framework. The T stands for time. Time identifies the specific times during the day the initiative will take place. I push leaders to carve out time in important meetings (e.g., leadership team meetings, curriculum meetings, team meetings) to execute the initiative and avoid making antiracism work ancillary. If we treat antiracism as ancillary by placing it after school or billing it as voluntary, we further marginalize it and portray antiracism as merely optional.

The A stands for accountability. I encourage leaders to decide from the onset which metrics of success will be used to measure the antiracist initiative. If the initiative is a curriculum change, then we need to develop a way to measure the impact on students, or this move is merely performative, not substantive.

The M stands for money. Akin to avoiding scheduling this work during ancillary times, this work should be compensated, not just voluntary. The most important work in school buildings is compensated; antiracism work should be no different.

Last, the E stands for energy. Which individuals will be charged with carrying the work forward? If the answer is everybody, that means nobody. It is critical to identify specific individuals who are expected to lead antiracism and carry it through execution.

School districts are typically well equipped and accustomed to providing time and money for antiracist initiatives, in the form of scheduling one-off professional developments or talks about diversity, equity, and inclusion. This is low-hanging fruit because all it requires is for educators to show up and feign engagement for a set amount of time with no concrete expectation that they apply the new learning to their work.

In my experience, schools and school districts start to fall off when it comes to energy, especially when partnering with an outside expert. Schools will often engage in the work as long as the outside provider is present.

However, once the partnership comes to an end, the work often ends too, because it was never decided at the onset of the relationship who would own the work once the expert is gone.

While energy is a bugaboo, the Achilles heel of antiracism work in schools is accountability. This is such a tough item because leaders all too often do not have clear outcomes for antiracist initiatives—they just want to do something. Leaders must sit at the table for as long as it takes to develop systems of accountability. This process often involves engaging in new learning and formulating new processes and procedures for measurement. Systems of accountability must be well-defined in order for antiracist initiatives to be successful, effective, and replicable.

TRUTH AND RECONCILIATION

I often say to my clients, "The best gift we can give each other on our antiracism journey is truth." My experience in Littletown taught me a lot regarding how to more effectively engage with schools and school districts around antiracism.

The teacher in me recognizes that I need to own a significant portion of the failures in our partnership. I entered the partnership assuming a modicum of racial literacy in the superintendent and her cabinet, that we shared a common definition of and dedication to antiracism, and that there would be a high level of willingness among school leaders to engage in the difficult and uncomfortable work of usurping white supremacy. None of my assumptions held true, and by the time I recognized we were getting off track, I lacked the skill and ability to call an audible and change tactics. A skilled educator differentiates for their students, meets them where they are, and finds a way to encourage and empower their learners to engage in the work. As a learner myself in the work, I hold each failure close in order to learn better how to become a highly skilled antiracist educator of adults.

This experience led me to a re-envisioning of what highly effective antiracist education and professional development should be. Now I lead an antiracism leadership institute that changes the paradigm on ineffective, normative modes of professional development. I have recommitted to the work in a way that provides leaders with the holding environment to deepen their racial literacy, develop plans for self-improvement, T.A.M.E. their antiracist initiatives, and receive support when implementing antiracist initiatives in their organization. This approach has, and will continue to, help leaders develop the skill, will, and ability to do the work themselves and not to rely on outside providers to be the experts bringing the work in.

The renewed approach aligns to a quote I live by: "Be the change you wish to see in the world." I see far too many highly ineffective approaches to antiracism in schools that placate white liberals but don't create the necessary change. I am working every day to be the change that our students and teachers of Color desperately need.

REFERENCES

Anderson, C. (2016). *White rage: The unspoken truth of our racial divide*. Bloomsbury Publishing USA.

Benson, T. (2020). "The plague of performative anti-racism in education." *Medium*. https://traceybenson.medium.com/the-plague-of-performance-anti-racism-in -education-127ebd4d23a1

Benson, T., & Fiarman, S. (2019). *Unconscious bias in schools: A developmental approach to exploring race and racism*. Harvard Education Press.

DiAngelo, R. (2018). *White fragility: Why it's so hard for white people to talk about racism*. Beacon Press.

Heifetz, R., & Linsky, M. (2017). *Leadership on the line, with a new preface: Staying alive through the dangers of change*. Harvard Business Press.

McIntosh, P. (2007). White privilege: Unpacking the invisible knapsack. *Race, class, and gender in the United States: An integrated study*. https://psychology.umbc .edu/wp-content/uploads/sites/57/2016/10/White-Privilege_McIntosh-1989.pdf

Sullivan, S. (2014). *Good white people: The problem with middle-class white antiracism*. SUNY Press.

CHAPTER 7

"We Aren't Going There Today!"

Unpacking and Challenging White Liberalism, Racial Silence, and What Kids Are "Ready" for in the Early Childhood Classroom

Andréa C. Minkoff and Katherine Wood

"But what about police officers who shoot people of Color?"

A 3-year-old child in an early childhood education center in a metropolitan area in Southern California asked this question during a morning circle discussion on community helpers. The class had already discussed teachers, doctors, nurses, and firefighters, and had turned to law enforcement. In the face of ongoing police brutality and violence against communities of Color, the child asked an important question, one that he wanted to process with his learning community as he tried to engage in a meaning-making process around how police officers could be considered community helpers in the face of numerous reports of the loss of Black life at the hands of police. Instead of leaning in, meeting the child where he was, and engaging in a critical dialogue, the teacher simply responded, "We aren't going there today," silencing the child, and moving on.

The above scene took place in 2015 at an early childhood education center in Southern California. What could have been an extraordinary opportunity to engage a class of young learners in critical dialogue was lost when the teacher effectively dismissed and silenced the child who asked the question. We offer this vignette as a starting point to explore the ways elements of white liberalism, including racial silencing for the preservation of white racial comfort, contributes to the repression of critical conversations around issues of race and racism in early childhood contexts.

We begin by situating children's development and meaning-making processes around race within a context that privileges whiteness and normalizes anti-blackness. We then position early childhood educators as significant facilitators of children's development and unpack the literature on race, racism, and early childhood education. Then we turn our attention to the significance of white liberalism in the early childhood classroom, with specific attention on racial silence for the preservation of white comfort. In our analysis, we recognize the ways white liberalism in the classroom may reinforce problematic power dynamics and suppress student expressions of emotion discourse around race. Finally, we conclude by discussing ways to move forward by challenging white liberalism in early childhood education.

The opening vignette offers us a chance to explore children's developing understanding of issues of race and racism in context. Despite common beliefs that children are not developmentally ready to discuss complex issues of race at a young age, research informs us that children begin perceptually processing physical differences in infancy (Katz & Kofkin, 1997). Visual preference tasks suggest that 3-month-olds exhibit preferences for faces of their own race (Bar-Haim et al., 2006) and 9-month-olds are able to categorize faces according to race (Anzures et al., 2010). As children grow, racial differences shift from being perceptually salient to being psychologically salient (Bigler & Liben, 2007). By the time they enter preschool, most children have developed associations between racial groups and positive and negative traits (Dunham et al., 2013; Hirschfeld, 2008; Newheiser et al., 2014; Olson et al., 2012; Perszyk et al., 2019), and utilize those associations to make inferences about racial group members (Katz & Kofkin, 1997; Park, 2011). Further, by preschool, children are prepared to act on those associations through discriminatory practices, such as excluding peers from play activities, establishing dominance, and engaging in power negotiations on the playground (Feagin & van Ausdale, 2001).

Despite what research tells us about children's developing conceptualizations of race, adults often delay talking with children about race and racism because they underestimate children's abilities to understand (Sullivan et al., 2020). This is the case with parents or adults at home (Hughes & Chen, 1999) as well as educators (Kelly & Brooks, 2009). In this chapter, we focus on race in the early childhood classroom and consider the impact of this reluctance to engage in critical dialogue around race with young learners. If we refuse to engage children's inquiries and ideas, the silence results in the legitimization and maintenance of whiteness (Castagno, 2008) and a further normalization of anti-Blackness (Nxumalo & Ross, 2019). Additionally, discourses of presumed childhood innocence that prevent adults from engaging in critical conversations on race with young children often occur at the expense of children of Color, and Black children in particular (Bernstein, 2011).

WHITE LIBERALISM, WHITE FRAGILITY, AND RACIAL SILENCE

We engage critical race theory (CRT) (Ladson-Billings, 1998; Sleeter, 2016; Solorzano & Yosso, 2001) and critical whiteness studies (Aronson & Ashlee, 2018; Matias & Mackey, 2016) as explanatory frameworks for understanding the centrality of race and racism, as well as the emotional investment in whiteness, in schools and society. From a critical race and critical whiteness lens, we problematize and explore racial silence as a vehicle of white liberalism in early childhood contexts. In unpacking the mechanisms behind implicit racial silence, we turn to the literature on white fragility, a response elicited by even minimal amounts of racial stress (DiAngelo, 2018). According to DiAngelo (2018):

> Though white fragility is triggered by discomfort and anxiety, it is born of superiority and entitlement. White fragility is not weakness, per se. In fact, it is a powerful means of white racial control and the protection of white advantage. (p. 20)

Working from this definition, we position white fragility as a state that has the potential to ignite reactionary silencing of those who disrupt white racial comfort (DiAngelo, 2018). White fragility can be triggered in a number of situations, including transgressing white taboos of talking openly about racism, undermining white solidarity, challenging white racial innocence, and countless other conditions that invoke a sense of racial stress for dominant group members (DiAngelo, 2018).

In our opening vignette, the question "But what about police officers who shoot people of Color?" activated white fragility in the teacher by challenging the white taboo of engaging in critical dialogue on race in a public space. The question about police brutality toward people of Color was probably especially emotionally provoking for the teacher if she did not anticipate that a young learner in her class would frame law enforcement as anything other than community helpers. Thus, feeling that the critical inquiry by the student set off the potential for racial stress, the teacher reactively silenced the conversation with her response, "We aren't going there today," to restore (white) comfort at the expense of the young learners in the class. Instead of engaging in a collective process of critical inquiry and opening the possibility for dialogue, it was made clear that questions that explored racialized dynamics of power and privilege were not welcome within the white liberal discourse of the preschool classroom (Zembylas, 2013).

Not only does this type of racial silencing deny the reality of systemic violence against communities of Color, it also contributes to the creation of classroom spaces where "the pain [of] people of Color is still secondary to the discomfort to whites" (Matias, 2016, p. 203). In exploring the emotional frameworks that undergird the maintenance of whiteness in educational spaces, we argue that white fragility (DiAngelo, 2018) is a marker of white liberal thought that results in the repression of critical conversations around issues of race and racism in early childhood contexts.

WHITE LIBERAL RACIAL SILENCING IN THE EARLY CHILDHOOD CLASSROOM

Early childhood learning environments may be particularly susceptible to white liberal racial silencing due to reductionist ideas about the types of topics with which children are developmentally ready to engage. In reflecting upon the dominance of Piagetian thought on the development of early childhood curricula and pedagogies, Ramsey (2004) states:

> Many principles of early childhood education (and by extension parent education) are based on the theories of Jean Piaget, who provided some wonderful insights into how children's thinking changes as they get older. However, child developmentalists and early childhood educators—certainly including myself—have traditionally focused on children's cognitive limitations at each stage. (p. 29)

Ramsey (2004) goes on to problematize deficit discourses about children's capabilities, asserting that "foregrounding children's cognitive limitations may provide an excuse to avoid difficult and complex issues" (p. 29). While sociocultural (Park, 2011; Vygotsky, 1978) and sociocritical perspectives (Gutiérrez, 2008; Gutiérrez & Rogoff, 2003) on development offer more contextual perspectives on the meanings that children attach to race and racism as they learn and grow, it is still important to grapple with ways the paradigms to which educators subscribe reinforce or challenge false ideas of children's racial innocence.

It is also important to attend to the ways teacher enactments of racial silence reinforce problematic power dynamics within the classroom. By saying "We aren't going there today," the teacher chose to suppress what could be framed as curious, emotional discourse regarding police brutality from students, thus establishing and reinforcing hierarchical classroom power relations (Chubbuck & Zembylas, 2008). Consequently, this establishes norms for the classroom in which the teacher controls emotional reactions, beliefs, and actions (Zembylas, 2007). This results in a division that embraces those with similar emotional reactions and excludes those who do not feel comfortable within the white liberal norm (Chubbuck & Zembylas, 2008). In this instance, those who exhibited white fragility or a negative emotional reaction due to the conversation regarding police brutality would automatically become members of a specific emotional category. By asserting dominance and attempting to manage the emotional energy of her students, the teacher's actions encourage students to navigate the space in ways that are consistent with white liberalism by engaging in racial silence.

The norms established in this interaction reinforce white liberalism by suggesting that conversations that trigger racial anxiety do not belong in the early childhood classroom. White liberal racial silence situates the emotional needs of students of Color and critically conscious students as the lowest priority in the classroom and sets the stage for emotional resources such as support, solidarity, patience, and trust, to be bestowed upon students who subscribe to the same white liberal norm. This emotional capital manifests into resources that students can use to mobilize, boost confidence, improve relationships in the classroom, and much more (Zembylas, 2007). The hidden curriculum of navigating emotion rules and categorizations perpetuate white liberalism in preschool classrooms.

White liberalism is so deeply ingrained in early childhood schooling that it may go unnoticed by white teachers and students, as well as teachers and students who embrace ideologies of whiteness, despite the detrimental effects it has on students and teachers of Color (Matias & Mackey, 2016). Further, practices like racial silence that reinforce white liberalism enable teachers who experience racial anxiety to stifle critical dialogue and think they are engaging developmentally appropriate practice when, in fact, these practices intensify inequality and mask whiteness (Grinage, 2020). If educators want to enact transformative and equitable teaching strategies, they must actively acknowledge the privileges associated with whiteness and make antiracism, not non-racism, a continuous practice in the classroom. This begins, but does not end, with critical reflection on being a social justice change agent in and out of school contexts (Gorski & Dalton, 2020).

Emotions and their outward representations play a subtle yet powerful role in the classroom. Enacting socially just and critical teaching can unknowingly induce overwhelming emotions for an educator, which range from passion and excitement to disillusionment, anger, and fear (Chubbuck & Zembylas, 2008). As stated earlier, these emotions are projected as real and tangible investments or divestments toward students of Color in the form of emotional capital (Zembylas, 2007). Educators must closely examine their own emotions to better express themselves and provide equitable investments in their students. Ongoing emotional examinations can expose hidden personal biases and privileges that aid individuals in enacting transformative resistance.

Keeping a journal with daily reflections on emotional encounters that trigger racial anxiety may be helpful throughout this process. Here, an educator can point out each instance in which powerful emotions surrounding race emerged in the classroom and reflect on their reaction, as well as the impact their reaction had on students. Utilizing a case analysis process (Gorski & Pothini, 2014), one may critically reflect on how to better manage their emotional triggers around race and consider short- and long-term responses and policy and practice adjustments to encourage accountability to action.

CHALLENGING WHITE LIBERALISM, RACIAL SILENCE, AND WHAT KIDS ARE "READY" FOR IN THE EARLY CHILDHOOD CLASSROOM

Critical emotional reflection is an important first step toward disrupting the fragility that gives way to white liberalism. That being said, reflection in and of itself is not enough. Teachers need to be accountable for their own emotions and impact when it comes to engaging in and disengaging from race in the early childhood classroom. Dismantling white supremacy cannot be dependent solely on students and educators of Color (Matias & Mackey, 2016). White teachers must utilize their privilege, not as white saviors but as accomplices to stand in disruptive solidarity with fellow educators and students of Color (Jackson, 2018). Without consistent critical reflection combined with active and continuous opposition to injustice, early childhood educators may sustain the current hegemony of whiteness and white liberal practices (Hyland, 2010).

In addition to reflecting upon one's own fragility and the ways it may pave way for white liberalism to take hold in the classroom, early childhood educators must also reflect upon and unlearn many of the ways they have been socialized to think about children in both schools and society. Souto-Manning and colleagues (2019) assert:

> These critiques [of the limitations of child development theories] and related findings point to the need for the field of child development to more fully interrogate the theoretical centrality of Whiteness to its conceptualizations of developmental appropriateness or quality teaching practices and to (re)position the linguistic and cultural assets of intersectionally minoritized communities foundationally in and through early childhood teaching. (p. 264)

This push to de-center whiteness creates space for the voices, experiences, histories, and inquiries of children, families, and communities that have been marginalized from the white liberal discourse of the early childhood classroom (Souto-Manning et al., 2019). As a way to "(re)center quality away from dominant norms" (Souto-Manning & Rabadi-Raol, 2018, p. 217), early childhood educators must be mindful of how power and privilege manifest in both schools and society, and actively work to challenge them.

A shift like this requires "going there" in response to critical inquiries about issues of race and racism instead of engaging white liberal practices, such as racial silencing, that promote white comfort at the expense of children of Color. We must create classroom environments where children can authentically be in community, ask critical questions about social and racial inequities, and challenge dominant perspectives to create more racially just classrooms for young learners.

REFERENCES

Anzures, G., Quinn, P. C., Pascalis, O., Slater, A. M., & Lee, K. (2010). Categorization, categorical perception, and asymmetry in infants' representation of face race. *Developmental Science*, *13*(4), 553–564. https://doi.org/10.1111/j.1467-7687.2009.00900.x

Aronson, B. A., & Ashlee, K. (2018). Holding onto dread and hope: The need for critical whiteness studies in education as resistance in the Trump era. *Journal of Critical Scholarship on Higher Education and Student Affairs*, *3*(3), Article 8.

Bar-Haim, Y., Ziv, T., Lamy, D., & Hodes, R. M. (2006). Nature and nurture in own-race face processing. *Psychological Science*, *17*(2), 159–163. https://doi.org/10.1111/j.1467-9280.2006.01679.x

Bernstein, R. (2011). *Racial innocence : Performing American childhood from slavery to civil rights*. New York University Press.

Bigler, R. S., & Liben, L. S. (2007). Developmental intergroup theory: Explaining and reducing children's social stereotyping and prejudice. *Current Directions in Psychological Science*, *16*(3), 162–166. https://doi.org/10.1111/j.1467-8721.2007.00496.x

Castagno, A. E. (2008). "I don't want to hear that!": Legitimating whiteness through silence in schools. *Anthropology & Education Quarterly*, *39*(3), 314–333. https://doi.org/10.1111/j.1548-1492.2008.00024.x

Chubbuck, S. M., & Zembylas, M. (2008). The emotional ambivalence of socially just teaching: A case study of a novice urban schoolteacher. *American Educational Research Journal*, *45*(2), 274–318. https://doi.org/10.3102/0002831207311586

DiAngelo, R. J. (2018). *White fragility: Why it's so hard for white people to talk about racism*. Beacon Press.

Dunham, Y., Chen, E. E., & Banaji, M. R. (2013). Two signatures of implicit intergroup attitudes: Developmental invariance and early enculturation. *Psychological Science*, *24*(6), 860–868. https://doi.org/10.1177/0956797612463081

Feagin, J. R., & van Ausdale, D. (2001). *The first R: How children learn race and racism*. Rowman & Littlefield.

Gorski, P. C. (2011, December 30). Complicating "white privilege." www.counterpunch.org/2011/12/30/complicating-white-privilege

Gorski, P. C., & Dalton, K. (2020). Striving for critical reflection in multicultural and social justice teacher education: Introducing a typology of reflection approaches. *Journal of Teacher Education*, *71*(3), 357–368. https://doi.org/10.1177/0022487119883545

Gorski, P. C., & Pothini, S. G. (2014). *Case studies on diversity and social justice education*. Routledge.

Grinage, J. (2020). Singing and dancing for diversity: Neoliberal multiculturalism and white epistemological ignorance in teacher professional development. *Curriculum Inquiry, 50*(1), 7–27. https://doi.org/10.1080/03626784.2020.1754114

Gutiérrez, K. D. (2008). Developing a sociocritical literacy in the third space. *Reading Research Quarterly, 43*(2), 148–164. https://doi.org/10.1598/RRQ.43.2.3

Gutiérrez, K. D., & Rogoff, B. (2003). Cultural ways of learning: Individual traits or repertoires of practice. *Educational Researcher, 32*(5), 19–25. https://doi.org/10.3102/0013189X032005019

Hirschfeld, L. A. (2008). Children's developing conceptions of race. In S. M. Quintana & C. McKown (Eds.), *Handbook of race, racism, and the developing child* (pp. 37–54). John Wiley & Sons.

Hughes, D., & Chen, L. (1999). The nature of parents' race-related communications to children: A developmental perspective. In L. Balter & C. S. Tamis-LeMonda (Eds.), *Child psychology: A handbook of contemporary issues* (pp. 467–490). Psychology Press.

Hyland, N. (2010). Social justice in early childhood classrooms: What the research tells us. *Young Children, 65*(1), 82–90.

Jackson, T. A. (2018). We don't want no trouble: Inspiring white accomplices and solidarity in the age of all lives matter. In K. J. Fasching-Varner, K. J. Tobin, & S. M. Lentz (Eds.), *#BRokenPromises, Black deaths, and blue ribbons: Understanding, complicating, and transcending police-community violence.* (pp. 67–70). Brill | Sense. https://doi.org/10.1163/9789004378735_017

Katz, P. A., & Kofkin, J. A. (1997). Race, gender, and young children. In S. S. Luthar, J. A. Burack, D. Cicchetti, & J. R. Weisz (Eds.), *Developmental psychopathology: Perspectives on adjustment, risk, and disorder* (pp. 51–74). Cambridge University Press.

Kelly, D. M., & Brooks, M. (2009). How young is too young? Exploring teachers' assumptions about young children and teaching for social justice. *Equity & Excellence in Education 42*(2), 202–216. https://doi.org/10.1080/10665680902739683

Ladson-Billings, G. (1998). Just what is critical race theory and what's it doing in a nice field like education? *International Journal of Qualitative Studies in Education, 11*(1), 7–24. https://doi.org/10.1080/095183998236863

Matias, C. E. (2016). "Why do you make me hate myself?": Re-teaching whiteness, abuse, and love in urban teacher education. *Teaching Education, 27*(2), 194–211, https://doi.org/10.1080/10476210.2015.1068749

Matias, C. E., & Mackey, J. (2016). Breakin' down whiteness in antiracist teaching: Introducing critical whiteness pedagogy. *The Urban Review, 48*(1), 32–50. https://doi.org/10.1007/s11256-015-0344-7

Newheiser, A. K., Dunham, Y., Merrill, A., Hoosain, L., & Olson, K. R. (2014). Preference for high status predicts implicit outgroup bias among children from low-status groups. *Developmental Psychology, 50*, 1081–1090. http://dx.doi.org/10.1037/a0035054

Nxumalo, F., & Ross, K. M. (2019). Envisioning Black space in environmental education for young children. *Race Ethnicity and Education, 22*(4), 502–524. https://doi.org/10.1080/13613324.2019.1592837

Olson, K. R., Shutts, K., Kinzler, K. D., & Weisman, K. G. (2012). Children associate racial groups with wealth: Evidence from South Africa. *Child Development*, *83*(6), 1884–1899. https://doi.org/10.1111/j.1467-8624.2012.01819.x

Park, C. C. (2011). Young children make sense of racial and ethnic differences: A sociocultural approach. *American Educational Research Journal, 48*(2), 387–420. https://doi.org/10.3102/0002831210382889

Perszyk, D. R., Lei, R. F., Bodenhausen, G. V., Richeson, J. A., & Waxman, S. R. (2019). Bias at the intersection of race and gender: Evidence from preschool-aged children. *Developmental Science, 22*(3), e12788. https://doi.org/10.1111/desc.12788

Piaget, J. (1951/2013). *Sociological Studies*. Routledge.

Piaget, J., & Inhelder, B. (1966). *La psychologic de l'enfant*. Presses Universitaires de France.

Ramsey, P. G. (2004). *Teaching and learning in a diverse world: Multicultural education for young children* (3rd ed.). Teachers College Press.

Sleeter, C. E. (2016). Critical race theory and the whiteness of teacher education. *Urban Education, 52*(2), 155–169. https://doi.org/10.1177/0042085916668957

Solorzano, D. G., & Yosso, T. J. (2001). From racial stereotyping and deficit discourse toward a critical race theory in teacher education. *Multicultural Education, 9*(1), 2–8.

Souto-Manning, M., Falk, B., López, D., Cruz, L. B., Bradt, N., Cardwell, N., McGowan, N., Perez, A., Rabadi-Raol, A., & Rollins, E. (2019). A transdisciplinary approach to equitable teaching in early childhood education. *Review of Research in Education, 43*(1), 249–276. https://doi.org/10.3102/0091732X18821122

Souto-Manning, M., & Rabadi-Raol, A. (2018). (Re)centering quality in early childhood education: Toward intersectional justice for minoritized children. *Review of Research in Education, 42*(1), 203–225. https://doi.org/10.3102/0091732X18759550

Sullivan, J., Wilton, L., & Apfelbaum, E. P. (2020). Adults delay conversations about race because they underestimate children's processing of race. *Journal of Experimental Psychology: General, 150*(2), 395–400. http://dx.doi.org/10.1037/xge0000851

Vygotsky, L. S. (1978). *Mind in society: The development of higher psychological processes*. Edited by M. Cole, V. John-Steiner, S. Scribner, & E. Souberman. Harvard University Press.

Zembylas, M. (2007). Emotional capital and education: Theoretical insights from Bourdieu. *British Journal of Educational Studies, 55*(4), 443–463. https://doi.org/10.1111/j.1467-8527.2007.00390.x

Zembylas, M. (2013). Critical pedagogy and emotion: Working through "troubled knowledge" in posttraumatic contexts. *Critical Studies in Education, 54*(2), 176–189.

WHITE LIBERALISM IN CURRICULUM AND INSTRUCTION

CHAPTER 8

White Teachers' Black Historical Consciousness

Can We Teach Black History?

Brianne Pitts, Daniel Tulino, and Greg Simmons

So, when you want to know good white folks in history where Black people are concerned, go read the history of John Brown. That was what I call a "white liberal." But those other kinds, they are questionable.

—Malcolm X

CAN "GOOD" WHITE LIBERALS TEACH BLACK HISTORY?

Within Malcolm X's concept of who are "good" white[1] liberals of history—the "race traitor" John Brown, abolitionists Lucretia Mott and William Lloyd Garrison, the Weather Underground—where do we, the authors of this article and educators of children, position ourselves? Have we been the "questionable" ones in our teaching of Black history without addressing the impacts of its inherent whitewashed narratives? As three white scholars—two social studies educators and one ELA professor—our experiences with racism against people of Color and the racially oppressive systems that sustain it are impacted by our own whiteness. Our collective years of teaching Black history have found us questioning both systems of power and individual practices in schooling. Yet, is it enough to simply question? How can we act as "good white liberals" in the realm of education, let alone the world?

While we recognize limitations in our perspectives, we argue in this chapter for using the tool of Black Historical Consciousness (BHC) (King, 2020) to confront the consequences of racism and oppression within U.S. public school instruction. In the act of writing this chapter we challenge our own (and others') white liberal practices in teaching Black history in U.S. schools, implementing the critical lens of BHC to highlight the potential for transformative educational experiences.

Using our own experiences, we explore how we grapple with white liberalism in Black history instruction, and attempt to remediate its impacts through a BHC framework espoused by LaGarrett King (2020) that conceptualizes Black history instruction as a means to challenge assumption. King does not assert that BHC will *ipso facto* disrupt white liberalism; instead, he presents it as a lens through which to understand the richness of Black humanity so often excised from (white) school instruction. As a catalyst, BHC themes and principles confront white liberalism via a critical analysis of Black history instruction, revealing the many perspectives from which all students will benefit.

PURPOSE AND DEFINITIONS

The white middle-class background from which most U.S. teachers (NCES, 2019) hail compounds the ignorance of their miseducation (Woodson, 1933/1998) and racial isolation. Such miseducation is manifest as the "hidden curriculum of whiteness" (Matias, 2016, p. 7) across all subjects, but perhaps especially in that of Black history, wherein subjective evaluations are based on Eurocentric perspectives. The resulting texts and teaching materials provided to teachers for Black history instruction, which currently exists in the national curriculum as a one-month segment, exacerbate an already whitewashed topic. Therefore, to teach a more accurate Black history, our nation's teachers must delve into territories many of us who are white have not yet explored: Black pain, resistance, culture, and joy.

As Dagbovie (2018) posits, "A major challenge . . . revolves around how K–12 educators decide to handle Black History Month and approach the study of African American life during the school year" (p. 75). While Black History Month is widely accepted as a part of the instructional canon, in our years of teaching the subject, we've found the experiences of people of Color in Black history instruction as routinely absent in K–12 classrooms while white teachers assume the role of white ally through interpreting the subject through their own eyes. For example, many white educators appear to feel their allyship is attained through simply hashtagging #BlackLivesMatter. In the context of "living in the afterlives of slavery, sitting in the room with history, in a lived and undeclared state of emergency" (Sharpe, 2016, p. 100), such "liberal" non-action perpetuates prevailing racism by failing to disrupt the status quo. As white teachers we need to reach beyond the hashtag, so to speak, and center Black voices in Black history instruction.

Consider Mills's (2017) definition of "white liberalism":

> White liberalism is the actual liberalism that has been historically dominant since modernity: a liberal theory whose terms originally restricted full personhood to whites (or, more accurately, white men) and relegated non-whites to an inferior

> category, so that his schedule of rights and prescriptions for justice were all color-coded. (p. 31)

Ergo, left unchecked, white liberalism can permeate the instruction of Black history by people who are socialized by Eurocentrically dominated school systems. We might call white liberal obfuscation of the Black historical record "dysconscious racism," which is defined by Joyce King (1991) as "a form of racism that tacitly accepts dominant white norms and privileges" (p. 133). This acceptance not only fails to reorient "palatable" instruction, it silences the resistance, power, and joy infused in the Black historical record. As white liberalism is understood in the context of both dysconscious and overt racism, so must be frameworks designed to disrupt it. LaGarrett King's (2020) BHC tool can play a role by (de)radicalizing the traumatic histories of people of Color and centering them in the instruction of Black history.

Again, we look to the scholarship of King (2020), who details the impacts of a "white epistemic logic" in Black history wherein white teachers' versions of the subject are

> predicated on how white people wish to see or imagine Black people to be through history education. They represent an effort to sanitize the ugliness, diminish achievements and contribution, ignore the diversity of Blackness, and pigeonhole Black people as monolithic in an effort to continue to empower, not offend, or assuage white people about America's legacy. (p. 337)

Without grounding Black history in a Black epistemic framework, dysconscious racism remains, protecting a white-washed normative Black history narrative. By positioning the feelings of white people above the truth of Black people, these narratives become examples of "educative psychic violence" wherein predominant white narratives of Black history, and slavery in particular, are enacted in reductive ways that negate the humanity of Black people (King & Woodson, 2017).

The concepts of educative psychic violence, dysconscious racism, and white liberal Black history are not synonymous, but they are intricately entwined. Love (2019) explains:

> Racism is not exclusive to one political party or particular type of white person. White, well-meaning, liberal teachers can be racist too. Therefore, understanding how racism works and understanding how white privilege functions within our society does not bring us any closer to justice, and it certainly does not undo educational survival complex. Knowing these truths is the first step to justice, but it's only a start. (p. 51)

BHC moves teachers from naively enacting a white liberal Black history to actively redirecting the narrative to a Black perspective. It engages teachers in discussions beyond white liberal retellings of Black heroes and heroines; recognizes the power, humanity, and liberatory dreams of Black communities in the United States; and offers a fuller understanding of the complexity of the African Diaspora, Black enslavement, and the protracted racism levied against Black people.

EXAMPLES IN PRACTICE

When a white liberal version of Black history does address Black pain and suffering, it is often silent on Black agency. Likewise, in failing to provide a Black-centered view of this history, we perpetuate both the failed narrative *and* our own racism. For many white teachers, the reluctance to truly examine this phenomenon relates to the fact that we are hard pressed to unlearn the heroic stories in our own Black history education. Yet, as educators, we must come to realize that failing to interrupt whitewashed Black history pushes Black humanity further into the margins, perpetuates the inaccurate portrayals that limit all students' perceptions, and omits truer stories of heroism, resolve, and antiracist successes. If white educators do not take up this challenge, then we perpetuate violent historical misrepresentation.

To understand how a white liberal Black history manifests in the classroom, consider the words of Mrs. Evans, a white elementary teacher:

> We did a Black history program two years ago that was pretty fun, but I think we talked basically about the "Core" of, like, Dr. King and Jackie Robinson. To be honest, I don't know a lot beyond the standard Black History Month people. Just 'cause I am white and I grew up in white middle-class suburbia. (Pitts, 2020)

Author Brianne Pitts remembers offering similarly simplistic instruction when teaching Black history in her own classrooms, focusing on admirable men and women without addressing the systemic oppression and racism that necessitated their actions. These monolithic narratives occur when teaching a person or an idea rather than a movement or system; examples include learning about Malcolm X as an anti-white Black Nationalist, Rosa Parks as a tired seamstress, and Dr. Martin Luther King Jr. as a pacifist preacher. These one-dimensional presentations fail to connect to the broader intersections and contexts of Blackness, the African Diaspora, and institutionalized socioeconomic disparities, racial profiling, and other forms of racial oppression.

To challenge this whitewashed version of Black history, we call on all teachers to implement BHC by exploring King's (2020) six central themes. Engaging students in discussions of (1) *systematic Black oppression* and the ongoing violence Black people experience will promulgate a connection to (2) *Black agency, resistance, and perseverance* (King 2020). Instruction must incorporate a focus on the (3) *African Diaspora*, wherein millions of Africans were sold into slavery for the economic benefit of European countries' western colonies, which will elicit students' understanding of (4) *Black identities and experiences* in a context beyond white-washed heroism, a context that includes (5) *Black pain and contention*, but also (6) *Black joy*.

FROM BHM TO BHC

During February, many teachers expose their middle school students to the "hard history" of the slave trade and the Jim Crow era through the construct of "Black History Month." At its introduction to the U.S. curriculum in the 1970s, Black History Month was considered a tool by which to "uplift" Black students by providing them role models to which to aspire. When this is done through a white liberal perspective, it's also infused with white saviorism, perhaps less naively sustaining white authority. For example, Mrs. Evans explains why her "Core" Black history instruction was "beneficial": "I'm not saying it's just African American kids, but a lot of [the students] have not the greatest role models, so seeing that they can do something good with their lives is good too" (Pitts, 2020). Mrs. Evans names the "white savior" perspective that many white teachers perpetuate: by teaching Black history because "they need it," or focusing attention on the white heroes in Black history, or celebrating the "right" (i.e., nonviolent or integrationist) way versus a "wrong" (i.e., violent or nationalist) way of advocating for Black freedoms, the Black historical record has been revised to ensure white safety, white ideals, white saviorism. This saviorism manifests on two levels: white teachers as all-knowing given their status of power over students, and white teachers bestowing heroes onto their students.

BHC realigns this approach to center Black experience. Texts like *From Slaveship to Freedom Road* (Lester & Brown, 1998) and videos such as *The African Americans: Many Rivers to Cross* (Gates & Yacovone, 2013) can be effective BHC tools in exposing all students to Black voices.

But educators must also specifically consider the impact these resources have on their Black students; although they are important to their students' sociopolitical development, the inclusion of these resources could speak of the horrific events affecting Black people today. So, while centering Black voices is important, a balance between Black people's struggles with oppression in history and "Black agency and resistance" (King, 2020) is important, too. Author Dan Tulino (2021) faced this problem during his time teaching middle school. For many years he focused on "exposing" his students to the horrors that not only impacted many of his students' ancestors but also unearthed many of the oppressive forces impacting their present lives. Although making these connections between history and the present conditions was an important aspect of teaching through BHC, he also needed to make room to showcase stories and examples of Black agency, Black resistance, and Black joy. After reflecting on his practice and finding support, Tulino created a more Black-centered curriculum based on the writings of James Baldwin, Frantz Fanon, bell hooks, and others.

Tulino (2021) recounts witnessing one middle school social studies teacher engage in reflective practice by asking questions of himself and his 8th-graders, questions that required more than names and dates. The teacher, Mr. Devers, who was a white man, acknowledged to his students, who were racially diverse, his complicity in what he described as the "residue" of U.S. history, those problematic moments that continue to negatively affect our social fabric. Mr. Devers allowed his students to see him as complex and vulnerable. Meanwhile, his use of Black perspectives on topics such as slavery, Reconstruction, and the Civil Rights Movement, and the connections he made to present-day racism and oppression, enabled them to understand Black history more deeply. Devers and his students engaged in dialogue and critical literacy (Freire, 1970/1996; Shor, 1999) wherein the students and teacher learned together about how best to approach and disrupt forms of systematic racism, such as mass incarceration, police violence, and the wage gap. Through the lens of BHC, these 8th-graders were given the opportunity to explore their own identities, whatever their racial identities, in relation to one another, to their actively learning teachers, and to U.S. society at large.

Use of BHC through the themes of Black identity and the African Diaspora (King, 2020) will protect against white saviorism and help ensure a Black-centered Black history. This approach to Black history begins at and extends from the African continent, highlighting the intersectionality of Black people and Black experiences through multiple Black voices and points of view.

Certainly, white people using the BHC themes can expect to feel uncomfortable; this is part of the BHC process and ultimate success. Using a BHC outline enables teachers to assess white responsibility and idealism in equal parts, to choose more relevant content from truer voices, and to more effectively teach Black history. Regardless of white discomfort, however, our vulnerability as white educators teaching a more appropriate Black history pales in light of the impact the white liberal Black history curriculum might have on Black students. Unintentional or not, we, as white teachers, perpetuate racism when we fail to teach liberatory Black history.

ENACTING THE BHC FRAMEWORK

Table 8.1 outlines the six BHC themes that redirect white liberal pedagogies, offering solutions for how to confront and reframe Black history instruction.

To answer our question, *Can white liberal educators teach Black history?*, we reply, "Yes, but with several important caveats." Before white

Table 8.1. Confronting White Liberalism through Black Historical Consciousness (King, 2020)

White Liberal Approach to Black History	Themes of Black Historical Consciousness
Recognize this sanitized history as "happy" stories of heroes and heroines (King, 2018) who triumph over challenge. Instruction focuses on "safe" topics and individuals, failing to name racism as a significant factor.	1. **Power and Oppression:** Center the lack of justice, freedom, equality, and equity Black people experience. Examine how Black people have been victims of racism and white supremacy, as well as of individual actions.

Confront white liberalism as Mills (2017) suggests, using a model that "registers rather than obfuscates the non-ideal history of white oppression and racial exploitation" (p. 36). Using BHC to engage in discussions of systematic Black oppression and continued white responsibility, teachers can own the miseducation they likely experienced and commit to learning about Black history beyond what they were taught as a child.

Recognize that the narratives of subjugation, enslavement, and traumatic experiences are passive and do not focus on agency.	2. **Black Agency, Resistance, and Perseverance** are Black histories that show how, although Black people have been oppressed, they are not one-dimensional victims.

Confront white liberal Black history by recounting instances of Black agency, resistance, and perseverance in every time period because "history tells us that dark folx's humanity is dependent on how much they disobey and fight for justice" (Love, 2019, p. 71).

Recognize that white liberal approaches to Black history are limited to a North American viewpoint, failing to acknowledge global and ancestral contexts.	3. **Incorporating Africa and the African Diaspora** contextualizes the narratives of Black people within the horrors of losing homeland and family, and being stolen, sold, and enslaved.

Confront the white liberal view by exploring Black histories that begin and extend from the African continent, contextualizing Black experiences historically and globally.

Recognize that focusing on Black pain and suffering reinforces "always already weaponized Black bodies" (Sharpe, 2016).	4. **Black Joy** consists of narratives that focus on Black people's resolve, endurance, and triumph.

Confront assumed norms with BHC and teach Black history through and with Black joy. Build on the joy in students' lives, inviting the diversity of Black joy.

Recognize liberal white pedagogy as monolithic narratives and singular experiences that fail to consider intersectional perspectives of Black history.	5. **Black Identities** comprises a focus on a more inclusive history, one that uncovers the multiple identities of Black people through Black history.

(continued)

Table 8.1. (continued)

Confront with BHC through inclusion of multiple Black voices, experiences, and points of view, using texts by Black people.

Recognize that whitewashed Black history shies away from difficult histories, especially those suggesting white people's responsibility in the present.	6. **Black Historical Contention** is the recognition that all Black histories are not positive; they are complex and difficult, yet should not be ignored because they are part of the history writ large.

Confront with BHC by teaching complex Black histories, even the hard parts, and owning the benefits white liberals gain from a white supremacist society.

educators engage in attempts to help revise this entrenched project, they must look inward to confront their own whiteness and racialized belief systems. This is difficult and uncomfortable work. White teachers need to be conscious about their identities and positionalities in the classroom, while fostering an atmosphere of community, openness, and safety in grappling with issues like white supremacy, racism, and other forms of oppression revealed in the teaching of Black history. Love (2019) suggests these "abolitionist teachers must process and respond in some meaningful way to the lives of our students and their own lives as well" (p. 125). Before becoming experts of Black historical content, they first need to be experts on their own racial experiences and be willing to share their understanding of them with their students.

Second, once a white teacher's eyes are open to how white liberal ideologies impact schooling, they need to reconsider *what* they teach as Black history and *how* they do so. As King (2020) points out, Black history cannot be a "traditional history course in 'Blackface'" (p. 340). Pedagogical approaches to Black history should center Black experiences and include depth that transcends Eurocentric visions of history instruction.

Third, with a particular emphasis on how Black history content is taught, white teachers must teach *through* Black folks, not merely *about* Black folks (King, 2017). Teachers of Black history must use resources by Black people so that Black human experiences are expressed by Black voices.

Last, we remind all white teachers that developing a better Black history curriculum is an iterative process. Teachers must remain students of and connected to Black history as they continue to learn, grow, and develop capacities that positively impact their knowledge of the subject. For white teachers, this "continuing education" needs to be built upon the excavation of their own inherent assumptions about race and white supremacy.

The enormity of national, state, district, and school directives that mandate what, how, and when teachers teach adds an even heavier burden to this work, especially when, in our experience, very few teachers receive formal training on how to teach and learn Black history. This is where teacher education and professional development can pave a road to a better Black history curriculum. Some examples already exist of quality of this programming for teachers. The annual conference by the Carter Center for K–12 Black History Education is a prime example of how educational researchers, teachers, students, administrators, activists, and community leaders are coming together to provide rich and substantial resources. The continuous practice of learning new pedagogical approaches to Black history and engaging in critical self-analysis is necessary for the growth of practicing and developing teachers, particularly and importantly for those who are white.

CONCLUSION

To end his biography of John Brown, the preeminent scholar of Black history W.E.B. Du Bois (1909) noted that Brown's life and actions had significant value in the modern age, and that "the cost of liberty is less than the price of repression" (p. 287). Through Brown's example, Du Bois demonstrated that the United States, vis-a-vis white liberalism, has been more willing to pay the cost of racism than the cost of freedom for Black people. The legacy of Black history reveals how entrenched racial oppression and white supremacy are in U.S. educational programs and institutions. Brown literally armed himself to pay the cost of Black freedom. As educators, we likewise need to equip ourselves in the fight for racial justice; we just need better tools such as a Black historical consciousness that bring to the fore the truer realities of the battle we are fighting.

White educators must be willing to conspire in an intellectual, pedagogical, and ontological rebellion against the white liberal version of Black history. They must step outside of themselves to understand how their racialized identities impact their work in the classroom. By adopting a BHC, these teachers will be better able to teach Black history by understanding that "what is historically significant to white people may not be historically significant to Black people" (King, 2017).

REFERENCES

Dagbovie, P. G. (2018). *Reclaiming the Black past: The use and misuse of African American history in the twenty-first century*. Verso.

Du Bois, W. E. B. (1909). *John Brown*. Jacobs & Company.

Freire, P. (1970/1996). *Pedagogy of the oppressed*. Continuum.

Gates, H. L., & Yacovone, D. (2013). *The African Americans: Many rivers to cross*. Smiley.

King, J. E. (1991). Dysconscious racism: Ideology, identity, and the mis-education of teachers. *Journal of Negro Education*, 60(2), 133–146.

King, L. J. (2017). The status of Black history in U.S. schools and society. *Social Education, 81*(1): 14–18

King, L. J. (2018). Interpreting Black history: Toward a Black history framework for teacher education. *Urban Education, 54*(3), 1–29.

King, L. J. (2020). Black history is not American history: Toward a framework of Black historical consciousness. *Social Education, 84*(6), 335–341.

King, L. J, & Woodson, A. (2017). Baskets of cotton and birthday cakes: Teaching slavery in social studies classrooms. *Social Studies Education Review, 6*(1), 1–18.

Lester, J., & Brown, R. (1998). *From slave ship to freedom road.* Dial Books.

Love, B. L. (2019). *We want to do more than survive: Abolitionist teaching and the pursuit of educational freedom.* Beacon.

Matias, C. E. (2016) *Feeling white: Whiteness, emotionality, and education.* Sense.

Mills, C. (2017). *Black rights/White wrongs: The critique of racial liberalism.* Oxford.

National Center for Education Statistics (NCES) (2019). *Status and trends in education of racial and ethnic groups: Indicator 6: Elementary and secondary enrollment.* https://nces.ed.gov/programs/raceindicators/indicator_rbb.asp

Pitts, B. R. (2020). *Black History month in suburban schools: An examination of K–12 pedagogies* (Publication No. 27964129). [Doctoral Thesis, University of Wisconsin Madison]. ProQuest.

Sharpe, C. (2016). *In the wake: On Blackness and being.* Duke University Press.

Shor, I. (1999). What is critical literacy? *The Journal of Pedagogy, Pluralism and Practice, 1*(4).

Tulino, D. (2021). "Embracing the kaleidoscope: Four teachers' journeys toward sociopolitical development." *Theses and Dissertations.* 2876. https://rdw.rowan.edu/etd/2876

Woodson, C. G. (1933/1998). *The mis-education of the Negro.* Africa World Press.

CHAPTER 9

Overpromising and Underdelivering
White Liberal Narratives in Arts Education

Alina Campana and Amelia M. Kraehe

The art world is a bastion of white liberalism. Whether in art museums or commercial galleries, symphonic concert halls or popular music productions, on Broadway or in Hollywood, whiteness functions as an invisible yet dominant framework for the arts. When schools incorporate the arts, it is often part of a strategy of inclusion that stems from the notion that the arts are inherently good. Among progressive educators working with Black and Brown students, the arts hold the power and promise of elevating those students intellectually, culturally, and emotionally. This promise of the arts is persuasive because it appeals to white liberalism in ways that we explore in this chapter. Specifically, we show how white liberal narratives seem to promise educational and social progress, but actually mediate curricular and pedagogic decision making in ways that perpetuate racial and colonial histories. In the end, we argue that if the arts are to contribute to, rather than thwart, social justice in education, we may need to reimagine some of our most deeply held beliefs about the arts.

Liberalism is a European philosophy from the Enlightenment that revolves around the ideals of freedom and equality. Though these ideals developed in non-European societies well before the European Renaissance, the liberalism that is common in the United States today is a product of white European male philosophers. Their specific formulation was motivated by ancient social hierarchies they wished to abolish to make way for a new, more egalitarian social order. These philosophers—among them Immanuel Kant, a pioneer of Western aesthetics—envisioned a more developed and just civilization in which laws would protect individual freedoms and equality of man (Mills, 2017). Liberalism was considered an ethical stance, one that sought economic advancement and social progress through a new set of ideals. These ideals were never intended to apply to all human beings, though. "Man" was a category that referred only to white males of a particular socioeconomic standing.

The liberal thought leaders of Europe espoused supremacist views. Kant's (1983/1795) writings, for example, helped to establish pseudo-scientific rationales for modern racism. He elaborated a theory of race before scientists had widely bought into the idea (Eze, 1997). He (falsely) argued for the natural origin of racial differences and the inherent goodness and superiority of so-called white people, concluding that "our continent [Europe] . . . will probably legislate eventually for all other continents" (Kant as quoted in Bernasconi, 2002, p. 4). Importantly, these original racial-colonial imaginings of Europe did not disappear when they crossed the Atlantic. They remain attached to Western liberal thought even now. We use the term *white liberalism* to make whiteness and colonial desire visible markers of liberal identity.

The white liberal ideal is a society of free individuals. They make their own choices, speak freely, and participate in private enterprise. It is a society of laws advanced through order and civility. The arts help to animate this white liberal vision in the United States in ways that run counter to the freedom dreams of non-white people. For example, the arts were used to erase the cultural knowledge of Indigenous people and assimilate new immigrants seeking freedom into white ways of being.

The arts continue to serve a "civilizing" function. For the white liberal, civility is often the answer to society's ills. Indeed, in response to protest movements for social justice, white liberals frequently call for civility. But what if civility and courtesy do not further equity and change, but rather evade and delay it (Nyong'o & Tompkins, 2018)? In institutions where white norms are privileged, civility often is a veneer that disguises, in Hughey's (2018) words, "racialized policing that stems from (and thereby reproduces) a belief in the person, ideal, or object's lesser value and virtue" (p. 528).

If, as we have said, the arts serve a civilizing role in education, who then is seen and elevated, and who is invisible and dismissed? And conversely, if racial equity is the goal, how can educators dislodge the arts from white liberalism in schools to further that work?

Trained in the arts and with classroom teaching experience, we, the authors, now work with pre-service and in-service teachers who want to improve the education of all children through the arts. Alina identifies as white and is an independent scholar. Her work at a state department of education includes leading an initiative that supports schools to use the arts as a tool for transformation. Amelia, who is Black/biracial, taught art in diverse school, museum, and community settings and now is a professor and researcher of race in art education. Because our professional lives are devoted to understanding and supporting liberatory arts experiences for young people, we offer this chapter in the spirit of commitment to racial justice and as a step in our own journey toward reimagining the arts in education.

We begin with a vignette. Its purpose is to bring to life the narratives that tether the arts to white liberalism. There are many layers and dynamics at play in the scene. For the sake of space, we examine two narratives that are widespread in education. We focus on the more recent socio-emotional learning narrative and the perennial arts-bridging-differences narrative because the gaps between what they promise and what they deliver can be vast, the consequences of which, at the very least, undermine inclusive class-rooms and efforts to abolish racism in education. We conclude with strate-gies for avoiding the pitfalls of these narratives and re-envisioning the arts beyond white liberalism.

A VIGNETTE

The bell rings, and six teachers settle into a circle in the social studies room at a Title I school. Their students are Black and Asian, and most qualify for free and reduced lunch. The 6th-grade team has invited the art and music teachers to their professional learning community (PLC) meeting because they are rethinking their annual field trip and want additional creative in-put. They have 20 minutes to brainstorm and arrive at a new plan.

After chatting about a couple of "high-flyers," Pam, the music teacher, shifts the conversation by asking how they can help. "Well, we usually go to the science museum for the big 6th-grade outing," answers Joe, the sci-ence teacher. "I'm all for it, but most of these kids don't get excited about the trip. We want it to be learning, for sure, but fun, too. We're thinking something a little more artsy, entertaining."

"I think our kids would really benefit from more exposure to culture," said the language arts teacher, Sarah. "I've always been a big believer in the arts' ability to lift people up and help them grow. And I can think of a few kids"—she smiles wryly at the group—"who could use some joy and beauty in their lives. They just go through so much at home, you know?"

"Oh my goodness, you are really speaking to my heart!" responds the art teacher, Lisa. "The arts are perfect for social emotional learning. When I was in school, the art room was my safe space. I'd eat lunch there. It was a place where I could actually be myself, express myself, you know? Some kids who don't get love at home come to my room to be loved. I think you're onto something."

"Do you have any ideas for where you'd want to go?" Pam asks. "I have connections at the orchestra. That's good for self-regulation and stay-ing quiet. You know, good decision making."

"I've read that the arts can help students build resilience and grit, too," says Frank, the math teacher. "And we all know our kids could use more of that. It's like pulling teeth to get most of them to do anything in my class." He sits back, rolling his eyes.

"How about visiting an orchestra or art museum to expose them to the masters?" responds the social studies teacher. "But I was also thinking about a hip-hop artist residency or something. You know, connect with our kids' lives in a real way."

"For sure," exclaims Lisa. "The arts are a perfect place for building bridges across differences! In the art room, it doesn't matter who you are or where you're from. Everyone can learn to use color, line, and shape. It's probably the same in music. Everyone can play Beethoven, right? Art is a great way to understand yourself and other people. We can tell our stories and listen to others through the arts."

"Yup, the arts are definitely culturally relevant. It's natural for us," Pam beams. "So what are our next steps? Lisa and I can check with the orchestra and the museum. And I can email a few people about hip-hop residencies. Does that sound good?" Everyone nods and thanks Lisa and Pam.

"I'm so inspired by this conversation," Sarah exclaims. "Our kids need so much. And I want to give them so much. We can't go wrong with the arts for our kids."

*   *   *

There is much that could be explored from the vignette. However, we focus on two common narratives about the arts in education that we see championed by white liberalism and so many who have been schooled in its thinking. In doing so, we hope to create space for more racially and socially just approaches to the arts in education.

THE "ARTS TEACH SOCIAL EMOTIONAL SKILLS" NARRATIVE

A widely held belief is that the arts are a healthy outlet for emotional expression. Lisa hints at this, speaking of her experience in the art room as a student: "It was a place where I could really be myself, express myself." Beliefs about expression and the arts are rooted in Romantic notions of art as "uniquely capable of facilitating emotional expression and spiritual transcendence" (Farrington et al., 2019, p. 19). These beliefs run throughout our society, and are one basis for the common assumption that the arts are a natural way to provide kids better social emotional learning (SEL).

However, the arts do not automatically have a positive impact on social and emotional well-being. For some people, the arts induce fear and anxiety. From an early age and throughout school, some students get regular and consistent (though often unintended) messages that the arts are not really a place for them and others like them.

Furthermore, how do we define what positive and healthy expression of emotions looks and sounds like? Who decides? There are many ways to define SEL, and that is one of the movement's challenges. Often definitions highlight skills and competencies, such as having a healthy self-image, managing emotions, setting and achieving goals, cultivating empathy and healthy relationships, and encouraging responsible decision making. Of course, a definition is just a starting point. Implementation and beliefs regarding SEL vary widely from school to school and educator to educator.

We commonly hear interpretations of SEL, who it is for, and how the arts facilitate it that are well intentioned yet perpetuate a deficit mindset. Some of them are rooted in left-leaning liberal values that all humans have equal worth and are entitled to the resources necessary to flourish. From there it is not far to perceiving some children as more in need, and identifying what they need as something that dominant white culture has. Frank exemplifies this when he says, "I've read that the arts can help students build resilience and grit, too . . . And we all know our kids could use more of that." This inspires well-meaning but assimilationist and often damaging actions by "white saviors" who believe they can help students they see as defined by what they do not have, be it materially, academically, or behaviorally. This impulse is common throughout education, and neither SEL nor the arts are immune. In fact, they both can help spread these harmful beliefs.

Another common assumption is that students lack social emotional competencies, and especially certain students. "Some kids who don't get love at home come to my room to be loved," Lisa says. If you imagine that certain kids need more SEL, who are those children? What do you believe, and what does our society tell us, about those children? Similar to the arts, many educators unquestioningly assume that there is a universal set of SEL skills and behaviors that students must have to be successful. In actuality, some conceptualizations and frameworks for SEL are grounded in dominant culture perspectives on behaviors, values, norms, and expectations. For example, self-regulation and strong decision making are skills often referenced as student deficit areas in schools where behavior referrals are high.

This damage-centered framing has the effect of placing full blame on students (and by extension, their families and communities) for their perceived deficits and absolving responsibility for the system and individuals within it (Tuck, 2009). Approached from this lens, SEL becomes about compliance and control, and perpetuates the racial hierarchy. It has the risk of becoming "white supremacy with a hug" (Simmons, 2020, para. 19–20).

If we pair SEL and the arts with an unexamined belief that they are good for kids, they may have the opposite impact of excluding, silencing, and invalidating students' lived experiences and ways of being. Neither the arts nor SEL is a magical cure; they are clay, and it is the educator that molds them.

"THE ARTS BRIDGE DIFFERENCES" NARRATIVE

In the planning session, the arts are described as a bridge. This metaphor is about connection; the arts bring people together and create understanding across cultural differences. Thus, the arts are the answer to social division. Although this idea is appealing, it obscures two troubling assumptions.

First, the mental image of a bridge is meant to suggest transportation and freedom of mobility. The bridge invites students to partake freely of different styles of music, storytelling, dance, objects, and images, as though the arts were a cross-cultural marketplace. Turning to markets as the remedy for societal ills stems from a white liberal belief that conflict can be avoided and peace can be achieved through the logic of open markets and capitalist enterprise (Kant, 1983/1795). The bridge promises access to people and places unknown, turning the arts into commodities in a bazaar of oddities that stand in for immigrant, Black, Muslim, and other racialized communities.

This is best exemplified when schools implement a "foods and festivals" approach to the arts. Here the arts function less as a means for mutual understanding and more as exotic forms of entertainment that add some "spice" to a standardized curriculum centered on the culture, worldviews, and histories of white people. Students play the role of colonial travelers who traverse the bridge to encounter "the other," whose creative culture forms have been sanitized, packaged, and presented as a neutralized version of itself. White liberalism strips these artforms of the social contexts and human struggles that give them meaning. Encountering difference in this way ensures that white sensibilities remain intact, distanced from and undisturbed by "the other." A curriculum built upon this metaphor merely tolerates difference.

Another assumption is captured in Lisa's statement: "In the art room, in some ways, it doesn't matter who you are and where you're from—everyone can learn to use color, line, and shape. It's probably the same in music, everyone can play Beethoven, right?" Her assumption appears inclusive because it casts the arts as a universal language that anyone can understand despite differences in background. She assumes art is inclusive because elements such as color, line, and shape are present in artwork all around the world. Yet appreciating the arts primarily for their compositional elements misses the purpose of the creative practice, its meaning to the audiences for whom it was intended, and the social and historical circumstances that gave rise to it in the first place. The same problems apply to playing a musical score written by Beethoven or engaging with any artform.

A focus on composition without understanding the sociocultural contexts of artistic practices is not as inclusive as Lisa believes. It ignores and trivializes differences rather than bridging them. This is true in any cross-cultural situation. But in this case, the composition or surface features Lisa notes—color, line, and shape—are important to white modernist art practices. This was a movement that arose in Europe in the 20th century and was exported or carried by expatriates from Europe to other parts of the globe. Therefore, surface features are helpful when interpreting artworks created with a white modernist aesthetic sensibility, but that does not make them universally appropriate for making sense of all artistic works.

When a modernist framework is assumed to be a universal vocabulary for talking about all creative cultural practices, then white ways of perceiving and representing the world become the filter through which all creative cultural practices are understood and the standard against which they are judged. Centering whiteness in this way is a common form of aesthetic violence because it attempts to control and civilize expressions of difference from that which is considered white. It also masks the dominant culture's power by presenting itself as universal.

We need to question the assumption that anybody can access the symbolic meanings rooted in another group's experience simply by taking up its cultural style. When members of one social group benefit from copying the creative culture of another social group, it is called cultural appropriation. White supremacy and cultural appropriation go hand in glove. Nowhere is this clearer than in the popular 19th-century artform of minstrelsy, which as Wesley Morris explained on the 1619 Project podcast (Hannah-Jones, 2019), white performers appropriated by stereotyping the style and appearance of Black people: "Watching these white men in blackface make fools of black people, a white audience could feel cultured. They could feel civilized. They could feel superior to the people they were watching be made fun of." The appropriation of blackness generated social and emotional benefits for white audiences at the same time it financially profited the show's producers. The same dynamic is found in the so-called fine arts as well. Viewing Japan as less sophisticated, Vincent Van Gogh (1888) appropriated Japanese woodblock prints and cloaked his racist attitude in polite admiration characteristic of white liberalism, saying, "The Japanese draws quickly, very quickly, like a flash of lightning, because his nerves are finer, his feeling simpler" (para. 11). Educators fall into the same trap when we encourage students to learn about "the other" by, for example, copying totem poles using toilet paper cardboard tubes or wearing feathered headdresses while drumming in a Thanksgiving Day performance. Arts initiatives that begin with a white liberal desire to be inclusive can end up promoting white supremacist colonial relations through cultural appropriation.

RECOMMENDATIONS

The teachers in the vignette employed white liberal narratives to advocate for arts experiences for their students. The recommendations in Table 9.1 will help educators address pitfalls embedded in these narratives and engage the arts toward a more socially and racially just education.

The arts cannot be both civilizing and liberatory. White liberal narratives, like those we examined above, promise social and individual progress through the arts but are tethered to an exclusionary and oppressive racial-colonial imagination founded in a belief in the inferiority of non-white

Table 9.1. Recommendations for Avoiding White Liberal Pitfalls Engaging the Arts Toward Racial Justice

Pitfalls	Recommendations
Thinking that the arts are an easy and natural SEL magic bullet.	• Do not assume the arts have a positive SEL impact. • Be specific. Articulate clear intended outcomes for the combination of the arts and SEL. Intentionality is key. • Use a critical, equity-centered, antiracist lens. Rethink what SEL and the arts are and what combinations might work. • Listen to students, families, and community members. Build learning experiences around what you learn. • Be mindful of oppressive systems when combining the arts and SEL practices, to "facilitate healing from the effects of systemic oppression, build cross-race alliances, and create joyful, liberatory learning environments" (National Equity Project, 2020, para. 4).
Viewing students, families, and communities with deficit mindsets and seeing SEL as a way to save them.	• Deepen your self-awareness. Vigilantly work to see your own frames and assumptions at work in decisions you make. Use an antiracist lens to interrogate your beliefs and feelings about students. • Discard damage-centered narratives about groups of students. Start with students' SEL strengths and build from there. See children—all of them—as whole people. • Invest in your own social emotional growth, identifying strengths and growth areas. Question where your beliefs and expectations come from and what triggers different reactions. • Be open to difficult change. This might include reimagining your expectations around behavior norms, reactions to students, and how learning is structured. • Be sure you're focused on the actual problem. Is it that Black and Brown children need more SEL? Or do systemic barriers need to be removed (Love, 2019)?
Turning the arts into a universal language.	• Think of the arts as plural languages. Do not assume aesthetic frameworks from white dominant culture are universal to all artforms and creative practices. Learn aesthetic frameworks that are indigenous to the community cultures out of which creative practices arise. • Do not shy away from conflict. If the arts are the language of pluralism, then differences in outlook are sure to include dissenting ideas and tastes. • Decenter whiteness in the curriculum. Increase the range of racial and ethnic representation among artworks and artists featured throughout the year. Balance performance and artmaking activities with experiences that deepen understanding of other people's situations and concerns, accepting that those understandings will always be partial.

(continued)

Table 9.1. (continued)

	• Prioritize creative cultural practices that lean into more challenging contexts of racism and colonization. There is joy and goodness to be found in struggles for liberation, and understanding this provides a better scaffold for building solidarity.
Appropriating styles that differ from white norms.	• Teach the arts as meaning-making systems. Too much attention to style, techniques, and composition to the exclusion of what artistic works and cultural forms communicate or how they function in a society might produce interesting experiences but will not engender understanding, much less interpersonal or social change. • Humanize the people behind the cultural forms. Learn about the worldviews, desires, and struggles of the people behind the cultural forms. Modeling this for students is a way to stave off the white liberal propensity to oversimplify or stereotype identities or artistic works that do not resemble white norms. • Find inspiration in the ways nondominant racial and ethnic groups make meaning through creative activity, but do not mimic their look, style, or symbolic forms of expression if it is a group of which you are not a member. Just because you can copy (take) something someone else created does not mean you should.
Ignoring the collective to focus on the individual.	• Don't do this work alone. Find at least one other person with whom you can form a support group to help each other push past failure and resistance, celebrate progress, and hold each other accountable. • Engage, deeply, outside the school walls. Support collective action, listen to and learn from people outside your identity groups, and engage in critical conversations. • Connect with others to identify and replace policies and practices that create and sustain inequity with new structures and pathways to opportunities.

peoples and cultures. White liberalism is unlikely to deliver the racial justice Black and Brown people seek, and yet dominant narratives about the arts mask this.

If our hope is to abolish racism in education, we might need to abolish some of our deeply held beliefs about the arts. Arts advocates must be careful not to overpromise. We must separate the exciting potential of the arts to impact students powerfully and positively from the belief that the arts are inherently beneficial and benign. Only then can we collectively envision liberatory counternarratives about the arts and their place in schools.

REFERENCES

Bernasconi, R. (2002). Kant as an unfamiliar source of racism. In J. K. Ward & T. L. Lott (Eds.), *Philosophers on race: Critical essays*. Blackwell Publishers.

Eze, E. C. (1997). The color of reason: The idea of "race" in Kant's anthropology. In E. C. Eze (Ed.), *Postcolonial African philosophy: A reader* (pp. 103–140). Blackwell Publishers.

Farrington, C. A., Maurer, J., McBride, M. R. A., Nagaoka, J., Puller, J. S., Shewfelt, S., Weiss, E. M., & Wright, L. (2019). *Arts education and social emotional learning outcomes among K–12 students: Developing a theory of action*. Ingenuity and the University of Chicago Consortium on School Research.

Hannah-Jones, N. (Host). (2019, September 6). The birth of American music (No. 3) [Audio podcast episode]. In *The 1619 Project*. New York Times. https://www.nytimes.com/column/1619-project

Hughey, M. W. (2018). Four thoughts on Charles Mills "Black rights/White wrongs: The critique of racial liberalism." *Ethnic and Racial Studies, 41*(3), 523–531.

Kant, I. (1983/1795). *Perpetual peace and other essays on politics, history, and morals*. Translated by T. Humphrey. Hackett Publishing Company.

Love, B. (2019). *We want to do more than survive: Abolitionist teaching and the pursuit of educational freedom*. Beacon Press.

Mills, C. (2017). *Black rights/white wrongs: The critique of racial liberalism*. Oxford University Press.

National Equity Project. (2020). *Social emotional learning and equity*. www.nationalequityproject.org/frameworks/social-emotional-learning-and-equity

Nyong'o, T., & Tompkins, K. W. (2018). Eleven theses on civility. *Social Text Online*.

Simmons, D. (2020, October). SEL and equity. *The Learning Professional, 41*(5). https://learningforward.org/journal/supporting-each-other/sel-and-equity/

Tuck, E. (2009). Suspending damage: A letter to communities. *Harvard Education Review, 9*(3), 409–427.

Van Gogh, V. (1888). *To Theo van Gogh. Arles, on or about Tuesday, 5 June 1888* [Personal letter]. Van Gogh Museum.

CHAPTER 10

White Liberalism in the U.S. History Curriculum

Issues of Diversity and Accountability

Chris Seeger and Maria Gabriela Paz

INTRODUCTION

Across the United States, social studies teachers are becoming more interested in including diverse perspectives in the curriculum. However, our social studies standards continue to be framed through a white liberal lens that reproduces white supremacist historical master narratives. In this chapter we analyze the curriculum standards of three stereotypically liberal states: New York, California, and Massachusetts, and discuss some of the ways that white supremacy is maintained through a white liberal approach to diversity. Then we present a critical approach that can be used to guide the curriculum toward goals of racial and social justice.

The United States has no national social studies curriculum. Individual states and districts create their own curriculum standards. There is a good deal of overlap across states, with predictable units about colonial settlements, wars, and eras such as Westward Expansion and Industrialization/ Urbanization. Within these units, the historical narrative is overwhelmingly presented through the perspective of white male presidents, generals, and businessmen. For example, in Virginia's U.S. history curriculum, Thomas Jefferson is referenced more frequently than the combined total references to all Black and Indigenous women.

Our collective teaching of history has been centered on white male perspectives for so long that it has become normalized and expected. The American Tale is a Great White Man's story, with occasional appearances from white women and Black people who are fighting against mysterious forces of sexism and racism. Stories of diverse individuals and social movements have been added to the standards in some states, but as we demonstrate, simply adding people to the curriculum does not disrupt the problematic master narratives.

This critical analysis of the history standards began in Virginia, whose curriculum includes Confederate Lost Cause propaganda and deceptively softened language regarding racism and sexism (Jones, 2022). White individuals account for 75% of the people in the standards, and the narrative downplays the atrocities of slavery, Jim Crow, and westward expansion, while simultaneously portraying white Southerners as the victims of Northern aggression during the Reconstruction era.

Virginia's history curriculum is especially dubious given the state's role in the history of white supremacy and anti-Black racism. In 1619, the first enslaved people were brought to Jamestown; in 1865, Richmond was the capital of the Confederacy; and in 1956, Virginia's state legislature waged a *massive resistance* to school integration. If we used Virginia as the sole example for this chapter, it would be easy for non-Southern teachers to dismiss this as a Southern problem.

Instead, we expanded our analysis to look at the high school history standards of three states whose liberal reputations are so well known they have become synonymous with liberalism at large. California, Massachusetts, and New York evoke images of tree-hugging hippies, ivory tower know-it-alls, and pretentious city folk. These states thankfully avoid the Confederate nostalgia of Virginia's curriculum, but their standards remain centered on white male perspectives and an avoidance of white accountability.

In this chapter we have chosen to focus on white supremacy as it relates to anti-Black racism and oppression, while acknowledging that other forms of discrimination persist in the teaching of U.S. history. Considering ongoing realities, we believe that anti-Black racism is the most urgent social issue, and the process of delivering systemic justice to Black Americans will translate into justice for many other groups, just as the Black Freedom Struggle brought progress for other social justice movements in the 20th century.

THE DIVERSITY PROBLEM

From the 1980s to the 2010s, white liberalism cherry-picked MLK's dream of judging others by the content of their character and promoted colorblindness as a solution for racial injustice. Meanwhile, wealth and incarceration disparities continued to grow between Black and white Americans. Colorblindness is part of a larger pattern of liberalism that has allowed white people to profess themselves as allies for racial justice while opposing race-specific policies that would directly address racial inequality. In the 2020s, the more progressive branches of white liberalism have begun to reject racial neutrality in favor of an antiracism approach that encourages white people to see all things as either racist or antiracist, removing the option of *not racist* from the toolkit of white deference. In more moderately liberal organizations, such as corporations and schools, efforts to address racial disparities are pursued through initiatives of *diversity and inclusion*.

Diversity has increasingly become a catch-all term used within white liberal institutions to address a variety of issues stemming from white supremacy and socioeconomic marginalization. The white liberal conception of diversity is an additive approach that attempts to add small numbers of people from certain racialized and gendered groups into places where they had been excluded. When newcomers arrive, they are expected to conform to the white cultural norms of the school or workplace. An uncritical, additive model of diversity casts its gaze outward onto "other" racialized groups; it never critiques the systems that have maintained inequality and exclusion. From corporate workplaces to the social studies curriculum, white liberal diversity initiatives aim to bring formerly excluded people into settings and systems without addressing the exclusionary and unfair systems themselves.

In the history standards there are two primary problems related to diversity. The first is a basic issue of representation. Across the three liberal states, white people comprise the majority of individuals in the curriculum. The second problem is the unequal portrayal of racial groups. White people are almost always described as individuals, and rarely if ever described as a collective group. The opposite is true for Black people; they are more likely to be described as a group than as individuals. And when they do show up as individuals, their Blackness usually plays a central role in their description, something that never occurs for white people. Why do the standards writers feel compelled to label the identities Black people, Native Americans, Asian Americans, and other groups of Color, but not white people? When we think of people of Color as having only racialized identities, how does this affect the racial identity development of white people?

To be clear, diversity is a good thing, but we must diversify the curriculum through a critical lens that examines unjust systems, laws, beliefs, and actions. Teachers should be wary of white liberal diversity efforts that avoid a confrontation with whiteness and patriarchy, because doing so reinforces misleading ideas about the history of the nation. Racism, sexism, and class inequality are central themes of U.S. history, and avoiding those themes causes the curriculum to look more like white folklore than an honest inquiry of the past.

INDIVIDUAL VERSUS GROUP REPRESENTATION

What does diversity look like in the high school U.S. history standards of New York, California, and Massachusetts? Do these states use a white liberal additive model of diversity? Or do they use a critical model that disrupts the Great White Men master narrative?

In each state, we counted all the references to individual people in the standards, sorted them by race and gender, and found that white people comprise about 75% of the individual references (see Table 10.1). Although white people dominate the individual references, their representation is heavily skewed toward a male perspective, with white men appearing three to six times as often as white women. The same pattern of patriarchy is seen among Black individuals, with Black men appearing about three times as often as Black women. Kimberlé Crenshaw's (1990) concept of intersectionality is relevant here, as we see Black women marginalized by overlapping forms of discrimination due to both their race and gender.

Based solely on references to individual people, a white liberalism framework might describe these standards as sufficiently diverse because there are some references to white women and Black people. However, a critical approach to diversity would object to the continued dominance of white men as the heroes of history and the exclusion of women's perspectives across racial groups.

As we were counting the individuals in the standards, we noticed relatively few references to Black people as individuals; however, there were many references to African Americans as a group. We counted all the references to white people and Black people as racial groups, and a consistent pattern emerged in which Black people are portrayed far more frequently as a group in comparison to white people. New York's standards contain no references to white people as a group.

We then compared the individual and group references for white and Black people, and the resulting ratios of representation show us that white people are far more likely to be described as individuals than as a group (see Table 10.2). In California and New York's standards, Black people are more often portrayed as a group than as individuals. Massachusetts is the only

Table 10.1. Individual References by Race and Gender in the U.S. High School History Standards

	White Men	White Women	Black Men	Black Women
New York	33	9	8	3
Massachusetts	120	19	24	9
California	81	27	21	8

Table 10.2. Individual Versus Group Representation in the U.S. High School History Standards

	White Individual	White Group	Percentage of Representation as Individuals	Black Individual	Black Group	Percentage of Representation as Individuals
New York	42	0	100%	11	13	46%
Massachusetts	108	5	96%	29	16	64%
California	139	13	91%	33	37	47%

state in which Black people are portrayed as individuals more often than they are portrayed as a group. When Black people are described primarily as a group, their experiences become monolithic and oversimplified. When white people are almost never described as a group, they avoid accountability for the maintenance of white supremacy.

In California, most of the references to white people illustrate how economic progress was unevenly distributed at different points in history, such as: "For middle-class white Americans, the standard of living rose in the 1920s." Only one reference to white people is used to portray them as the perpetrators of racism and, even then, the standard uses softened language. White resistance to integration is described this way: "Many white Southerners committed their resources to pushing back against . . . an overly intrusive federal government regulating race relations." The avoidance of naming white people and white systems as the perpetrators of racism results in a dishonest historical narrative. When racism is portrayed as a mysterious force, there is no incentive for white people to critically reflect upon the social upholding of white supremacy.

THE PRIVILEGE OF INDIVIDUALITY

In the U.S. history standards, and across society, white people benefit from the privilege of individuality. The privilege of individuality protects white people, and especially white men, from bearing any negative stereotypes that limit their socioeconomic well-being. During our lifetimes we have witnessed countless mass shootings and unjust police killings committed by white men, yet we never see a rise in job discrimination or hate crimes targeting white men. Neither do we see increased police surveillance and harassment in predominantly white communities. White women often benefit from the privilege of individuality, but they are not as well-protected from race and gender-based stereotypes. There is no male equivalent of the b-word or *Karen*.

White liberal ideology encourages white people to use the privilege of individuality to distance themselves from things that are deemed racist, including other white people (that one racist teacher), organizations (schools), and systems (gentrification, voting suppression).

The othering of racist white people is a white liberal strategy for avoiding accountability. It is common to hear a white person talking about the racist behaviors of a white relative, a co-worker, or even Republicans at large. Within the antiracism binary, self-proclaimed *antiracist whites* position themselves as different from *racist whites*. When white people do this, they untether themselves from the problematic aspects of whiteness, a privilege that is not afforded to other groups. This untethering also occurs throughout the history curriculum.

AVOIDING ACCOUNTABILITY

In all three liberal states, the standards touch on topics of organized racist violence and socio-economic oppression. Black people are described as the collective victims of racism, but white people are not held collectively accountable as the perpetrators of racism. For a contextual example, look at how each state addresses the Jim Crow era. Consider the following questions while reading the standards:

1. Does the standard describe the race of the group that is victimized by racism?
2. Does the standard describe the race of the group that is the perpetrator of racism?

History Standards about the Jim Crow Era

New York	11.4a Students will investigate the ways individuals, groups, and government institutions limited the rights of African Americans, including the use of Black Codes, the passage of Jim Crow laws, the Ku Klux Klan, restrictions on voting rights, and Supreme Court cases including the Civil Rights Cases (1883) and *Plessy v. Ferguson* (1896).
California	The enormous barriers African Americans had to overcome in the struggle for their rights as citizens: legal statutes in place that prevented them from voting and exercising their rights as citizens, Jim Crow laws that kept them in a state of economic dependence, a system of violence and intimidation that prevented most African Americans from attempting to exercise power, and a legal system that was devoted to preserving the status quo. Life for African Americans at the century's mid-point was one of second-class status. (Ch. 16, p. 415)
Massachusetts	USI.T5 Analyze the long-term consequences of one aspect of the Jim Crow era (1870s–1960s) that limited educational and economic opportunities for African Americans (e.g., segregated public schools, white supremacist beliefs, the threat of violence from extra-legal groups such as the Ku Klux Klan, the 1896 Supreme Court decision in *Plessy v. Ferguson*, and the Court's 1954 decision in *Brown v. the Board of Education of Topeka*).

In New York, the standard blames "individuals, groups, and government institutions" for "limiting the rights of African Americans." Notice how the standard describes the race of the targets of racism, but not the perpetrators. The authors of New York's history standards should know that during the Jim Crow era, *white Americans* used violence, exploitation, and exclusion to inflict intergenerational harm upon Black Americans. Historian Rayford Logan (1954) describes the early part of the Jim Crow era as the nadir, or the lowest point of race relations in America. The horrors of Jim Crow are common historical knowledge, yet the New York standards use softened language to describe them as an issue of "limited rights."

California's standard says African Americans were victimized by "a system of violence and intimidation." Similar to what we see in New York, the California standard describes the race of the victim but not the perpetrator. The standard also says that African Americans lived as "second-class" citizens without describing the race of the "first-class" citizens who created and maintained a racial hierarchy.

Massachusetts is the only state to use the term "white" in their Jim Crow standard. They include "white supremacist beliefs" as one of the causes of "limited educational and economic opportunities for African Americans." The violence and exclusion of the Jim Crow era is too often pinned on a minority of whites, such as the Ku Klux Klan, which fails to account for white society's collective participation in the enforcement of Jim Crow during that time. Massachusetts' standards have made the most progress in terms of holding white people collectively accountable as the perpetrators of racism, but there is still room for improvement.

In recent years, governors in several states, including Virginia, Florida, Texas, and Arkansas, have enacted laws that censor the teaching of topics related to racism, sexism and other types of power differences. They claim that teaching about these topics makes a certain unnamed group of students feel uncomfortable or ashamed. This argument is a bad faith attempt to protect white supremacy because reckoning with racism threatens its continued existence. When done well, teaching about white supremacy does not cause shame or harm to any student. Such teaching engages students' minds and brings them to their growing edge, so they can better understand their own identities and the social issues of their lifetimes. Choosing to hide, soften, and manipulate the history of white supremacy serves only to maintain white supremacy.

TEACHING U.S. HISTORY THROUGH A RACIAL JUSTICE LENS

Where do we go from here? As individual teachers, we have little influence on our state's standards because each state's department of education contains dense bureaucratic barriers and a hierarchy of gatekeepers, including many white liberal people who proclaim to care about equity and diversity.

Many opportunities exist outside of the classroom, including teacher groups that work to expose their problematic standards on social media, in the hope that it will provoke the tide of public opinion. Exposing the problematic master narratives within each state's history standards can help to challenge the insufficient white liberal conception of diversity in the social studies. Realistically, we may never see the standards shake free from their white supremacist framing, so we can't wait for better standards. The remainder of this chapter will focus on things that U.S. History teachers can do to pursue racial justice in their classrooms immediately.

Living Black History

Our classrooms are a *sphere of influence* (Gorski, 2007). Within this sphere, we can disrupt the reproduction of the Great White Man version of U.S. history by teaching all units through diverse perspectives and holding white people accountable for white supremacy. Well-known eras such as the Civil War, Westward Expansion, and Industrialization should be retold through the perspectives of Black and Indigenous people of Color. What would that reveal? I recently posed a similar question to Dr. Derrick Alridge, the founding director of Teachers in the Movement, an ongoing oral history project that interviews Black teachers who taught in the south from 1950 to 1980. Dr. Alridge is an advocate of teaching history from the perspectives of everyday people, as opposed to a top-down approach that elevates powerful men as sacred heroes. He explained that when we look deeper into Black histories and the stories of everyday people, we get a very different history, and a whole new way to look at history.

The most radicalizing experiences in our journeys of understanding have come from reading novels written by Black authors that are set in the 19th and 20th centuries. Books like Toni Morrison's *Beloved*, Edward P. Jones's *The Known World*, Langston Hughes's *The Ways of White Folks*, and Ralph Ellison's *Invisible Man* all provide powerful historical counternarratives to the master narratives in our curriculum. For Chris as a white educator, these stories provoked a reconsideration of what it means to be a history teacher.

Rather than teaching history as a set of fixed events that happened a long time ago, we use an approach to historical inquiry that re-examines the myths and master narratives of our past and draws connections to the present. Historian Manning Marable calls this Living Black History, or the "core belief that powerful narratives we construct about the past have the potential capacity to reshape contemporary civic outcomes" (Marable, 2004). The goal of teaching history should not be to simply prepare students to participate in society as it exists presently but to transform our society into a more just version of itself through reflection and action.

For example, Living Black History helps students to understand how throughout U.S. history, racial justice progress has always been followed by an intense white supremacist backlash, which continues in modern times. The abolitionist movement faced the backlash of the Civil War; Reconstruction faced the backlash of Jim Crow; the Civil Rights Movement (also known as the Black Freedom Struggle) faced the backlash of white flight and mass incarceration; the election of the first Black president faced the backlash of an outspoken white supremacist president; and most recently, the BLM movement has faced the backlash of the MAGA movement.

In 1967, Nina Simone sang about the "Backlash Blues" in a song written by her friend Langston Hughes. When students hear Nina Simone singing, a voice from the past is inspiring children of the future, and they are experiencing Living Black History. By making these connections, students can see how the past is relevant to their lives today. The NPR podcast *Throughline* is another great example of how to connect the past to the present, and many episodes could also be used as curriculum resources to teach Living Black History.

Living Black History does not fit within the white liberal model of diversity; rather, it is a critical model that recenters the historical narrative onto the perspectives of diverse individuals and groups while also holding white people accountable as the enforcers and beneficiaries of white supremacy. Racial justice in the social studies can be achieved only by addressing the underlying issues of representation, narrative, and accountability in the curriculum. To do this, we must abolish the standards.

Abolish the Standards

What is the difference between abolition and reform? Consider the original abolitionist movement, which sought to remove the system of chattel slavery and provide full citizenship to Black Americans. The abolitionists did not seek to marginally improve the lives of enslaved men and women through regulation; they wanted a radical restructuring of society. There is a modern abolitionist movement in education, led by scholar Dr. Bettina Love and her Abolitionist Teaching Network. Her work is rooted in the scholarly tradition of Queer Black Feminism, and builds on the ideas of Audre Lorde, bell hooks, and Charlene Carruthers. Dr. Love (2021) and her co-conspirators have criticized white liberal equity initiatives in schools for being performative and shallow. She argues that we cannot wait for every white person to change their heart and mind before we begin to abolish white supremacy in our school curricula, pedagogies, policies, and hiring practices.

Another of Dr. Love's foundational messages has major implications for history teachers: We need to teach Black joy. In our history curriculum, Black people are almost always portrayed as the downtrodden victims of violence and oppression. While it is important to confront the history of racism, it shouldn't be the only time we discuss Black history in our classes. Throughout history, despite the ceaseless crush of white dominance, Black individuals and communities have found outlets for joy. Most Black joy occurs when Black people are unburdened by the white gaze. But sometimes we see public expressions of Black joy, and YouTube has become an extensive archive for Black joy in the performing arts. When students see Sam Cooke singing "You Send Me" in a black-and-white TV broadcast, or the Nicholas Brothers and Dorothy Dandridge singing and dancing the "Chattanooga Choo Choo" in a 1941 Hollywood movie, they are witnessing Black joy. To teach Living Black History, we must include the pain, resistance, and joy that have defined the Black American experience.

For social studies teachers, the commitment to racial justice cannot be a performative add-on each February. Reading books and displaying signs must be accompanied by a commitment to action. Going forward, we must abolish the racist standards, teach Living Black History, and hold white people accountable for white supremacy. It's never too late to join the many social studies teachers who already adapt their teaching to include diverse perspectives and counter-narratives, even in states that have outlawed such practices.

The analytical methods and critiques in this chapter can be used with any curriculum framework, at any grade level. After teachers have a clear idea of how individuals, groups, and master narratives are portrayed in their curriculum, they can develop a plan to abolish it and reconstruct a new curriculum through a lens of racial justice.

Special thanks to Dr. Kate McGrath for her thoughtful editing of this chapter.

REFERENCES

Crenshaw, K. (1991). Mapping the margins: Intersectionality, identity politics, and violence against women of color. *Stanford Law Review, 43*(6), 1241–1299.

Gorski, P. C. (2017). *Reaching and teaching students in poverty: Strategies for erasing the opportunity gap.* Teachers College Press.

Jones, B. L. (2022). Feeling fear as power and oppression: An examination of Black and white fear in Virginia's US history standards and curriculum framework. *Theory & Research in Social Education*, 1–33.

Logan, R. W. (1954). *The Negro in American life and thought: The nadir, 1877–1901.* New York: Dial Press.

Love, B. L. (2021, January 13). How to make anti-racism more than a performance (Opinion). www.edweek.org/leadership/opinion-empty-promises-of-equity/2021/01

Marable, M. (2004). Living Black History. *Souls, 6*(3–4), 5–16.

Part IV

WHITE LIBERALISM IN POPULAR PROGRAMS AND INITIATIVES

CHAPTER 11

Liberalism to Liberation
Reimagining Montessori Education

Daisy Han and Katie Kitchens

INTRODUCTION

Many liberatory practitioners are attracted to Montessori education. Like other alternative educational movements, the Montessori community presents itself as a more enlightened, humanizing option when compared with traditional educational practices. From a distance, this appears to be true: Montessori emphasizes education as the practice of freedom within limits. However, while Dr. Maria Montessori's radical-for-her-time approach underscores the potential for education to serve as a pathway for liberation, Montessori is often wielded as a shield to protect white liberal educators and institutions from facing responsibility for the ways they are perpetuating racism and upholding whiteness.

In this chapter, we will explore specific manifestations of white liberalism within the Montessori community, including (1) the deification of Dr. Montessori that extinguishes critique; and (2) the white liberal Montessori practices of assimilationist teaching, white saviorism, co-opting antiracism, and upholding white supremacy. These manifestations are barriers to antiracist educational practice; however, by pushing their good intentions to the forefront, alternative pedagogies like Montessori education often obfuscate their role in perpetuating systemic racism.

In an intentional practice of disrupting the white liberal Montessori tradition, we uplift and center the voices of Montessorians of the Global Majority, people of Color who globally comprise the majority of the human population. These practitioners have been using this pedagogy in culturally sustaining ways within their communities for decades. Their stories provide a vision for what racial justice and true liberation in Montessori schools can be.

As Montessori educators with a combined 21 years of experience in public, independent, and charter Montessori schools, we bring our unique perspectives from direct experience as Montessori teachers, teacher trainers, instructional coaches, and administrators to this analysis of Montessori education. Daisy Han (she/her) is a Korean-American social entrepreneur focused on equity, diversity, inclusion, and innovation. Above all, Han believes in the power of education in nurturing resistance and dismantling systems of oppression. Han founded the nonprofit organization Embracing Equity in 2017 to create affirming, equitable environments across the country through robust and interactive online learning programs.

Katie Kitchens (they/them) is a white, queer, nonbinary Montessori educator and teacher trainer. Katie is also a PhD student, studying the ways white children and families both resist and reify white supremacy culture. Currently, Katie serves as the English Speaking Elementary Guide at Keres Children's Learning Center and is an Embracing Equity facilitator and curriculum designer.

Daisy and Katie seek to work in coalition with other radical educators to reimagine Montessori education for liberation.

As two Montessori educators who have dedicated our lives to Montessori education, we offer this work as a labor of love. Love, as bell hooks conceptualizes it, is a commitment to our own and one another's spiritual development (hooks, 2000). We recognize that in this chapter we wrestle with some uncomfortable truths about the Montessori community, a community of which we are also members. This chapter is as much a reflection on our own practice as it is a call to action.

DR. MARIA MONTESSORI: THE HERO, LEGEND, AND RACIST

As educators who believe that education is a key lever for change, we feel a strong draw to Montessori environments. Like other educators striving for antiracist practice before us, we read liberation in the gaps left in our teacher training programs. In the descriptions of self-directed learning, dedication to community, reverence for the child, and educational freedom, we read *emancipation*.

In many ways, the Montessori Method articulated a pedagogy that embodied the liberatory aspirations that shaped our desire to become teachers. In Montessori's teachings, we found more space to ask questions and radically imagine a different possibility for schooling. What if we responded with curiosity rather than punishment? What if we built our relationships with our students rather than teaching from a pedestal? What if we viewed the child with reverence rather than with an expectation of compliance?

And yet, as we attended our teacher training courses, began working in Montessori schools, and networked with national Montessori organizations, we quickly realized that the pedagogy was steeped in the same racist, dominating behaviors that we hoped to dismantle. Despite Montessori educators' belief of the Montessori Method as inherently equitable and peace promoting, racial disparities persist in discipline practices in Montessori schools (Brown & Steele, 2015). Additionally, the majority of the existing Montessori teacher education programs are preparing teachers to serve in independent, affluent, predominantly white schools that have historically been limited to this narrow population. There is a compulsion to teach in the same manner as Maria Montessori did in the early 1900s (read: no computers), so little to no changes have been made in the training. However, the context is changing and teaching racially diverse students and in underserved communities requires a different kind of training on one's own social identities, mindset, socialization, and deep-seated beliefs. It requires rethinking everything from the classroom environment to academic instruction to family engagement to student discipline.

Black lives matter. Stop Asian hate. Water is life. We're here, we're queer, get used to it. We cannot be satisfied as educators with merely repeating these statements on social media or on protest signs. We must work to create curriculum and communities that speak these words through the topics we explore, the stories we uplift, and the relationships we build. Montessori teacher training does not equip most educators to confront these very real challenges—and without being able to do so, it is impossible to teach or serve or love all children. Claiming to do so is an affront to their humanity.

DEMYSTIFYING THE DEITY

The Montessori method is named for the woman who articulated it, Dr. Maria Montessori. Born to a middle-class family in a small, provincial town in Italy, Dr. Montessori eventually became one of very few women of her age to graduate from the University of Rome as a Doctor of Medicine. An advocate for the rights of workers, women, and children, Dr. Montessori began to create what would eventually become the Montessori Method in the State Orphrenic School in Rome, an institution that housed children with disabilities. By 1906, she opened the first *Casa dei Bambini*, or children's house, in an economically exploited area of Rome.

We Montessori educators proudly celebrate Dr. Montessori as an ardent feminist, a progressive, an advocate for children and for workers. While not entirely untrue, this narrative conveniently neglects the reality of Dr. Montessori's less savory ideologies, including deeply racist beliefs revealed in personal letters written to her father in 1915 (Hawthorne, 2017). This form of white feminism allows liberal white Montessori educators to feel adequately satisfied in their progressive intentions, while also serving as a tool for bypassing antiracism work.

Attempts to wrestle with Dr. Montessori's shortcomings are often met with resistance and defensiveness. This lack of willingness to truthfully confront the realities of bias, racism, and Eurocentrism that shape the

Montessori Method undermine its liberatory potential. In many ways, mainstream Montessori communities are built around exceptionalism bred through hero worship. Dr. Montessori is deified, recognized as singularly genius in her articulation of child development.

Recently, while in the middle of a global pandemic and national uprisings for racial justice that included calls for the removal of racist statues and redistribution of resources, the Montessori community prioritized raising funds to erect a statue of Maria Montessori in Perugia, Italy, in celebration of her 150th birthday. Children in Montessori schools create musicals about her life and effectively turn her existence into a multigenerational folklore. At any Montessori conference, one can purchase a variety of shirts, bags, or art emblazoned with Montessori's likeness.

The hero worship that defines Montessori educators' relationship with Maria Montessori is replicated in Montessori teacher education programs, which often have a single teacher trainer responsible for teaching all the required course areas. Montessori educators often proudly share the name of their trainers, who are ranked according to their proximity to Maria Montessori. The phrase "well, in my training . . ." is often used as a way to insulate oneself from critique or challenge, and exclude those perceived as having attended less authentic training programs.

Montessori's deification is further apparent in teacher education curriculum centered almost solely on the Montessori method, without credit to the many communities of Color who have been practicing affirming child-rearing for millennia. References to other educational theorists are few and far between, leaving Montessori trained teachers with a myopic vision of educational theory.

THE WHITE LIBERAL MONTESSORI PRACTICE

"I don't care if you're Black, white, yellow, or polka dot, and kids don't either," proclaimed one Montessori teacher trainer, brandishing an image of stereotypically depicted children in their ethnic clothing holding hands around the globe. While on the surface this appears to be inclusive, the sentiment effectively shuts down discontent and reinforces the narrative of the well-intentioned Montessori practitioner. Montessori teacher educators espouse the importance of a robust cultural geography curriculum that celebrates food and holidays, unintentionally othering the people they desire to celebrate and conveniently avoiding a deeper analysis of power and colonization.

Furthermore, a dangerous consequence of proudly claiming neutrality and objectivity and asserting that social identities do not influence one's teaching practice is defaulting to a narrow cultural standard that becomes the justification for a classroom environment that centers the dominant culture. In the United States, this means centering whiteness. Trisha Moquino

(2020), co-founder and education director of Keres Children's Learning Center (KCLC), questions the Montessori dogma of *following the child*, asking: Which image comes to mind when Montessori educators, the vast majority of whom are white, think about *the child*? Do they imagine an Indigenous child, like those served by KCLC? A Black child? Or does the image that arises in their mind reinforce the myth of the universality of whiteness?

The replication and reification of the characteristics of white supremacy culture in Montessori often begins in teacher education programs, bolstering the maintenance of white liberalism in the Montessori community. Montessori classrooms are defined by the purposeful buzz that fills a classroom of 24 to 30 children self-directing their work. The orientation toward children is that they were born whole and are capable of learning in an environment intentionally designed to support their development. The adult is decentered, acting as an observant guide who supports the children in their own self-construction. In a primary (3–6 year old) classroom, as one child completes a four-digit addition problem using golden beads, another will be reading a book, while yet another prepares a snack for themselves and a friend. The teacher might be tucked away in the corner presenting a one-on-one lesson to a child, or diligently observing the flow of the classroom.

Now step into many Montessori teacher education classrooms, and the experience will appear diametrically opposed. Montessori training centers have been known to rely on oppressive conventional educational approaches rooted in the banking method of treating students like empty vessels to be filled by their more competent and qualified teachers (Freire, 1970). A single trainer will lecture for hours at a time, while students furiously write down their every word. Between the two of us, we hold six different Montessori credentials, attained at different training centers around the country. As Montessori trainees we were expected to passively absorb the barrage of information dutifully dispensed by our teacher educators. Often, when we critiqued materials, lessons, or pedagogical approaches, we were both met with a refrain of the necessity of patience, the slowness of change, and the need to perform the lessons as they would be traditionally presented to pass our exams and receive certification.

We were instructed that once you have complied and received your certification entering into your own practice, only then is individual expression as Montessori teachers allowed. This sentiment shifts the burden for a commitment to decolonizing Montessori pedagogy and crafting culturally sustaining curricula from Montessori accrediting bodies to individual teachers. The essential structures of white dominance remain, sustaining the illusion of progressive inclusivity through the promise of freedom in the classroom.

But how much freedom can there be when administrators, colleagues, accrediting bodies, and families are consuming, and thus expecting, the implementation of a white centric curriculum that is upheld as the highest standard of authentic practice?

Montessori teacher education continues to struggle with disrupting white middle-class norms that dictate our ways of engaging in discourse and learning. Instead, we continue to promote systems that claim progressiveness but remain firmly rooted in the myth of white supremacy. As a result, our ability to cultivate the teachers needed to enact culturally sustaining pedagogy for liberation has been limited. Montessori teacher education must eliminate the tendency to pretend that Western European modes of thinking and doing are in fact universal. This critical analysis of power is a necessary step to culturally sustaining and revitalizing pedagogies that humanize students, their families, and their communities.

The Montessori Approach to Social Emotional Learning: An Assimilationist Tool and Weapon to Silence Discontent

Dr. Maria Montessori (1995) stated, "Considering the method as a whole, we must begin our work by preparing the child for the forms of social life, and we must attract his attention to these forms" (p. 121). Lessons, such as greeting someone and accepting or rejecting an invitation, help children learn social strategies so they may better navigate relationships with others. These lessons are a core component of Montessori education and are the social emotional learning approach referred to as the *Grace and Courtesy* curriculum. And yet, these social strategies often fail to consider the societal context and power dynamics in which grace and courtesy are practiced. Who gets to define what is graceful and courteous? Stemming from a white, European scholar, too often the standards for grace and courtesy are white normative practices that are tools for assimilating children into white culture to be respectable members of society operating within and maintaining the status quo.

Meanwhile, Black bodies are policed in the streets and in the classroom to fatal outcomes. Montessori education is not exempt from the racial disparities in discipline practices (Brown & Steele, 2015). Time and time again, research demonstrates that Black boys are viewed as 4 and 5 years older than they are and that racial disparities in school discipline exist in the most subjective of categories—"willful defiance," "insubordination," "disrespect" (Children's Defense Fund, 2011). This same subjective judgment applies to teachers and teacher candidates in training. When Black, Indigenous, people of Color dare to confront racist actions, policies, and lessons, *Grace and Courtesy* is weaponized to silence discontent. Rather, the desire to cling to the illusion of equality and peace violently and unironically trumps any real effort to achieve true equality and peace.

White Saviorism

Nigerian-American novelist Teju Cole (2012) coined the term "white savior industrial complex" to explain how white people are rewarded for "saving" those less fortunate, all while able to completely disregard the policies they have supported that have created and maintained systems of oppression. This white savior narrative is applauded, and indeed uplifted as aspirational, in many Montessori teacher training programs and schools.

White saviorism in Montessori education takes many forms. One of the most egregious examples is Educateurs sans Frontières (EsF), a division of the Association Montessori Internationale. EsF, unnecessarily in French (despite Dr. Montessori's Italian origin), is a network of Montessori practitioners who strive to "promote the rights of the child throughout the world, *irrespective* of race, religion, political and social beliefs" (Educateurs sans Frontières, 2011). This approach is devoid of historical context, social awareness, and critical analysis of power that has put in place these political borders and deeply inequitable outcomes. While EsF is committed to transcending borders to serve children, there is a profound lack of due diligence of what rich knowledge, culture, and history exist in these communities already. Rather than turning inward and reflecting on the ways in which the Montessori method upholds white dominance, well-meaning practitioners assert that the remedy for educational malpractice is greater access to *authentic* Montessori education.

Co-opting Antiracism and Upholding White Supremacy

Describing conventional approaches to inclusion of Indigenous cultures in public schools, Sabzalian (2019) noted that isolated cultural and language programs can reproduce the harmful reservation system, delineating which expressions of Indigeneity, pro-Blackness, and antiracism are acceptable to white liberal, settler-colonial schools. Initiatives, curriculum, and training that uphold the image of white liberal innocence and goodness are permitted, so long as they do not challenge the dominant, white-centric narrative of education.

This same process emerges in Montessori learning environments and national organizations, as these institutions meet demands for racial justice with the appointment of "Diversity Officers." When concerns arise regarding the rampant racism present in Montessori organizations, leaders can shrug their shoulders and point to the diversity officer, who acts as a scapegoat for their inaction. While touted as a revolutionary position that demonstrates an institution's commitment to seriously undertaking antiracism work, such positions functionally represent an *acceptable concession* because they do not disrupt the status quo. Funders are frequently eager to offer substantial grants for the creation of such positions, allowing schools and organizations to hide under the veneer of progressiveness. This financial incentive encourages organizations to hire for such positions regardless of whether they intend to earnestly dismantle institutional racism. This phenomenon is not unique to Montessori institutions, nor are these institutions immune to such bypassing of responsibility for true systemic change.

For instance, the American Montessori Society, the largest Montessori organization and certifying body in the world, has opted to create an additional, optional antiracism credential rather than interrogating their existing teacher-training programs. This expensive professional development program is separate from the already cost-prohibitive Montessori credentialing process, making this opt-in antiracist education even more unlikely. These accrediting bodies separate antiracism education into an acceptable, consumable box to check. This effectively allows Montessori teacher education programs to avoid any meaningful institutional change in decentering whiteness in the core components of Montessori teacher education, while appearing progressive. Such credentials absolve the Montessori community from actively interrogating racism in their work, thus upholding the systemic white liberalism that permeates mainstream Montessori thought, and dictates what is considered *authentic* Montessori practice. Instead of a collective community-wide commitment to intentionally emancipatory educational environments, the task of battling systemic racism falls on the shoulders of individuals (usually, People of the Global Majority) who are dedicated to liberatory practice.

WHAT IS LIBERATION?

Liberation sets free these theories into an embodied expression of freedom in the fullest form. Liberation is the creation of relationships and communities characterized by equity, fairness, and the implementation of systems that support the full participation of each human and the promotion of their full humanness (DeJong & Love, 2015). For liberation to exist, one must first become cognizant of the oppressive systems that dictate social relations. This consciousness illuminates the dynamics of oppression without giving into despair and hopelessness. Further, it enables humans to live outside the patterns of thought and behavior learned through an oppressive socialization process. A liberatory consciousness supports us in being intentional about our role in working toward transformation and the elimination of harmful, systemic, and internalized dynamics (Love, 2018).

People of Color are often under pressure to be *well-behaved* when talking about their struggles and are only allowed to do so in narrow ways that often continue to center white comfort. As Cole (2012) writes: "Marginalized voices in America have fewer and fewer avenues to speak plainly about what they suffer; the effect of this *enforced civility* is that those voices are falsified or blocked entirely from the discourse" (Cole, 2012). In this final section of our chapter, we will intentionally unblock and amplify three principles of antiracism in Montessori education. These principles are derived from how Montessori education has been a tool for liberation for decades. This legacy includes the work of leaders like Rosalyn D. Williams, who in 1964 founded the first Black-led Montessori teacher education program in the United States, and schools such as Malcolm X Montessori established around the same time in Los Angeles, California (Debs, 2019). Both founded their schools with the explicit purpose of using Montessori as a tool for liberatory practice, serving the spirits of Black children, a commitment to the community beyond the classroom, and an unrelenting dedication to dismantling racism.

Hakim Jamal, cousin of Malcolm X and founder of Malcolm X Montessori, urged: "If white people who always say they want to do something would raise some money for Montessori education aimed at eliminating racism, then America could really begin to move in a human family way" (Fein, 1968, p. 2). Though their stories are often marginalized, Montessorians of the Global Majority continue to imagine and enact liberatory, culturally sustaining educational environments, using Montessori in service of emancipation. As we close our chapter, we uplift three principles of antiracism, radically reimagining Montessori education: (1) Montessori as a Means, Not an End, (2) From Assimilation to Culturally Sustaining, and (3) Authentic Connection, Building Community.

Montessori as a Means, Not an End

In the Montessori community, there is often an emphasis on crafting *authentic*, Montessori environments (Basargekar & Lillard, 2021). This authenticity is lauded as the ultimate end goal of teacher practice, and the only pathway toward creating supportive classrooms. This distortion of Montessori education creates a worship of theory over practice, beliefs over people, and dogma over relationships. Emancipatory teaching requires reorienting ourselves—our end goal is not authentic Montessori practice as defined by the major Montessori organizations; our end goal is what Montessori (2007) called *universal liberation*.

High-fidelity Montessori practice—that which most closely resembles the teachings of Maria Montessori—is touted as the most effective method for teaching (Lillard & Heise, 2016). Amelia Allen Sherwood, founder of Sankofa Learning Center, describes a school established in a predominantly Black neighborhood in response to the community's desire for a Montessori program. This school hired white, Montessori-trained teachers, even though they were not members of the community, in order to have authentic Montessori practice. According to Allen Sherwood, shortly after helping open the school, the teachers "abandoned the work that they set out to do, which was mostly just to be white saviors, but they took their resources and materials with them." "I want to honor the Montessori-ish schools that are out there," Allen Sherwood continued, the ones "that *have to* be a hybrid of Montessori because materials and expertise are inaccessible."

Additionally, credentialing programs that most closely align with this narrow definition of Montessori education are considered the most prestigious, and are frequently the most inaccessible. The Indigenous Montessori Institute (IMI), the first Indigenous-led Montessori teacher-training program, resulted from a need to cultivate teachers who understand the importance of revitalizing Native languages and *the way Montessori is used in service to that goal*. As Trisha Moquino (Kewa, Cochiti, Ohkay Owingeh), the cofounder of IMI, describes:

> We needed a teacher training pathway for tribal communities and diverse popu-lations who have an urgency to revitalize and strengthen their languages and their cultures. There's an assumption that if you get Montessori certified, you will be prepared to teach in any community, but that is just not true. If you are teaching in an Indigenous community, you need to know the history, lan-guage, and culture of the children and their families. We need to prepare our adults with these values, this core knowledge, and how to practice decentering whiteness. Teachers need to know what it means to even decenter whiteness before they can know that they are perpetuating it, and Montessori Teacher Training does not do this. Thus, the Indigenous Montessori Institute provides a Montessori training center that centers the needs of Indigenous children and communities of color.

Liberatory Montessori environments recognize that Montessori pedago-gy is so much more than a destination; rather, it is one flexible and adaptable path to liberation. Reimagining Montessori from dogma to ethos allows us to embody Montessori orientation and values beyond the lesson plan. Through our wrestling with the pieces of Montessori pedagogy that limit and constrict, we find the answer is often in the process of wrestling itself.

From Assimilation to Culturally Sustaining

With fervent commitment to Montessori practice, training centers and schools both intentionally and unintentionally practice Montessori rituals that reify dominant white culture. In the United States, this includes centering English as the language of instruction, assessment, and prestige. For Indigenous com-munities, Trisha Moquino tells us, liberation is intimately tied to language. KCLC is both a language immersion (in the 3- to 6-year-old classroom) and a dual-language (in the 6- to 12-year-old classroom) school centered on lan-guage revitalization and culturally sustaining practice. KCLC is an intergen-erational learning environment that welcomes all generations, honoring and centering the wisdom of elders. As a concrete recognition of this wisdom, KCLC bases their pay structure not solely on credentials but also on the skills valued by the community, such as fluency in Keres.

Additionally, the Montessori lessons can be adapted to be truly cultur-ally sustaining to the children they are serving. At KCLC, the children do not have just a button frame to practice their fine motor skills and practical life skills. Rather, the children are also presented with moccasins that they learn to tie and clothing traditionally worn in their community. While many Montessori classrooms have puzzle maps of each country and continent, KCLC also has maps that represent the traditional and contemporary boundaries of Tribal Nations in the so-called United States.

Authentic Connection, Building Community

Reverend angel Kyodo williams tells us, "Without inner change there can be no outer change, and without collective change no change matters." This clarity and focus on collective, community-based action brings us to our final principle of antiracism: authentic connection and building community. Antiracism is not possible alone. It requires a deep relationship and trust. It necessitates vulnerability and intimacy. Finding the spaces and places where you can come together with others committed to antiracism in their own lives and practices is critical for building both resilience and accountability. Accountability—and specifically compassionate accountability—is a choice to recommit to community and to choose to be in integrity in our relationships.

For many Montessori practitioners, this kind of community is found in a nonprofit organization, Embracing Equity, founded by a Montessori educator (and one of the authors of this chapter). In 2017, while supporting teachers of Color in starting their dream Montessori schools, Daisy Han found that the very process of becoming a trained Montessori teacher was inadequate in preparing antiracist educators. Embracing Equity offers a learning community dedicated to unlocking the tools within ourselves through relationships and an emphasis on moving from intellectualization to embodying our antiracist practice. The Embracing Equity programs are designed to offer adults the kind of affirming Montessori environments they strive to create for children. Embracing Equity is a community where people, *often for the first time in their lives*, feel like Montessori students who are affirmed and guided in their self-directed learning journey for liberation.

Additionally, a group of Montessori educators and administrators banded together in 2014 to form Montessori for Social Justice (MSJ). As a group of founding board members, the organization offers an annual conference where Montessori educators can join together for an immersive, in-person experience that demonstrates what Montessori in service of justice could be like. At these conferences, new friendships are formed and new understandings of Montessori are found. For those of us who have been disrupting systems of oppression in Montessori classrooms and schools for years, the MSJ conferences helped us realize we are not fighting alone but have a supportive community to work alongside in a movement striving for greater liberation.

These spaces show us once again that, as Montessorians, as a community fiercely dedicated to the liberation of all children's potential, we have the capacity to bravely engage in this work in the same way our Montessori students do: Ask questions, listen to the voices of those learners who are marginalized or invisibilized, and use teaching as medicine and a concrete path for healing and restoring balance.

CONCLUSION

There are so many possibilities of Montessori education. We are two practitioners who deeply believe in the potential of Montessori for liberation. When we focus on ecosystems and move beyond the walls of the classroom, we can reimagine the boundaries of school to include community as foundational to antiracism education. We can move beyond a commitment to dogmatic replication of Montessori pedagogy as spoken by Montessori herself into a Montessori practice that truly serves the spirit of the child. We are grateful for the models of how this can be done and look forward to cheering on and contributing to this movement from white liberalism to liberation. Onward.

REFERENCES

Basargekar, A. & Lillard, A. S. (2021). Math achievement outcomes associated with Montessori education, early child development and care. https://doi.org/10.108 0/03004430.2020.1860955

Brown, K. E., & Steele, A.S.L. (2015). Racial discipline disproportionality in Montessori and traditional public schools: A comparative study using the relative rate index. *Journal of Montessori Research, 1*(1), 14–27.

Children's Defense Fund. (2011). Portrait of inequality 2011: Black children in America. Washington Research Project.

Cole, Teju. (2012, March 21). The white-savior industrial complex. *The Atlantic.* www.theatlantic.com/international/archive/2012/03/the-white-savior-industrial -complex/254843

Debs, M. (2019). *Diverse families, desirable schools: Public Montessori in the era of school choice.* Harvard Education Press.

DeJong, K., & Love, B. J. (2015). Youth oppression as a technology of colonialism: Conceptual frameworks and possibilities for social justice education praxis. *Equity & Excellence in Education, 48*(3), 489–508.

Educateurs sans Frontières. (2011). https://montessori-esf.org/what-is-esf/educateurs -sans-fronti%C3%A8res

Fein, D. (1968, November). *Montessori school attempts to free children of racism. New University,* 2.

Freire, P. (1970). *Pedagogy of the oppressed.* Continuum.

Hawthorne, B. (2017). Dr. Montessori's racism. *Montessori Life, 31*(1), 61.

hooks, B. (2000). *All about love: New visions*. William Morrow.

Lillard, A. S., & Heise, M. J. (2016). An intervention study: Removing supplemented materials from Montessori classrooms associated with better child outcomes. *Journal of Montessori Research*, 2(1), 16–26. https://doi.org/10.17161/jomr.v2i1.5678

Love, B. J. (2018). Developing a liberatory consciousness. In M. Adams (Ed.), *Readings for diversity and social justice* (pp. 129–132). Routledge, Taylor & Francis Group.

Montessori, M. (1995). *The absorbent mind*. Holt.

Montessori, M. (2007). *The formation of man*. Montessori-Pierson.

Moquino, T.L. [@indigenousChLdr]. (2020, June 16). https://twitter.com/indigenouschldr/status/1272916238969090051?s=27

Sabzalian, L. (2019). *Indigenous children's survivance in public schools*. Routledge.

CHAPTER 12

White Liberalism, Racism, and Restorative Justice in Schools

Crystena Parker-Shandal

Restorative justice in schools is a relatively new educational initiative. For some, the focus is on mitigating post-incident conflicts to reduce suspensions and expulsions. For others, it is about building a relational community. Conflicts are minimized and taken up differently when a community is strong. How administrators, teachers, and other school personnel take up restorative justice in education (RJE) shapes the process. In response to the structural inequities in handling post-incident conflicts in schools, RJE has become board-mandated in many schools worldwide.

Perhaps because of the rising popularity and need for institutions to name themselves as a "restorative school," the process has essentially become entrenched into school systems through a white liberal approach. This approach confines (often purposely) the possibilities for racial justice. White liberalism in RJE purports a procedural process that stifles the deep philosophical roots of restorative justice and the anti-oppression practices that contribute to building an authentic culture of care and connection.

Restorative justice is most known as a post-incident response to harm (Zehr, 2015). In its application in schools, the International Institute for Restorative Practices defines it as "a social science that studies how to build social capital and achieve social discipline through participatory learning and decision-making" (Wachtel, 2013, p. 2). RJE philosophy intends to draw communities together and foster connections to reduce conflicts and repair them proactively when harm has occurred (Bishop et al., 2015; Evans and Vaandering, 2016).

The practice of RJE is rooted in Indigenous and Afro-Indigenous communities and cultures (Davis, 2019). The revitalization of RJE as a cultural practice acknowledges Indigenous peoples' sociohistorical and contemporary contexts, interrupting a settler-colonial erasure (Lee & McCarty, 2017; Nxumalo et al., 2018). The peace circle, for instance, is a foundational element of any restorative process. Circles are an Indigenous approach to building relationships and a traditional RJE tool used to discern and exchange viewpoints constructively (Pranis, 2015; Stonechild, 2020; Wildcat, 2011). By drawing on principles rooted in building community and relationships, RJE has the potential to create a school culture in which all students may thrive.

RJE training, usually conducted over 2 to 3 days, typically involves teaching peaceful alternatives to managing conflict. The training itself is variable, and could be done by an external organization or within the school district or board. Still, it most often focuses on building a solid relational community and using restorative processes such as conferencing, class meetings, or peace circles instead of suspensions or detentions. RJE is used for post-incident problem solving (to repair conflict) or as proactive education (to reflect on conflicts and injustice).

Teachers trained in RJE may assume they have developed the necessary critical skills for addressing exclusion and racism. However, in my experience, many white teachers, including those who may see themselves as liberal and well intentioned, are oblivious to how their actions might perpetuate harm. This lack of racial justice consciousness perpetuates exclusion and bias through the processes meant to repair harm.

HOW RJE REPRODUCES RACISM THROUGH WHITE LIBERAL IDEOLOGIES

Engaging antiracism in restorative justice means taking a step back to acknowledge and respond to a legacy of colonization and racial injustice (Parker, 2020). Eurocentric priorities and perspectives have structured Western education systems. Thus, educational priorities have been misconstrued by the very systems meant to promote equity and inclusion. In this chapter, I describe how restorative practices, while celebrated as progressive and sometimes even antiracist, often reproduce racism in schools. I also discuss how we can embrace a more authentically antiracist approach to restorative justice.

Knowing the Language, but Not Knowing the People

White liberalism shows up when the hardworking leader who can't possibly be racist uses hackneyed blanket statements that speak to promoting a restorative school culture. Incidents of racism, whether subtle or explicit, are depicted as isolated incidents that do not reflect their school's culture. Too often, educational leaders believe they could advance their career by saying they're engaging in RJE when, in actuality, they continue to perpetuate harm. In this way, white liberalism in restorative culture allows people to feel safer in their fictitious definition of a culture that does not yet exist and cannot exist without explicit recognition of the struggles and conflicts that are preventing racial justice.

Many teachers or leaders, and at times students, have learned the language of oppression and of RJE. However, underlying their scripted language, they continue to dismiss how power, privilege, and identity are performed and executed in circle practices. They present as educated and aware because of their token appreciation for jargony words that demonstrate their alliance to a cause they don't fully appreciate. They may even have emotional outbursts because they are so shocked and confused that hate incidents occur. While it is common for circles to bring up deep emotions, when the outburst derails the dialogue, it becomes impossible to have a sustained conversation about these deep issues.

Many leaders in the field openly name racism as wrong, and with their level of experience in the field of RJE, they see themselves as antiracist. Yet, when asked tough questions about how to handle racist incidents, they could default to using the restorative process to lessen racist incidents but do nothing to address the harm. Frequently, white leadership constrains possibilities for deep dialogue, which both silences and harms BIPOC students (Romano & Arms Almengor, 2021). Many of these leaders openly speak of how racism is terrible but continue to be gatekeepers to protect themselves and their whiteness. Such leaders are full of feel-good bromides that create the illusion of addressing racism while avoiding the real issues.

Destructive Conflict Management

Addressing classroom management is a critical practice and often a time when white liberalism is exuded; in moments of stress, deep emotional pain, and chaos, it is too easy for teachers to engage in punitive systems of control. When a student is testing boundaries and breaking classroom guidelines, it makes it challenging for adults to take that breath and step back to see the whole picture—to see the reality of a hungry child, a child in pain, a child experiencing trauma at home or at school.

Many schools measure the success of restorative justice by dropout rates, suspensions, and expulsions, which reinforces a deficit view. These kinds of data are symptoms of economic injustice; they are "opportunity gaps," which might be better justified by examining how students have been "pushed out" of school and how generational injustice persists for many historically marginalized groups (Gorski, 2016, p. 383).

In schools, teachers' implicit, unconscious racial bias often contributes to racial discrimination in disciplinary decisions (Ispa-Landa, 2018). When teachers purposely seek to include traditionally marginalized students, their academic success and social inclusion increase (González, 2015; Utheim, 2014). Evidence does not show that punitive approaches to discipline prevent future infractions. However, strong evidence shows that when teachers have strong relationships with students of Color, they have far fewer disciplinary referrals and are more academically engaged (McCluskey, 2014). Some research has addressed how restorative processes might increase young people's sense of inclusion (Morrison, 2007; Winn, 2020). Still, relational strategies presented as race-neutral will not reduce school-discipline disparities (Davis, 2019; Parker & Bickmore, 2020).

When I visited a grade 8 class in my role as an RJE researcher, the teacher told me that the students would have an intense circle that day because there was an incident with discrimination. I excitedly took out my notebook, ready to learn how the process would proceed. I found myself, however, taking few notes, as the teacher chose to pose surface-level questions about respecting differences without ever naming the incident or the conflict directly. Most of the students decided not to respond and passed the talking piece; others shared generic responses about being kind and respectful.

When navigating conflicts about differences, teachers often create an illusion of justice by washing away the opportunities for antiracist learning. This is how some people facilitate white liberalism in RJE: by removing the antiracism and anti-oppressive nature of the process. This whitewashing of critical practices presents a neat program (often for students of Color) that could have an antiracist impact; however, the antiracism is canceled out (Ladson-Billings and Dixson, 2021).

In the end, the ideals of a liberal multicultural education—to persist in celebrating differences and encourage everyone else to be respectful of differences—triumphs to present an illusion of justice. The core issues in such a restorative process go unaddressed when race and the implications of racism are not named. Without critical attention to the impacts of racism, restorative justice is not possible because the *justice* is removed.

Sabotaging the Process Through Silos and Other Tools of Whiteness

Remaining in our silos, where a principal, child, and youth worker, social worker, or teacher independently practices circles in their office or classroom without buy-in from the community, curbs important dialogue. An example of silos is when the burden to execute the process is placed on one or two people. Not only is this inequitable, but it most certainly prevents transformation.

Silos are a tool of whiteness; isolating people prevents collaboration and relationship building. When students are sent to the office, their dialogic encounters are often hidden, limited to the school administration and frontline school staff. Others who don't want to be accountable work in their silos and refuse to work together to dismantle white supremacy. When people have difficult conversations, it is easy to revert to a place of comfort within their privileged world. The discomfort is part of the restorative process.

We need to have difficult conversations through RJE, or we won't be able to have the kinds of deepened relationships required to pursue the type of transformation that is possible. For instance, I observed a grade 2 class during Black History Month when an RJE-trained teacher planned to facilitate a restorative circle about Harriet Tubman. There were two Black students in this class. Tubman was celebrated throughout the circle, but the teacher did not consider the implications of racism and slavery. The teacher felt that, given their age, it was not a topic she felt comfortable engaging. Their circle focused on responding to information-gathering questions in the book, and then the lesson closed with the students coloring a picture of Tubman. These are day-to-day examples of well-intentioned white educators who want everyone just to get along. Still, we can't get there without critical discussions about race and the implications of their white complicity (Applebaum, 2010).

Not surprisingly, very few teachers trained in RJE use the circle process to dismantle racism while acknowledging their compliance in an oppressive system. This is often tied to prescriptive pieces of training that do not engage in antiracism. It also reflects how many assume that by using RJE practices, they don't need to attend to issues of racism and diversity because they are automatically facilitating inclusion through their use of particular pedagogies.

Some educators focus on proactive community building through restorative justice and building relationships through activities like dedicated circle time. However, too often, traditional disciplinary procedures are still enacted; for instance, the teacher who attempted to do a restorative conference only to align with their white administrator in the end, putting their own needs first to protect their position. Teachers, child and youth workers, social workers, and even administrators who are working in silos must often stick their heads out quite far to support racialized children. They might see the harm and know that it's wrong but are forced to stand by and do nothing because, to some extent, they need to protect themselves and their positions.

PRINCIPLES TO GUIDE ANTIRACIST RJE

All RJE practices need to engage with antiracism. This includes examining how antiracism and restorative justice challenge the perpetuation of racism and exclusion while examining how white liberalism impacts restorative justice through emotional, social, material, and spiritual damage often done by white people and white-dominated educational institutions who see themselves as racial justice advocates. It is usually in these very communities that RJE is used as a feel-good approach to perpetuate further harm.

Critically Examining Our Role in Perpetuating Racism

Calling out racism in any restorative process involves challenging societal structures that are in place to perpetuate racism. We must think critically about whether our actions are perpetuating racism and derailing the actual implementation of a restorative process.

While RJE is built on the premise that people need to be interconnected and have strong relationships, white liberal approaches to RJE damage relationships.

As challenging as it is, we need to collectively name white liberalism in RJE practices and connect with allies and other racialized people to discuss our experiences. It is only by naming and speaking about it that we can work toward change. Some people are not in privileged enough positions to talk openly and truthfully. They, unfortunately, need to endure in silence to continue to protect themselves. Those who have the freedom to work with others to facilitate social and political intervention need to use all of their capacities to do so. It's the only way we'll be able to address how white liberalism shows up in RJE so that we can work toward the deep structural change.

In our critical examination of whiteness, white teachers and administrators need to be preparing to respond and engage in conflictual issues, refusing to make it about ourselves. While it might be an emotional process for teachers, inciting anger, fear, or sadness, it is incumbent upon adult educators to not make the incident about ourselves. Drawing on restorative principles to focus on relationships and prioritizing a process of attending to the harm, and to those who have been harmed, conversations and dialogue must center the needs of BIPOC youth and families.

Collectively Calling Out Racism and Empowering Young People

Restorative community-building circles focus on social issues that allow young people to dialogue about conflictual topics (Parker & Bickmore, 2020). Some teachers might choose to rely on the spontaneous emergence of issues concerning race and exclusion, allowing students to guide the process and decide what to talk about and how to reflect on it. This may appear to be a process run restoratively. However, as educators and facilitators of a process that needs to guide and respond to antiracism, teachers must engage in purposely planning how their facilitation will work toward engaging with antiracism in classroom dialogue, activities, and philosophical choices in their pedagogy, allowing for emergent curriculum to be nurtured while also actively resisting and responding to anti-Blackness and settler colonialism (Dei, 1996).

Providing students with leadership opportunities, such as facilitating restorative circles, dialogue, or activities, builds their courage to navigate intense emotions that emerge from these conversations. Young people can readily articulate and name exclusion—they are keenly aware of who is left in and left out—even though these indicators may sound or look different in their youth vernacular. Applying socially constructed terminology to navigate what could presumably be generic social relation issues based on inclusion and exclusion could lead to their abilities to name how racism, sexism, and other oppressions permeate societies. For instance, as students discuss and potentially validate each other's feelings, they may also practice naming examples of oppression based on their peers' or others' behaviors. This process of empathy-building in seeking to understand and dissect each other's experiences furthers their capacities for anti-oppressive engagement. Such leadership opportunities also build their identities as allies.

Working With Intention to Cultivate an Antiracist Approach to Justice

Students' varying experiences and positions of marginality influence educators' choices to facilitate proactive restorative practices. It can be vulnerable, being a principal or teacher who is committed to restorative justice. This vulnerability increases in toxic cultures even when people are on board with sustaining a restorative school culture.

Restorative justice in education should not be focused solely on curbing suspensions or expulsions. It is about connecting with people's humanity. It means that adults are building relationships with young people to honor who they are and to allow them to bring their gifts into the world. It fosters and deepens peer relationships, building a community of people who interact with intention, building a culture of care.

This intentional work is about reconnecting with young people of Color, dismantling the the school-to-prison pipeline, and building a solid pathway for student success and civic engagement. However, most approaches for restorative justice in schools ignore students' diversities and prescribe a one-size-fits-all program, which ultimately reinforces exclusion and marginalization. RJE is a philosophical way of seeing the world and being with one another. It cannot be a program or a set of rules; it is certainly not a quick fix. Teaching restoratively in a controlled environment is exhausting. Attempting to build relationships in a climate that persists on being detached means pushing back against those standing still while you're just trying to walk by.

RJE, when implemented with its authentic and conscious intentions, deepens antiracist education, proactively addressing conflicts and exclusion embedded in the curriculum. However, teachers don't necessarily have the motivation or confidence for such integrated implementation—particularly teachers unwilling to do the necessary work to acknowledge their complicity in perpetuating racism. RJE training must prepare teachers with tools for stimulating dialogue and building relationships, making them and their students better prepared to explore contentious issues, including racism.

RJE should speak back to punitive, white supremacist frameworks—insisting on an alternative platform to engage with young people. In this way, much of what is typically identified as students "acting up" or "rebelling" could be reframed as productive behavior (Velez et al., 2020). These students aren't acting out; they're "hurting out" (Arms Almengor, 2020).

Disrupting the System of Whiteness With Allies and Activism

Dismantling structurally embedded approaches is a complex process and, of course, has stirred further conflict in the RJE community. This pushback and disagreement are necessary to interrupt the whitewashing and appropriation of an Indigenous process. The perpetuation of violence and othering of racialized practitioners and students is another way RJE has been co-opted and colonized. Racialized practitioners in the field feel this most strongly and may be stifled from speaking up because they are economically dependent on the very system producing the harm. This forces many antiracist RJE practitioners to tread softly in their attempts to preserve the essence of RJE. White allies are critical for calling out and interrupting these entrenched conditions.

This is not about scheduling one-time mix-it-up lunches or a so-called restorative intervention to convince people of how their commitment to whiteness has harmed others. Instead, it is about acknowledging this tension and working to address these harms. White allies are a critical part of this process.

However, there is always the elephant in the room when working with our white allies. For example, I have been in staff meetings in restorative circles where, for instance, people of Color need to carefully choose their words during a supposedly open dialogue to appease white "allies." Marginalized people have developed generations of grit that readies us to bear the burden of oppression. The psychological and social strain of internalizing this oppression is often invisible to white colleagues. It is something a white person would not be able to understand or have the capacity to carry.

Acknowledging that this elephant exists is part of the process of disrupting the system. Without this consciousness, we will continue to witness how restorative practices further instill colonial beliefs and white supremacy.

MOVING FORWARD WITH AUTHENTIC EFFORTS FOR RACIAL JUSTICE THROUGH RESTORATIVE JUSTICE

The reality is that people will engage in conflict, and we must figure out how to engage more peacefully and restoratively as a society. We want to teach young people to engage peacefully. We also want them to know how to stand up and intervene when they witness racism. This is the difference between negative and positive peace: functioning within the complicity or consciously acting out against it. We need to create spaces of liberation to empower young people to become leaders and social activists; this is the goal of restorative justice: to learn to operate through a race-conscious lens.

In sum, there are various ways in which RJE practices are racist, reflecting white liberal tendencies. In one approach, democratic work is performed within extremely imperfect and unjust spaces. In another, injustice is reinforced within restorative justice practices.

This is not to say that teachers, administrators, and parents don't have room for mistakes when practicing such approaches. They need to make mistakes; as educators attempt to inculcate and implement these values, further injustice will be perpetuated, and the potential for harm is precarious. However, how these mistakes and critical incidents are taken up and reflected upon will shape what RJE looks like. We might find ourselves raising our voices or letting our egos take hold of the process, but it's how we catch ourselves and model to our children and youth what mistakes look like that will matter. Glossing it over without naming and discussing the polarizing experiences reinstitutes harm.

REFERENCES

Applebaum, B. (2010). *Being white, being good: White complicity, white moral responsibility, and social justice pedagogy*. Lexington Books.

Arms Almengor, R. (2020). Women colorizing restorative justice in white-led institutions. In E. Valandra (Ed.), *Colorizing restorative justice: Voicing our realities* (pp. 131–141). Living Justice Press.

Bishop, P., Picard, C., Ramkay, R., & Sargent, N. (2015). Restorative and reconciliation processes. In *The art and practice of mediation* (Ch. 10). Emond Montgomery.

Davis, F. E. (2019). *The little book of race and restorative justice: Black lives, healing, and US social transformation*. Simon & Schuster.

Dei, G. (1996). *Anti-racism education: Theory and practice*. Fernwood.

Evans, K., & Vaandering, V. (2016). *The little book of restorative justice in education: Fostering responsibility, healing and hope in schools*. Good Books.

González, T. (2015). Reorienting restorative justice: Initiating a new dialogue of rights consciousness, community empowerment and politicization. *Cardozo Journal of Conflict Resolution, 16*, 457–477.

Gorski, P. C. (2016). Poverty and the ideological imperative: A call to unhook from deficit and grit ideology and to strive for structural ideology in teacher education. *Journal of Education for Teaching, 42*(4), 378–386.

Ispa-Landa, S. (2018). Persistently harsh punishments amid efforts to reform: Using tools from social psychology to counteract racial bias in school disciplinary decisions. *Educational Researcher, 47*(6), 384–390.

Ladson-Billings, G., & Dixson, A. (2021). Put some respect on the theory: Confronting distortions of culturally relevant pedagogy. In C. Compton-Lilly, T. Lewis

Ellison, K. H. Perry, & P. Smagorinsky (Eds.), *Whitewashed critical perspectives: Restoring the edge to edgy ideas*, 122–137. Routledge.

Lee, T. S., & McCarty, T. L. (2017). Upholding Indigenous education sovereignty through critical culturally sustaining/revitalizing pedagogy. In H. S. Alim & D. Paris (Eds.), *Culturally sustaining pedagogies: Teaching and learning for justice in a changing world* (pp. 61–82). Teachers College Press.

McCluskey, G. (2014). "Youth is present only when its presence is a problem": Voices of young people on discipline in school. *Children & Society*, 28(2), 93–103.

Morrison, B. (2007). *Restoring safe school communities: A whole school response to bullying, violence and alienation*. Federation Press.

Nxumalo, F., Vintimilla, C. D., & Nelson, N. (2018). Pedagogical gatherings in early childhood education: Mapping interferences in emergent curriculum. *Curriculum Inquiry*, 48(4), 433–453.

Parker, C. (2020). Who's in and who's out? Problematizing the peacemaking circle in diverse classrooms. In E. C. Valandra, W. W. Hoksila, & A. Goffe (Eds.), *Colorizing restorative justice: Voicing our realities*. Living Justice Press.

Parker, C., & Bickmore, K. (2020). Classroom peace circles: Teachers' professional learning and implementation of restorative dialogue. *Teaching and teacher education*, 95, 103–129.

Pranis, K. (2015). *Little book of circle processes: A new/old approach to peacemaking*. Simon & Schuster.

Romano, A., & Arms Almengor, R. (2021). It's deeper than that!: Restorative justice and the challenge of racial reflexivity in white-led schools. *Urban Education*. https://doi.org/10.1177/0042085921998419

Stonechild, B. (2020). *Loss of Indigenous Eden and the fall of spirituality*. University of Regina Press.

Utheim, R. (2014). Restorative justice, reintegration, and race: Reclaiming collective identity in the postracial era. *Anthropology & Education Quarterly*, 45(4), 355–372.

Velez, G., Hahn, M., Recchia, H., & Wainryb, C. (2020). Rethinking responses to youth rebellion: Recent growth and development of restorative practices in schools. *Current Opinion in Psychology*, 35, 36–40.

Wachtel, T. (2013). Defining restorative. International Institute for Restorative Practices, 12. www.iirp.edu/images/pdf/Defining-Restorative_Nov-2016.pdf

Wildcat, M. (2011). Restorative justice at the Miyo Wahkotowin Community Education Authority. *Alberta Law Review*, 48(4), 919.

Winn, M. T. (2020). *Justice on both sides: Transforming education through restorative justice*. Harvard Education Press.

Zehr, H. (2015). *The little book of restorative justice: Revised and updated*. Simon & Schuster.

CHAPTER 13

Seeing Systems

The Case for Systemically Trauma-Informed Practice Instead of White Saviorism

Debi Khasnabis, Simona Goldin, and Addison Duane

INTRODUCTION

We begin with a dialectic.

Trauma-informed practice (TIP) is potentially transformational.

And, white liberalism operates through common approaches to TIP, most especially through white saviorism.

Too often, proponents of TIP weaponize an approach that holds promise for liberatory work in schools with young people.

Our concerns about and awareness of this dialectic have grown over time, as we have heard educators use the buzzword "trauma" more and more frequently. Teachers would say to us, "Well, you know, our kids have a lot of *trauma* at home, so that explains it." We have heard professional development facilitators profess, "Teachers, resiliency comes from the deep belief that at one time you really mattered to another human—that could be you." The statements came from educators who professed an interest in supporting our most vulnerable children, but in veiled ways that blamed children, and especially children of Color, their families, and their communities while perpetuating white liberalism. In these statements, educators invoked racist tropes, tokenizing and minimizing, often without explicitly naming race. If race was inherent to the issue, why was it not being named? Why was it not being examined? Even more importantly, why weren't educators pointing to the racist *systems* creating the trauma, or the strengths of the children they were pathologizing?

The answer, we believe, lies in the ways that white liberalism is entangled in our work in schools.

In this chapter, we examine how white liberalism weaponizes the concept of trauma-informed practice, and we explore suggestions for reclaiming the work. We begin with a narrative of a 9-year-old child, Khang. Throughout the chapter, we highlight how Khang and her trauma might be seen by her teacher through the smog of white liberalism. We then pivot to a visionary space, imagining how we can enact racially just systemic teaching practice, and how TIP can be transformational rather than re-traumatizing.

MEETING KHANG

Khang is a 4th-grader at a local public school and has three younger siblings. Both of her parents work long hours and leave the house before 5 a.m. each day to start their jobs. Because they are not paid a living wage, they frequently must work overtime. Each morning, Khang is responsible for waking herself and her siblings, and getting everyone dressed, fed, and out the door for school in time to be picked up by their grandma, who lives nearby, and does her best to get there on time. Khang's grandmother, who is a first-generation Hmong immigrant, is dedicated to driving her grandchildren to school, but also torn because her own and her children's experiences inside this school have been painful. Because of this, she drops the children off at the end of the street and sits in her car watching while they walk the rest of the way to school. Given the history of disinvestment and redlining, there is no sidewalk for the four children to walk on. Khang leads her siblings down the side of the road to get to campus, where they stop to pick up tardy slips. She then walks each one of her siblings to their classes. When they arrive at the classroom door, Khang hugs them tightly and says things like "Make good choices," "Be nice to your friends," "Read a lot." Afterward, she walks to her own class and prepares to start her day with her white teacher, Ms. Miller. Khang has never had a teacher of Color, much less a teacher who is Hmong.

We invite readers to reflect on Khang when prompted throughout this chapter, to imagine how a teacher might support Khang through their teaching practice.

UNDERSTANDING SYSTEMS AND TRAUMA-INFORMED PRACTICE

Psychological trauma is a complex concept with no simple definitions (Venet, 2021). It refers to the response to experiences that cause physical or emotional harm (SAMHSA, 2020). Research estimates that more than two-thirds of U.S. children experience at least one trauma before turning 16 (SAMHSA, 2020). Various fields, including medicine, social work, and psychology, have responded to these data and joined the trauma-informed care movement, which has grown roots in education over the last 20 years. However, in a review of 2 decades of trauma-informed education literature, Thomas and colleagues (2019) found that there is no one formally agreed-on framework for trauma-informed practice, nor are there consistent determinants of effective implementation.

We attend to a critical omission: Much of the work on TIP discounts the role of racism and overlooks the school as a source of trauma itself. Gorski (2020) illuminates this, pointing out that students are drowning in traumas within trauma-informed schools. He charges educators to attend to the practices, policies, and aspects of institutional culture that traumatize children *at school*. We echo this call, along with others, seeing school-based trauma as a systemic problem that is produced at all levels (e.g., administration, staff, students) (Petrone & Stanton, 2021).

Trauma is pervasive across demographics *and* exacerbated or caused by high levels of stress and inequality. But everyone does not experience stress equally. Instead, U.S. society is plagued by inequalities such as housing and food insecurity and unequal access to critically important resources such as employment opportunities, health care, mental health services, high-quality early childhood programming, and highly qualified teachers. Bias and racism infuse these inequalities. Housing insecurity, for example, intersects with race and racism through histories of housing discrimination. Unequal access to highly qualified teachers intersects with race and racism; recent research shows that the percentage of uncertified teachers in schools with high enrollments of students of Color is, on average, four times higher than in schools with low enrollments of students of Color (Cardichon et al., 2020). So, while stress is pervasive, it also compounds in ways that are exacerbated by racism.

Currently, TIP is incorporated in school settings from early childhood to higher education. From introducing classroom calm corners to "build inner resilience" (C. Thompson, 2021, p. 5), to offering explicit training on the trauma response (Petrone & Stanton, 2021), educators seek to incorporate these practices into their teaching. Still, these particular practices fail to recognize causal elements of racism and systemic oppression and reinforce harmful white liberal narratives.

WHITE LIBERALISM AND TRAUMA-INFORMED PRACTICE

Like any educational movement, TIP is not immune from white liberalism. Gorski (2014) describes white liberalism as the notion of being "so self-involved in my white goodness, that I am unable or unwilling to bear the rightful vitriol pointed at racism by people of Color without making myself its victim." A key idea, then, is that being seen as "good" (Gorski, 2014; Hayes & Juárez, 2009) takes priority over threatening racism (Gorski, 2020).

White liberalism also claims moral superiority, fueling an unwillingness to implicate the self in educational inequities (Lalik & Hinchman, 2001) while disguising racism as benevolence, saviority, and heroism (Matias,

2016). By subscribing to this line of thinking, educators promote themselves as "heroic liberal warriors who will save students of Color from failing" (Matias, 2013, p. 54) while neglecting to realize *their own racial culpability in upholding whiteness* (Matias, 2013).

We elaborate here how white liberalism manifests in TIP in the following ways: (1) attending only to the individual; (2) framing students and their communities with a deficit lens; (3) expecting children and communities to "be resilient" without disrupting systemically constructed injustices; and (4) performatively casting teachers as saviors. We will revisit Khang and her teacher, Ms. Miller, throughout to illustrate our argument.

Attention Only at the Individual Level

White liberalism suffuses TIP by promoting a narrow focus on individual children. TIP workshops often follow a familiar script, focusing on individual-level challenges and emphasizing brain-based deficiencies. Typically, a white presenter, usually from social work or counseling, begins by detailing the brain science of trauma, showing graphs of stress levels and images of shrunken brains. She lists trauma types stemming only from homes and communities, such as abuse, neglect, and gun violence, while omitting institutional trauma, school-based trauma, and oppressive historical trauma. From there, she does a deep dive about the ways trauma impacts students, listing cognitive deficits like working memory and attention, physical deficits like fine motor skills, physiological symptoms like headaches and stomachaches, and behavioral challenges. She walks through levels of arousal, stress responses, fight or flight, and sometimes mentions nerves that shut off during trauma.

Coupled with this exploration of behavior problems will be "practical classroom suggestions" like changing classroom color schemes to avoid triggering the visual cortex, keeping a calm tone of voice when de-escalating a child, and meeting children's "basic needs." Woven throughout the entire presentation is an emphasis on relationships, with suggestions to "connect before you correct," emphasizing "relationships over everything." The presentations almost always end on a feel-good note, by exploring the topic of resilience and how, as teachers, we can be "the one caring adult" in a child's life.

This individual level focus can be used to pathologize and cause harm to students, in particular when those individuals are children and families of Color. Some would likely refute this, given, for example, the push for professionals to move away from asking trauma-affected students, changing "What is wrong with you?" to "What happened to you?" While this reframing is intended to challenge pathologizing, it is insufficient. "What happened to you?" still locates the pathology or deficit in the *individual* no matter its cause. This is especially problematic when we consider the role of racism and other forms of systemic oppression in the production of trauma.

In Khang's case, attention only to the individual level could lead Ms. Miller to take a myopic view of her student. She might focus exclusively on Khang and Khang's needs to learn. During math, for example, Ms. Miller may notice Khang struggling with completing her math classwork. She may think, *I remember Khang's social worker mentioning that they've had a death in their community. In my trauma-informed trainings I learned how trauma impacts the brain and working memory. Khang's brain is probably so overwhelmed! I'll make sure she knows our classroom is a family, now that she's lost a member of hers. I should also implement a sticker chart to help motivate her to remember her math facts.* Ms. Miller might feel confident that she has used a "trauma-informed" approach to support Khang. After all, she has seen and named Khang's trauma, and thought about shifts to make based on that trauma.

But in this example, Ms. Miller *only* sees Khang through her individual symptoms and the deficits trauma might cause. She connects traumatic grief to Khang's inability to complete classwork and makes assumptions about Khang's community of support, without interrogating her own teaching.

Deficit Framing Children and Their Communities

The influence of white liberalism on TIP can result in a myopic view on the child, one that does not substantively acknowledge the stress and inequities that plague the child's community, family, school, and classroom. This can lead to a pathologizing orientation in which children are blamed and named as being "behind," "at-risk," "struggling," or "deficient," and educators are framed as saviors who can protect children from harm, as seen in the following examples, the sorts of things we often hear from educators who have bought into traditional TIP models:

> *My students have cognitive impairments. So sometimes they lie. Yesterday my student told me some crazy story about how his brother died. But I'm sure he's just acting out.*

> **Tweet:** *My heart goes out to the children who are having to stay at home within homes that are unstable and unable to sustain balance throughout this crisis. Let's get ready to help them once school is back on!*

> **Painted on wall of a school:** *Even on your worst day in the classroom you are still some child's best hope.*

This thinking is flawed and dangerous. It positions children and families as having deficits, challenges, limitations, constraints, or pathologies, and does so without acknowledging the systemic oppression that impact children and families. Further, this thinking holds those children and families responsible for overcoming these problems. These statements are often spoken by white saviors, frequently cueing children of Color, though race is typically not explicitly named.

From this lens, Ms. Miller might judge Khang's family as uninterested in her education. Ms. Miller might blame Khang's family for their lack of participation in school-sanctioned events. She may raise the issue with a colleague: "I just really can't understand where Khang's family has been all year. It's March and they haven't shown their faces once. I know they both work multiple jobs, but it's weird that they haven't made more of an effort to find one job that pays the bills so they can come to more school events. They clearly don't care about their daughter's success in 6th grade. It's just so frustrating. I spend more time with Khang than they do. Did you know one day at recess she called me mom? I feel like I know her better than her parents."

Expecting Children and Communities to "Be Resilient" Without Disrupting Systemically Constructed Injustices

When systemic injustices are unacknowledged in TIP-focused spaces, they are often referred to as traumas that students must overcome through the development of resilience. TIP focuses heavily on building social emotional learning (SEL) skills such as resilience, purporting that trauma-affected students come to school with significant deficiencies and in need of opportunities to develop SEL skills. The promotion of resilience—the capacity to "bounce back" after damage or disruption—places responsibility on individuals to manage their own internal state of equilibrium, such that damages can be covered and (re)covered (L. Thompson, 2021).

A popular TIP film, "Resilience" (2016), lauds the notion of resilience as an "answer" to the crisis of pervasive trauma. At one point in the film, Dr. Jack Shonkoff highlights the hope that resilience offers while holding families responsible for their lack of resilient capabilities: "We need to do more than give parents information and advice: we need to build their capabilities." The statement situates the problem of trauma within individual children and families, blaming them for systemically constructed injustices. This white liberal framing allows white educators to feel good about the benevolence of saviorism, in this case through teaching resilience, while obscuring racial injustices.

Simmons (2021) elaborates:

> SEL that fails to address our sociopolitical reality and combat racial and social injustice . . . SEL alone will not keep politicians from making laws that disenfranchise BIPOC communities. SEL alone will not keep educators from suspending BIPOC children at disproportionate rates. SEL alone will not keep teachers from having low expectations for BIPOC students. SEL alone will not prevent cops from killing BIPOC people.

Simmons's critiques of SEL apply to the teaching of resilience within TIP. Children *can* learn to be resilient (and if they are surviving are they not already resilient?), but should they need to manage systemic injustice? As educators, our focus should be on dismantling systemic injustice—not on teaching children to better cope with it.

Returning to Khang and her teacher, we see that Ms. Miller spent the second half of her TIP conference learning about resilience. She knows the topic well and chooses to focus most of her stand-alone SEL lessons on teaching her students how to build resilience. They even have a catchy class jingle about "bouncing back."

Despite Ms. Miller's efforts with the sticker chart, Khang is still "struggling." Her behavior is shifting and she's more withdrawn. Ms. Miller assumes there's trauma at home for Khang. She starts pulling Khang for lunch with the teacher to teach her more strategies for building resilience, as she believes that Khang just doesn't know *how* to navigate hard moments. She teaches her breathing techniques and a few affirmations to say to herself. She cheerily tells Khang, "If you could just be more resilient, things will get so much better for you! And, by the way," she adds, "feel free to teach your parents and siblings any of these strategies. They probably need them too!"

Performatively Casting Self as Savior

As the field has become informed about trauma, educators are acknowledging the role of trauma on their students' lives and the need for TIP. This has come with a cost: Roused by white liberalism, educators are operating on the assumption that they must be the ones to address and correct for the impact of trauma on their students' lives, that they are "the only one they have." This reproduces white saviorism, where teachers internalize the need to "save" children from adversity and trauma. TIP reinforces this concept. One TIP trainer once said, "Explicitly say and repeat often 'our class is a family' and do things like have family lunch, and keep food and snacks, soap and clothes, combs, brushes, and bobby pins in the room. . . . The classroom must become the home."

In our case narrative, Ms. Miller prides herself on receiving a TIP certificate. She is now ready to take her learnings back to her colleagues and is delighted when her administrators ask her to lead a staff meeting. She wants to highlight the most important element of being trauma-informed: relationships. She believes that she is the only adult who cares for Khang, as evidenced by the supposed "lack of familial involvement" for the past year. She has done everything she knows how to do to love and care for Khang. She's even started purchasing snacks for Khang to take home with her to her "empty house." She believes that she is the one caring adult who is changing the trajectory of Khang's life.

Ms. Miller plans to start the session by telling Khang's story, detailing her trauma, and explaining how her work has changed Khang's life for the better. She chooses her presentation title: "When we're all they have: trauma-informed classroom practices."

All of these practices create the illusion that teachers are doing something positive by promoting themselves, as Malcom X (1963) said, as a "friend" of people of Color intent on solving problems. They claim to be "trauma-informed." But the reality is that these practices cause harm for students, especially children of Color, while perpetuating white liberalism.

FROM SAVIOR TO SYSTIP

So, how can educators harness the potential transformative power of TIP and push back against the ways that white liberalism is weaponizing? Below we elaborate a method for moving from savior to SysTIP—systemically trauma-informed practice (Khasnabis & Goldin, 2020). In contrast to the four ways that we have outlined above that white liberalism manifests in TIP, SysTIP calls for educators to complement individual-level responses with systemic awareness and action. We illustrate this by showing how Ms. Miller might move from savior to SysTIP, reframing her response to Khang.

While we have raised questions about a solitary focus at the individual level, it is true that trauma-informed practice draws urgently needed attention to the individual's need to heal psychologically from the trauma they have endured. This is important, and we echo calls for this need to be met in schools and in communities by increasing mental health resources available to children and adolescents (Herrenkohl et al., 2019).

However, we do not call for teachers to save children. We have often heard teachers say, "How am I supposed to get my students to pass the state test when they have so much trauma and when I have to be so much more than a teacher? I have to be a teacher, a parent, a social worker, a therapist, and so much more!"

This stance is not professionally warranted. Insisting that teachers take on all these roles is unrealistic and minimizes other professional knowledge. It also minimizes the teaching profession's own bodies of knowledge and expertise. To this point, Venet (2019) calls for role clarity: "While teachers play many roles in students' lives, psychologist should not be one of them. . . . Clear boundaries and roles help students establish a sense of safety in relationships. If we dig too deeply into explorations of trauma with students, at best we create a confusing dynamic. At worst, we can impede a student's healing journey by providing uninformed counsel or treatment" (p. 3).

Educators *should* ensure appropriate professional care to individual children; and they should complement this with a systemic lens. They should learn to recognize the inequitable impacts of trauma on people who have varied levels of access to resources such as health care. To experience trauma and then to be denied mental health resources, whether due to limited access, finances, time, transportation, or other barriers, makes healing from that trauma more difficult. Suggesting that teachers should, or even can, take on this charge does not address the inequity. If anything, it can exacerbate the inequity by suggesting that a quick fix is possible. Schools must be staffed with well-qualified mental health care providers. Teachers must educate themselves about who these providers are, if not in the school, then in the community, and work to connect their students with them.

A systemic lens is also needed to stimulate systemic action and push against white liberalism, because societal contexts deeply impact teachers' work. For example, communities and families are nested within our racist and unequal society. Schools are located within those communities that are also plagued by stress and racial inequity. Finally, the classrooms in which academic teaching and learning occur, and the students themselves, are located within those schools. Recognizing the role of stress and racial inequity in children's lives, and the way that these forces accumulate and exacerbate or cause trauma, is critical to understanding the students in classrooms and their needs as learners.

SysTIP requires that educators consider the ways that trauma presents at each of these levels and make efforts to intercede at *each*, rather than enact a savior orientation at only the individual student level. Educators must not only see racism and call out flawed systems but must also act in ways that name and leverage the strength, assets, and skills of children who have experienced trauma. We flesh out how Ms. Miller can move from savior to SysTIP here, and in Table 13.1, which shows how we pull apart the nested contexts to ensure attention to systemic injustice at each level.

When Ms. Miller acts systemically, she engages in sensemaking that does not begin and end at the individual level. At the societal level, she pays attention to local community conditions of disinvestment and historical redlining, and is aware that many families, including Khang's, are living in poverty because caregivers are not paid a living wage. Ms. Miller acts on this understanding by voting for politicians who advocate for the needs of the community and by herself advocating for better wages and more investment in neighborhood infrastructure.

When Ms. Miller attends to the community level, she engages critically, wondering why Khang's grandmother may not be entering the school, and whether she may be uncomfortable there due to ongoing tension between the school and community. She utilizes her district's home visit resources and offers to meet and connect with Khang's family at her home or in the Hmong Community Center. She also sees the vast resources and cultural capital (Yosso, 2005) that exist within Khang's community and assumes

Table 13.1. Bringing Theory to Practice: Attending to the Nested Causes of Trauma

SysTIP Level	Society of Pervasive Stress & Inequality	Communities & Families	Schools	Classrooms	Students
Khang's Reality	*Khang's parents are not paid a living wage and work overtime. Disinvestment and redlining contributed to neighborhood disrepair.*	*Khang's grandmother avoids school because of her own "ghosts in the classroom" (Laurence-Lightfoot, 2004).*	*Khang's chronic tardies can contribute to low citizenship marks on her report card, absences, and suspensions.*	*Khang misses morning meeting and the opportunity for social connection with her peers.*	*Khang comes quietly through the classroom door late every morning, watching her teacher for cues.*
Ms. Miller's SysTIP-focused practice	I pay attention to local politics and vote for a higher living wage and for city council members who aim to redistribute local taxes to benefit the community infrastructure.	I look for authentic moments to express appreciation for Khang's grandmother's role, offer home visits and additional parent–teacher conference times outside of the school and in the Hmong community center.	I engage in creative non-compliance (Venet, 2020), not reporting Khang's tardies, resisting the school-to-prison nexus.	I design my morning instruction to include multiple opportunities for social connection as the children engage in academic learning.	I greet Khang warmly and notice her curiosity about the classroom activity.

connection, not deficiency, when thinking about what Khang goes home to each day.

When Ms. Miller attends to the school level, she critically analyzes the attendance policy. It requires that students' tardies are to be documented as an absence for every five tardies and that students are to be suspended after 10 absences. Furthermore, excessive tardies result in lower citizenship scores on report cards. In the short term, Ms. Miller engages in creative non-compliance (Venet, 2021) and doesn't report Khang's tardies. She understands the school-prison nexus and resists a school policy that she knows has the potential to harm Khang. In the long term, Ms. Miller talks with her administrators about transformative justice during her mid-year evaluation. She joins other teachers who begin organizing for change at the school and district level.

When Ms. Miller attends to the classroom level, she recognizes that Khang is regularly missing the morning meeting routine and not receiving opportunities to connect with her peers. Ms. Miller does not blame Khang or her family for this missed opportunity; instead, she recognizes the systemic barriers that make timely arrival at school difficult for Khang. She decides to provide multiple opportunities throughout the morning for her students to connect socially during academic activities. That way, Khang can connect with her peers whenever she arrives. She also establishes an entrance procedure that clearly supports Khang's success when she walks in the door, practicing with her class and posting visuals, so that Khang, or any other student, is welcomed in with a predictable routine and can quickly join the lesson.

Finally, Ms. Miller pays attention to Khang as an individual. She views her with an asset lens and sees her slip quietly into the classroom every morning, seeking not to disrupt the class and watching her teacher for cues to figure out what the class is working on. Ms. Miller values Khang's observant nature, greets her warmly, and capitalizes on Khang's interest and curiosity by guiding her to the current activity.

CONCLUSION

TIP has been weaponized in the U.S. education system by white liberalism. It need not be this way.

We have named here the ways that white liberalism focuses teachers' eyes on children and their families' perceived deficits, pushing educators to work to embody the role of many other professionals, and to reduce academic expectations, only further inhibiting children's access to liberatory schooling experiences. Teachers can push against the ways that white liberalism twists TIP to focus only on individual-level traumas, and instead stitch the promise of TIP together with a critical lens trained on systemic racism and inequality. When we do this, we can work in profoundly important ways. When both teachers and students can recognize and act upon flawed and harmful systems, then we have arrived at a morally just purpose of schooling: education for liberation.

REFERENCES

Cardichon, J., Darling-Hammond, L., Yang, M., Scott, C., Shields, P. M., & Burns, D. (2020). Inequitable opportunity to learn: Student access to certified and experienced teachers. *Learning Policy Institute.* www.semanticscholar.org/paper/Inequitable-Opportunity-to-Learn%3A-Student-Access-to-Cardichon-Darling-Hammond/3e6953e20abb3e5b035992da8bf413b74ed7f1d4

Gorski, P. (2014). White liberalism, violence, and the delusion of solidarity. Least harm / most good: A social justice blog by Paul C. Gorski. http://lehamogo.blogspot.com/2014/12/white-liberalism-violence-and-delusion.html

Gorski, P. (2020). How trauma-informed are we, really? *Educational Leadership,* 78(2), 14–19.

Hayes, C., & Juárez, B. G. (2009). You showed your whiteness: You don't get a "good" white people's medal. *International Journal of Qualitative Studies in Education,* 22(6), 729–744.

Herrenkohl, T. I., Hong, S., & Verbrugge, B. (2019). Trauma-informed programs based in schools: Linking concepts to practices and assessing the evidence. *American Journal of Community Psychology,* 64(3), 373–388.

Khasnabis, D., & Goldin, S. (2020). Don't be fooled, trauma is a systemic problem: Trauma as a case of weaponized educational innovation. *Occasional Paper Series,* 2020(43). https://educate.bankstreet.edu/occasional-paper-series/vol2020/iss43/5

Lalik, R., & Hinchman, K. A. (2001). Critical issues: Examining constructions of race in literacy research: Beyond silence and other oppressions of white liberalism. *Journal of Literacy Research,* 33(3), 529–561.

Lawrence-Lightfoot, S. (2004). *The essential conversation: What parents and teachers can learn from each other.* Ballantine Books.

Matias, C. E. (2013). On the" flip" side: A teacher educator of color unveiling the dangerous minds of white teacher candidates. *Teacher Education Quarterly,* 40(2), 53–73.

Matias, C. E. (2016). "Why do you make me hate myself?": Re-teaching whiteness, abuse, and love in urban teacher education. *Teaching Education,* 27(2), 194–211.

Petrone, R., & Stanton, C. R. (2021). From producing to reducing trauma: A call for "trauma-informed" research(ers) to interrogate how schools harm students. *Educational Researcher,* 50(8). https://journals.sagepub.com/doi/abs/10.3102/0013189X211014850?journalCode=edra

SAMHSA. (2020). Understanding Child Trauma. Substance and Mental Health Services Administration. www.samhsa.gov/child-trauma/understanding-child-trauma

Simmons, D. (2021). Why SEL alone isn't enough. *Educational Leadership,* 78(6), 30–34.

Thomas, M. S., Crosby, S., & Vanderhaar, J. (2019). Trauma-informed practices in schools across two decades: An interdisciplinary review of research. *Review of Research in Education,* 43(1), 422–452.

Thompson, C. (2021). *The impact of a classroom calm down corner in a primary classroom*. Northwestern College, Iowa. https://nwcommons.nwciowa.edu/cgi/viewcontent.cgi?article=1304&context=education_masters

Thompson, L. (2021). Toward a feminist psychological theory of "institutional trauma." *Feminism & Psychology, 31*(1), 99–118.

Venet, A. S. (2019). Role-clarity and boundaries for trauma-informed teachers. *Educational Considerations, 44*(2). https://files.eric.ed.gov/fulltext/EJ1206249.pdf

Venet, A. S. (2021). *Equity-centered trauma-informed education*. W. W. Norton.

Yosso, T. J. (2005). Whose culture has capital? A critical race theory discussion of community cultural wealth. *Race, Ethnicity, and Education, 8*(1), 69–91.

X, Malcom. (1963). *Digital history: Malcolm X speech*. Digital History. www.digitalhistory.uh.edu/disp_textbook.cfm?smtid=3&psid=3619

CHAPTER 14

Interrupting the White Liberalism of Social Emotional Learning

Jennifer C. Dauphinais and Jenna Kamrass Morvay

INTRODUCTION

Social emotional learning (SEL) curricula in schools has been offered as a cure for a variety of social problems (Durlak et al., 2011). Many schools have decided to implement state learning standards for SEL. We argue that this is in part because pushing SEL curricula is a seemingly simple "fix" for economic and social problems created by racism and capitalism; it appeals to the "white savior industrial complex" (Cole, 2012). With respect to SEL, white liberalism encompasses several mindsets, which have many damaging consequences for marginalized youth. These mindsets, examples, and consequences are detailed in Table 14.1.

As two white-presenting professors in an SEL certificate program for education professionals, we have seen this white liberal desire to "fix" Black and Brown children in many of our educators. Many begin our program understanding SEL as a process of teaching "coping skills" to children who are lacking them, usually using prepackaged curricula from white-owned companies. Those enrolled in our program represent a trend of white teachers, who are often not thinking about what skills their students already possess, and who do not turn to their students' communities for resources.

In letters that mirror in-person, phone, text, and email conversations that the two of us have had, this chapter navigates white liberal conceptions of SEL and its purposes. We offer approaches for moving education professionals away from shallow liberal ideals of "equality" that require students who are marginalized to assimilate into white ways of existing in the world, and toward enacting racially just SEL practices.

Table 14.1. Ways That White Liberalism Operates in Social Emotional Learning

Mindset	Examples	Consequences
White saviorism	Using SEL as a way to discipline students.	Denies agency of students (and teachers).
	Declaring that SEL will help save students from "broken homes," "bad neighborhoods," and being "at-risk."	Students' feelings, needs, and behaviors are constructed as problematic, and it is the job of liberal white educators to fix those problems.
	Using SEL as a way to address the so-called achievement gap.	Obscures the understanding of the historical context of the "opportunity gap."
Not acknowledging knowledges of racially marginalized communities	Not seeking community input about cultural practices that are used for self-care or self-soothing, especially if they are practices not based on white models of what is normal.	Students are implicitly told that their practices of social emotional health are not valuable or appropriate, and that white norms are the only ones worth emulating.
	Assumption that white norms are the only valid norms.	
	Insisting that SEL practices are colorblind and have no racial dimensions.	
Colorblindness	Insisting on "common language" before being willing to address racism.	The feelings of white educators are prioritized over the experiences of racially marginalized students.
	Colorblind state SEL standards surrounding self-regulation as part of "college and career readiness."	White educators do not need to acknowledge that using market-based language to justify SEL is drawing on an economic system that is racialized.
	Teaching discrete SEL "strategies" without attention to sociopolitical contexts.	White educators are protected from acknowledging their own racism.

LETTERS

Dear Jenna,

I am really happy that you'll be joining our teaching faculty for the Social Emotional Learning Certificate Program. As I mentioned when we last spoke, my experiences as a classroom teacher and SEL trainer in public schools presented some complex issues and concerns. There were contradictions between the goals of SEL programs, and what at the time was deemed multicultural education. I also observed how the tools and strategies proposed by contemplative programs and SEL curricula became synonymous with methods of student discipline in schools. From my perspective, as culturally responsive pedagogies became more widespread, SEL instruction, and the mindsets that make SEL enticing to educators, did not keep pace.

I began to understand that we, as educators, are not necessarily filtering SEL through an antiracist framework. We're thinking about SEL through a mindset of whiteness, and as educators committed to dismantling white supremacy, we are responsible for addressing that, just like we are responsible for instituting racially just teaching practices.

So many teachers have been working and learning in environments where deficit thinking and supremacist mentalities are normalized, and don't question whiteness as the "correct" social and emotional ways of being. My vision for this program has been to provide a space where educators can grapple with questions about what kind of SEL instruction, if any, could work in support of larger movements toward diversity, equity, and inclusion. One way we have been doing this throughout our courses is to question some of the ways that practitioners may be thinking about SEL due to the overarching influence of the deficit thinking shaping the education field, such as concerns about the "achievement gap," which is really a gap in opportunities.

You're faced with an additional challenge, since your course is the first in the sequence that introduces these ideas. I am grateful for the opportunity to work together as we both work with our educators to consider how they can move beyond whiteness to implement racially just SEL, and also continue to examine our own complicity in liberal whiteness.

—JCD

Research shows that SEL initiatives and interventions are commonly used as a frame for the social conditioning of racially marginalized students into whiteness (Au et al., 2016). This means that, in the name of diversity and equality, SEL can function to ask students to develop "self-awareness," to "self-manage," to be "resilient," or to display "grit." If students would only learn these traits or skills, they could then close the achievement gap, go to college, find a well-paying job, and live a life that looks like what many liberal white educators may find normal or desirable. In order to guide their students toward this vision of a good life, educators and policymakers have encouraged liberal-seeming programs such as contemplative pedagogy, trauma-informed teaching, and SEL approaches to school change. These strategies, under the umbrella of character education, are designed to help students develop skills of self-awareness, self-management, resilience, and grit.

Though these programs have been implemented in schools across social and racial demographics, the original research on these programs involved them being implemented as intervention tactics with students who have been labeled "at-risk" (Brown, 2016), with a focus on finding positive behavior outcomes. In other words, "at-risk" students, who are often presumed to be students of Color, display problematic behaviors, and it is the job of a mostly white educator force to fix them.

Results of the research on SEL interventions are often given as a percentage of reduction in what are viewed as "at-risk" behaviors, but do not actually include responses from the students who supposedly are "fixed." This is a reflection of the white savior industrial complex discussed earlier, where predominately white researchers, administrators, and teachers impose their values on Black and Brown communities, and declare success when students adhere to these values. These studies do not attend to the fact that issues such as poverty, food insecurity, toxic racial stress, and high incarceration rates were symptoms of systemic racism and white supremacy (Cole, 2012), and take for granted that Blackness and Brownness are traits that need adjustment.

Since this point of view is one that is, in our experience, shared by many white educators, it is often difficult for us to recognize, and then engage with, the fact that the underlying assumptions of SEL research and practice are structured by norms of whiteness. We have seen in our courses that the differences between new or novel SEL approaches and the existing discipline and accountability ideology are blurred for many educators. Pairing the promises that SEL can help students succeed through self-management with existing educational agendas for marginalized students remains problematic in that it presents an approach to social and emotional development in schools that is also structured by white supremacy. It is imperative for white teachers who want to move beyond the mentality of fixing things, and engage in racially just and equitable teaching practices (Gorski, 2016), to examine what systems are in place that are leading to or creating these behaviors and conditions, and to be aware of them, rather than assuming that individual students are at fault and need to overcome individual shortcomings to be successful.

Dear Jennifer,

First, I want to say that I am so happy to be teaching in this program! It's really necessary work, and you're right, there are so many underlying assumptions about how white ways of existing are the only right ways of existing. I'm working really hard to help the educators in my course recognize these assumptions.

You are absolutely right about the ways people see SEL as a disciplinary solution for "bad" student behaviors that are reactions to problems caused by white supremacy and often enacted by white educators. I keep hearing from the teachers and principals taking my class about how their students come from "broken homes" and have "discipline problems" as a result. They think that implementing some sort of standardized SEL curriculum will miraculously fix those broken homes and discipline problems. They also talk about using SEL strategies to end disproportionate punishment of Black kids in their schools, and it's great that they are thinking about that, but they won't consider the biases they have that lead to this level of disproportionate punishment. They seem to think that meditation, or mindfulness, or daily morning meetings will solve all disciplinary problems, which they seem to think are failings of the students, and not of the structures of school and society.

In addition to having the educators in my class identify how norms of whiteness have affected how they see their students, I'm trying to encourage them to find out how their students are already capable of social emotional skills, rather than assuming that their students lack them. Last week, I asked them if they had asked their students or families about what helped them calm down, and they didn't seem to know how to respond. Drawing upon the knowledge and resources about SEL from their communities never crossed their minds, because since the communities they work in aren't white, they see the communities as defective.

I get it. I had a similar mindset when I started teaching, and I was incredibly lucky to have mentors who helped guide me toward the critical self-examination of my own whiteness, which helped me start to dismantle the thoughts and practices of being a white savior. I hope I can help our educators change their mindsets in the same way.

—JKM

Social emotional learning has replaced "zero tolerance" disciplinary policies, where student misbehavior was punished with immediate suspensions or expulsions, as a reflection of the desire to make incremental shifts toward equality. That incremental shift approach is a key characteristic of white liberalism. The language used about student discipline has changed from detentions, suspensions, and rule violations to competencies, mental health, and trauma-informed care. This reflects the increased attention to the school-to-prison pipeline, and how students who were suspended or expelled from school were significantly more likely to be court-involved and imprisoned later in life than students who were not. This is undeniably an important shift. However, the underlying mindsets—that students are lacking skills because of their race, and that a predominantly white educator force is responsible for giving them those skills—have not changed. A focus on changing language and outcomes is an excellent start for teachers who want to effect social change. However, shifting mindsets that grasp onto the idea that students are defective and need to be fixed is necessary for making that change.

One action that white educators can take in confronting structures, rather than correcting individuals, is to stop teaching SEL in a vacuum. Scholar Dena Simmons (2019) notes that "educators often teach SEL absent of the larger sociopolitical context, which is fraught with injustice and inequity and affects our students' lives which includes topics like poverty, gun violence, racism, sexism, homophobia, transphobia, and other forms of injustice that many students, particularly our most marginalized, experience daily" (p. 2). Morning meetings, guided meditation, and mindfulness strategies, without attention to context, will not fix the injustices students counter in their lives. Further, white educators need to be aware that our students already possess the "competencies" they think their students are lacking. Bettina Love (2019) points out that Black Americans have exhibited grit and resilience throughout the history of the United States, in their continued survival of enslavement, Jim Crow, and police violence.

An educator who desires to implement racially just SEL must reflect on multiple aspects of whiteness. We need to recognize and identify the larger social systems of white supremacy that are assumed in current SEL curricula. We also need to think more locally about how our own privileges—which may not only encompass racial privileges, but also how those racial privileges work with our gender, economic, and sexuality privileges—influence our own practice of social emotional learning. As part of this process, it is incredibly important for us to acknowledge that our experiences with any kind of social emotional skills or processes are not universal. For instance, an educator who is a white woman and has experienced privileges of being upper class may find meditation valuable, but fail to realize why some students may *not* find it similarly valuable. This is why it is important for us to pay attention to the contexts in which our students exist. Rather than assuming that students do not already have social emotional skills, racially just social emotional learning requires turning to the communities in which we teach to find out how they practice, and always have practiced, resilience, self-awareness, and other skills.

Hi Jenna,

Your reflections remind me of something that came up in my classes recently. Like you, I have noticed how some educators take up SEL as a lens for developing a strong pedagogical commitment to antiracism and schooling equity. They earnestly put SEL practices in conjunction with DEI initiatives and student supports that are focused on student and staff wellness. They also grapple with what their reflections reveal as they work through descriptions of their personal and collective feelings, stressors, responsibilities, and dynamics in our coursework.

In my courses, I noticed that teachers will often get hung up on the idea of sharing common language for emotional and behavioral expectations with their colleagues. We unpack the idea that even though we are saying the same thing, such as "being mindful," we may not be doing the same thing. This realization seems to frustrate teachers who thought that the use of common language for emotions, for example, would create instructional continuity and streamline regulation of student behaviors.

Instead, I've noticed how teachers come to understand the varied ways in which emotions and social skills can be interpreted and taught. Oftentimes, this realization allows them to see how whiteness is implicated in the decision making around preferred language and dispositions that are determined by their majority white teaching and leadership staff. Sometimes, though, this is a distraction from actually addressing racism.

Throughout both times teaching this course, I have also noticed that teachers felt trapped in a different way. They are aware of working in the complex grooves of systemic injustices and are aware of the inequities that were present in their school district and the lives of their students. Yet, they were also deeply affected by the discourse about being "mindful," "toxically positive," and "socially just," which are examples of popular educational jargon that lends itself to stress and tension in their personal and professional lives.

My hope in continuing to work together is to further reveal how these concepts can be connected to whiteness. I want them to leave with the understanding that SEL created solely by white educators, even if they are well-intended and diversity-minded, is problematic.

—JCD

Emotionality and emotional literacy have been a large part of the broader conversations about SEL. While the concepts of self-awareness and self-management that make up many SEL curricula are supposedly about helping students manage their feelings, there is a darker side to centering emotionality. The strong emotions attached to discussing race in educational settings can often prevent white educators from engaging with the ways SEL initiatives are structured by whiteness (Matias et al., 2016). Most often, educators tend to bypass these emotions for the sake of good intentions or personalize them to avoid the emotional labor required. When confronted with discussions about race and SEL, some white teachers display emotions such as anger, frustration, defensiveness, or sadness. These emotions redirect discussions of race and racism toward assuaging these feelings, thus assuring that white teachers are not forced to confront their own past and present racist actions or behaviors.

Other white educators may display their emotionalities by refusing to have the conversation, and instead insist on discussing topics that do not touch on race at all. We have encountered several educators who insist that the most important subject to address is not how whiteness is a problem, but the lack of "common language" surrounding what different SEL skills or concepts mean. While this tactic of avoidance may mean some educators prevent themselves from having to think about how white supremacy is a problem, it does help other educators understand that linguistic norms about SEL that are created by other white people may have good intentions but do not accomplish the goals of teaching children to be self-aware.

We are aware that this white liberal emotionality comes from the difficulty of confronting the idea that our racial identity, and all the norms and values that come with it, is itself antithetical to contributing to student success with social emotional learning. The importance of sitting with these emotions, facing them, and moving past them to move toward enacting racially just SEL cannot be overstated. While these are certainly complicated pieces of information for white teachers to explore and manage, a focus on words, rather than on changing mindsets, makes racially just SEL impossible to implement.

Dear Jenn,

Your work with our educators on how to grapple with a white identity did some good, and I'm feeling really excited as I mentor some of our educators through their capstone projects. Perhaps some of what we and our colleagues taught them about more traditional SEL programs are shaped by whiteness has really struck them. I see how they're moving toward reflecting on thinking about SEL as something other than a one-size-fits-all disciplinary mechanism, and how they're thinking through race, rather than operating as "colorblind."

Since you're not going to get to see their work up close the way I am, I want to share with you some of the ways in which teachers in our program are moving toward more racially just implementations of social emotional learning that aren't structured by white liberal ideas about what calm and discipline look like. One educator created a community survey that was sent to students, parents, and teachers, asking each of them what they felt their or their students' or kids' social emotional strengths were, asking where they thought SEL skills needed work, and asking for suggestions for how to make that happen. I really appreciated the combination of looking at SEL from a strengths-based perspective, and asking students and their families for their contributions. She said she was surprised by the responses, and that they were going to help inform her school's SEL practices. It really solidified how important it is to get community input, rather than assuming that the experiences of white people are universal.

Another teacher created a really cool project in which she talked to her elementary students about things that make them upset or anxious, and strategies that they already have to calm down. They all worked together to create a class system to practice their social emotional skills, where students teach each other strategies that they use for calming and self-regulation. Again, I was really pleased with the way she positioned her students as being knowledgeable and already having these skills, rather than assuming they lacked them.

Of course, plenty of our educators have a lot more work to do with respect to reflecting on how their whiteness is affecting the way they do SEL work in their classrooms—as do I, and as do you. It's an ongoing process, as we both know. But I am so encouraged by the work some of the educators in our program have done, and that they continue to do. Let's keep up our own.

—J.

In our letters to one another, and in the explanations between them, we have talked about how values of white liberalism are foundational to the way SEL initiatives and curricula are often designed and implemented. Some well-intentioned educators and policymakers approach SEL as a set of skills designed to correct children considered to be "at-risk," often because of their race. Black and Brown students are portrayed as lacking SEL skills and attributes, including self-awareness, self-management, resilience, and grit, without an acknowledgment of what skills or knowledge about these topics Black and Brown students already possess (Love, 2019).

We have also pointed out the difficulties that many white liberal educators have with the important work of both recognizing how values of whiteness structure the way SEL is conceptualized, and also starting to recognize how their own privileges affect the ways they approach SEL with their students. Understanding how they have thought of themselves as white saviors, or thought of themselves as helping their students achieve what they perceive to be a good life, can bring on some difficult emotional reactions, and sometimes these reactions prevent educators from making the necessary changes to their mindsets and practices.

RECOMMENDATIONS

For white educators who are able to push beyond these overwhelming and difficult emotions, and who do not need to be reassured that they are good people with good intentions, there are important actions that can move us toward a racially just paradigm of social emotional learning. We have seen educators who move through our program become more aware of their own whiteness, and take these steps to change their thoughts, their attitudes toward their students, and the ways they approach the social emotional curricula they implement.

First, white teachers who are moving toward this paradigm take the time to understand and unpack how whiteness operates. They think about how Black and Brown students are implicitly framed as being "at-risk" through research on SEL that focuses on reductions in particular behaviors. They consider whether using strategies taught in social emotional learning curricula as a replacement for punitive discipline actually creates desired changes. We have seen this with several students, many of whom start out saying that SEL should not be connected with race because racism is a subset of bullying, or who believe that talking about whiteness means that we see them as individually bad people, although they have good intentions. When they stop prioritizing their own emotions in favor of thinking critically about systems, they become more aware of some of the self-work they need to do.

Because of this, a second step that more successful practitioners of racially just SEL take is to critically examine their own mindsets and assumptions about their students. It can be incredibly uncomfortable to realize that what you thought were good intentions for your students are actually drawn from assumptions that are rooted in white supremacy. An example of this is a teacher in our program who realized that her frustrations with students not sitting still during mindfulness exercises were rooted in a presumption that stillness is synonymous with mindfulness. Furthermore, because most social structures in the United States, including schools, assume whiteness as normal, some white educators struggle to understand that their own experiences are not universal. This was made clear to one of our teachers when she talked about how she found meditation to be calming, and another teacher said that she felt most calm when engaging in physical activity. Understanding that the intersections of race, class, gender, ability, and sexuality can shape experiences with social emotional learning, and that white experiences cannot be generalized, is a step toward racially just SEL practices.

Third, educators who presume that the students and families in the communities where they teach already have skills and competencies, and who ask for input, discover they are surprised by the responses. Educators whose capstone SEL projects were structured around valuing community input seemed to have more success with creating SEL curricula that were not centered on white ideas of what self-awareness and self-management should be. Conversely, those whose projects continued to use SEL as a form of discipline, or as an intervention for students who they viewed as having behavioral deficits, seemed to struggle to obtain their desired results.

CONCLUSION

We want to point out that thinking about SEL as a racially just enterprise is not a linear process, and for those of us who are white, it is a continuous process of unlearning the values of stillness, individuality, and compliance that we were socialized to believe are the correct ways of being. As much as we are working with the educators in our program to reconceptualize what social emotional learning can look like through their own self-work, we are also constantly re-learning about ourselves and our views on the world. We hope that by sharing our experiences, others can begin or continue their own work to make SEL an enterprise of racial justice rather than white liberalism.

REFERENCES

Au, W., Brown, A. L., & Calderón, D. (2016). *Reclaiming the multicultural roots of US curriculum: Communities of color and official knowledge in education.* Teachers College Press.

Brown, K. D. (2016). *After the "at-risk" label: Reorienting educational policy and practice.* Teachers College Press.

Cole, T. (2012, March 21). The white-savior industrial complex. *The Atlantic.* www.theatlantic.com/international/archive/2012/03/the-white-savior-industrial-complex/254843

Durlak, J. A., Weissberg, R. P., Dymnicki, A. B., Taylor, R. D., & Schellinger, K. B. (2011). The impact of enhancing students' social and emotional learning: A meta-analysis of school-based universal interventions. *Child Development, 82*(1), 405–432.

Gorski, P. (2016). Poverty and the ideological imperative: A call to unhook from deficit and grit ideology and to strive for structural ideology in teacher education. *Journal of Education for Teaching, 42,* 378–386.

Love, B. L. (2019). *We want to do more than survive: Abolitionist teaching and the pursuit of educational freedom.* Beacon Press.

Matias, C. E., Montoya, R., & Nishi, N. W. M. (2016). Blocking CRT: How the emotionality of whiteness blocks CRT in urban teacher education. *Educational Studies, 52*(1), 1–19.

Simmons, D. (2019). Why we can't afford whitewashed social-emotional learning. *ASCD Education Update, 61*(4), 2–3.

CHAPTER 15

White Liberalism, Positive Behavior Supports, and Black, Indigenous Students of Color

"We're Teaching Them How to Do School"

Jeanne Connelly

This chapter represents my experiences as a white woman elementary educator, my present understanding of structural oppression within schools, and my future hope for an education system that humanizes Black, Indigenous Students of Color (BISOC). Much of my work involved supporting BISOC students and their families when the child's behaviors were deemed problematic by school. White colleagues often told me my "liberal" approach meant I was enabling them, that I failed to make BISOC students accountable for their poor choices. These statements reveal the following unspoken expectations for BISOC: They are to comply with adult directives to assimilate to the school's white normative expectations of behavior.

As I collaborated with other white educators, I heard statements such as, "We need to treat everyone equally" and "We need to build positive relationships." We described our work with BISOC by saying, "We're teaching them how to do school." However, what was hidden in those statements was the erasure of other ways of being and behaving. School expectations that fail to acknowledge other cultural ways of being exact a toll on BISOC when they learn to "do school." We did not examine the role of power found in whiteness in the education of BISOC. Teaching BISOC "how to do school" reinforces white cultural norms of behavior (Broderick & Leonardo, 2016) and comforts white teachers.

This chapter challenges white educators to move to a zone of discomfort to interrogate how positive behavior interventions and supports (PBIS) serve whiteness (Bornstein, 2017) through white liberalism. Implementing PBIS uncritically allows well-intended white educators to remain in the comfort zone of whiteness while maintaining an image of charitable caretakers of

BISOC. Implementing PBIS critically challenges white liberalism by explicitly naming power dynamics and examining whiteness built into schools.

The purpose of this chapter is to facilitate deep reflection and move toward challenging systems that harm BISOC. I will begin with my understanding of white liberalism and whiteness within schools. I then share a case study of one school's implementation of positive behavior interventions and supports. Finally, I introduce DisCrit pedagogy and solidarity from Annamma (2018).

WHITENESS AND WHITE LIBERALISM IN SCHOOLS

In U.S. schools, academic subjects, children, and families are implicitly, if not explicitly, placed in hierarchies of highly regarded/disregarded and good/bad (Leonardo, 2013). In my experience, white educators who screen and sort BISOC students for "at risk" behaviors are comforted by identifying ourselves as helpers. The consequences of targeting BISOC students when their behaviors don't fit norms of whiteness are not acknowledged. When BISOC students are targeted, intersectional deficit-based identities of race, ability, and goodness limit their opportunities (Broderick & Leonardo, 2016). When white educators categorize and construct deficit-based identities for BISOC using recommended educational practices of whiteness to determine what is normal, this is the "pedagogy of pathologization" (Annamma, 2018).

My conception of liberalism, developed through lived experience, has been steeped in whiteness. I see liberalism as the expectation that public institutions care for vulnerable people and work toward true freedom for all; education is a basic right. However, this is white liberalism because public institutions such as schools serve whiteness. Whiteness is a social concept and means of organizing society: It is a system of ideas, structures and practices that support an avoidance of race and racism, a denial of racist legacies of social policies, and a common-sense understanding of white superiority (Leonardo, 2002).

White liberalism, then, is an extension of whiteness: It creates groups of superior and inferior people and allows the realities of racism to be avoided, thus protecting the status quo (Oviedo-Torres, 2020). White liberalism centers the needs of white people and their good intentions, while failing to name structural racism, ableism, and goodness. Therefore, white liberalism allows white educators to claim we are helping the less fortunate, while never interrogating our own power and privilege.

I can identify with white liberal educators (WLEs) because in my decades in elementary schools, I was one. Only when I moved out of the elementary school system was I given access to knowledge and skills for critical analysis of schools' norms of practice. Moreover, to move toward transformative practices, I must consistently remind myself to disrupt the comforts of whiteness built into educational systems. Therefore, I include myself as a WLE within this chapter.

CASE STUDY: CULTURALLY RESPONSIVE PRACTICES AND POSITIVE BEHAVIOR SUPPORTS

After entering my doctoral program, I completed a case study with classroom teachers from my former school to examine connections between culturally responsive teaching practices (CRPs) (Gay, 2018) and PBIS (Horner, 2016) in a suburban school. This study was approved by my university Institutional Review Board in December 2017. I refer to the school and the PBIS program using "ours" or "we" because prior to studying the school I had been employed there. Six teachers volunteered: Three participants were white women, two identified as white and Asian women, and the sixth participant was a South Asian woman. I do not generalize the term WLE to this group.

CRPs include designing culturally relevant curriculum, building caring relationships with students and families, creating an inclusive environment, and building intercultural communication skills (Gay, 2018). Behavior management systems such as PBIS are systematized to ensure order and safety for students and staff, as well as to assure that the environment is conducive to learning. The culture of the school is embedded in the implementation of traditional schoolwide PBIS, which involves (1) creation of a cohesive learning environment, (2) direct instruction and reinforcement of behaviors and social skills to support learning and relationships, and (3) systematic supports of increasing intensity (Tiers I, II, and III) for students who do not meet behavioral expectations (Bal et al., 2012).

More recently, culturally responsive PBIS (CR-PBIS) has been developed. CR-PBIS recommends building reciprocal relationships with families and community members, monitoring office referrals by racial category, and integrating culturally responsive practices (Bal et al., 2012).

The school I studied was implementing traditional PBIS. Interviews and focus groups primarily involved discussion of CRP within PBIS that aligned with the district's intercultural competency training. When teachers described the behaviors of BISOC, they talked about differences from white cultural norms, rather than naming the behaviors as problematic. For example, Ellie, a South Asian 1st-grade teacher, described a student's behavior as "overlapping communication" rather than "interrupting" or "blurting out": "You can have the biggest overlapping communication style you want, as long as it's allowing other people to learn and you're engaged with what we're actually talking about." Teachers in the study also described high expectations and persistence in caring for their students. Mia, a white-Asian teacher, described talking to a student: "I'm doing this because I care about you, I'm telling you this because I know you can do it. We just have to figure out a different way. I'm willing if you're willing . . . just saying that sometimes, a million times."

Our PBIS team used office disciplinary referrals (ODRs) grouped by race for decision making. ODRs were used to screen for students needing more intensive interventions. We formed groups of "target students" and added supports such as informal mentoring with a chosen adult, additional choices for social time, or extra communication with parents. During the study, we noticed the PBIS team had celebrated a decreasing number of ODRs for Black students but had missed the increase of ODRs for non-white Hispanic students. The school was following implementation guidelines, yet the gaps in who was benefiting from our efforts were not acknowledged or addressed. The teachers in the study noticed an inclination by our faculty to implement conventional practices with greater intensity in response to identified problems, rather than to attempt to innovate or critique the system.

TENSIONS BETWEEN PBIS AND CULTURALLY RESPONSIVE PRACTICES (CRPS)

PBIS is applauded as the replacement for harmful discipline policies that disproportionately exclude BISOC from the learning environment. The number of schools implementing PBIS continues to increase (Horner, 2016), yet our research study team noted tensions between PBIS and CRPs in our school. PBIS implementation impacted CRP within data informed decision making and sending students out of the room. Our traditional PBIS implementation was lacking in ways to engage BISOC and their families, and we had never noticed the role of whiteness.

Data-Informed Decision Making

We struggled with questions about what other type of data could lead to more holistic thinking about the child: Our data-informed decision making focused on the BISOC's deficits in behavior without considering sociocultural or historical factors. Toward the end of our study, I wondered aloud about how our school could be so invested in CRP and PBIS without ever explicitly connecting the two. Karen, a white kindergarten teacher, replied, "We were following directions." When we were following directions, as we were trained to do, we weren't being critical consumers. We stayed in our comfort zone and operated from the white liberal view that schools are the great equalizers and focused on our good intentions rather than our impact.

Sending Students Out of the Room

PBIS attempts to define measurable behaviors to reinforce and to determine when an ODR is necessary. However, in our study, we noted that in 6 years of implementation, common definitions of problem behaviors had never been developed. Also, teachers have discretion in using ODRs and processes for monitoring for teacher bias are not built into the system. Teachers in the study saw the ODR process of removing a student from the learning environment as harmful to their relationship with BISOC and to the BISOC's belonging in the community. They rarely or never used ODRs and created workarounds within the system. Ellie, the South Asian 1st-grade teacher, said, "With Roy . . . in terms of him, [being] extremely disruptive, [I] never once kicked him out of the classroom. Never once, because it is his job to be part of this community and in this classroom." The teachers acknowledged that the workarounds required ongoing explanation to administration and white families, as well as ongoing practice in restoring relationships with all students in the classroom.

Engaging Families

CRPs center positive reciprocal relationships with families as well as each student. Each teacher in the study described CRPs that helped them build and maintain positive relationships with BISOC families, regardless of behavioral differences. They listed practices such as random phone calls just to check in, listening to family members rather than reporting out problems, and asking families to share their parenting tips for their child. On the other hand, Colleen, a white 6th-grade teacher, described her issues with administrative recommendations to make a set number of documented calls per month. In her view, that made the relationship seem transactional, rather than authentic:

> That relationship with the family, and I think we try to make that so systematic and, "Oh, you're going to make three positive phone calls . . . And if something happens, here's what you do." I think it's so relational that when you make it systematic, families don't feel cared about.

During the study, we discussed ways that family power in our school was weighted heavily toward white, middle-class families who had purchased their homes in this neighborhood because of the "good schools." For example, we had not included any BISOC families on our PBIS team or in our CRP professional development. We discussed examples when teachers were supporting a BISOC whose behavior didn't fit white norms, and the white families' needs were prioritized over the BISOC by colleagues or the administration. Any attempts at disrupting this power dynamic were minimized or blocked. The system was never named as problematic for BISOC; faculty members named individuals with difficult personalities as the problem. Systemic whiteness remained intact.

Noticing Whiteness and Goodness

In our focus groups, the teachers described how examinations of white power and privilege had been avoided among the faculty at our school. Race was a topic that made people uncomfortable, so it was never explicitly discussed; we talked about culture instead. Their first opportunity to discuss white cultural norms and whiteness within our PBIS implementation was during the research study. We critiqued our behavioral expectations matrix, noting how the culture we were creating privileged and comforted white educators while marginalizing other ways of organizing, communicating, and behaving. We had believed that sharing the behavioral matrix meant that we were helping and redistributing power by sharing information; we hadn't noticed that we had constructed a program that maintained white authority.

Furthermore, WLEs within a traditional PBIS system may implement the system while we call ourselves helpers and never name our role in a system that harms BISOC. *Goodness* from Broderick and Leonardo (2016) is another important concept to consider when asking critical questions of white liberalism in PBIS. Behavior norms based in whiteness influence methods of instruction, assessment, and behavior management, which in turn construct a performative, cultural, and ideological system that defines what is normal and good within the school. Goodness is "inextricably intertwined in the creation of good (and not so good) people" (Broderick and Leonardo, 2016, p. 57). Once a child has been placed on the goodness scale, power and privilege is granted or denied, which determines who gets to learn and belong in the classroom. White liberalism accepts this hierarchy uncritically and encourages educators to operate as if this is the right and best way to serve BISOC.

Uncritical Implementation of PBIS

As we discussed our PBIS implementation, we acknowledged that we had implemented the system uncritically. Teachers are expected to remove certain students from the learning environment—removing the "bad" kids to protect the "good" kids (Broderick & Leonardo, 2016). Each of us had heard WLEs justify excluding BISOC from the classroom because "they need the extra help" for their behavior, yet we had not challenged them. We had remained focused on fixing the student. PBIS is one of the structures that results in the sorting and pathologizing of BISOC and gives permission for teachers to define behaviors of BISOC as deviant, or criminal (Bornstein, 2017). Importantly, the labels on behavior can then be used to label the BISOC.

While PBIS can be effective at reducing ODRs for BISOC (Horner, 2016), deficit ideologies created within the system are rarely examined. Our lack of critical questioning allowed the comfort zone of whiteness to remain intact, which impeded structural change. Whiteness was not named as the school moved toward CR-PBIS. White educators who examine their PBIS implementation acknowledge privilege and power within the school system; if we are able to endure discomfort and disrupt systems that heretofore have been implemented uncritically, we can become critical consumers of systems like PBIS.

TRANSFORMATIVE PRACTICES: BISOC

White educators who want to transform systems need to step out of whiteness' comfort zone. This means being open to publicly discussing mistakes and omissions while acknowledging systemic harm to children. While PBIS supports our comfort, a discomfort zone involves asking questions such as, "What do white people get out of the current system?" or "What/who is missing?" In the PBIS case study, we noticed we had rated our school's implementation as "with fidelity" in 4 of 5 years without evaluating whether there were corresponding academic or social gains. Moreover, the standardized program evaluation didn't consider racial disparities or cultural responsiveness. We hadn't been critical consumers. We weren't expected to acknowledge that the system comforted us and promoted the deficit narratives of BISOC. This myopia kept us in our comfort zone, and we didn't go further in evaluating our PBIS program.

Discomfort Zone

White educators are positioned with power in systems that are built to maintain whiteness so there is an "overwhelming disincentive" for us to disrupt the system (Leonardo, 2013, p. 102). The comfort zone of white liberalism allows us to avoid emotions like shame, sadness, and defensiveness, which protects institutions that harm BISOC (Matias, 2016). From that position of superiority and power, educating BISOC can be considered charity work. This perpetuates the story that BISOC and their families require fixing. Deficit stories of BISOC whose behaviors are constructed as problems are so common that we may never challenge them (Connelly, 2021) and can avoid paying attention to our privileges (Leonardo, 2013) or our role in a dehumanizing system (Annamma, 2018).

On the other hand, discomfort is part of growth. We need to recognize that our schools, profession, and practices may comfort us, yet they are not perfect, so we need to get into our discomfort zone (Applebaum, 2017;

Matias, 2016). White educators who develop a mindset and skillset to manage their cognitive dissonance and defensive emotional reactions can disrupt systemic racism within PBIS. Whiteness has protected our feelings, so we've got to be ready to have our feelings hurt without expecting people of Color to comfort us (Matias, 2016). Just as we teach our students, we are in control of our responses; we can choose to be open to listening and wrestling with our discomfort when systems that have historically validated our practice are challenged. Operating in humility will help us see that BISOC and families have knowledge that we do not possess, and that their behaviors are not deficient (Annamma, 2018). By stepping into our discomfort zone and refusing to run when things get difficult, we are more likely to effect meaningful change.

Systems Change

Changing school culture is a complex process. Schools need to be "recultured" beginning with critical reflection and changes to practices that produce harmful outcomes for BISOC and disabled youth (Bal et al., 2012, p. 7). Transformation extends beyond charitable acts to social justice. My understanding of justice work involves directly interrogating systems that are implemented uncritically, such as PBIS. Systemic change requires us to acknowledge structural problems and deficit mindsets. Such transformation depends on three crucial factors: (1) time and resources for broad community participation in critical reflection, with open dialogue among participants; (2) supported opportunities to recognize the gaps in our understanding of how white social norms operate in schools; and (3) explicit discussion of the hierarchies of superiority and inferiority in schools. White educators who transcend liberal approaches and participate in transformative reflection and action can become resistors in the system that tells us our role is to "label, surveil, and punish" BISOC youth who engage in school using their own strategies of resistance; this requires spending our valuable resources of "time, commitment and energy" to transform the system and our role within it (Annamma, 2018, p. 146).

TRANSFORMATIVE OPPORTUNITIES IN DISABILITY CRITICAL RACE THEORY

Annamma's (2018) vision for the future uses Disability Critical Race Theory (DisCrit) to frame the transformation of school discipline systems and teacher practices. DisCrit recognizes that (1) race and ability are constructed by cultural institutions and systems, (2) race and ability are intertwined in our society, and (3) both of these social constructions are used to exclude people because hierarchies of power and privilege maintain white people whose ability is considered "normal" at the top. Further, when discussing how students behave, the concept of *goodness* is added into this hierarchy: how BISOC behave determines their value. DisCrit theory discusses how the social norms of whiteness, smartness, and goodness combine to construct an idea of *normal*, and systems are enacted to fix people who don't fit into *normal*.

DisCrit provides a framework for analyzing programs like PBIS that may pathologize BISOC. As an example, when BISOC are excluded using ODRs and targeted for intervention, they are seen as broken or *less than*. Policies and practices within the system that protects whiteness hide this deficit thinking. White educators who see themselves as well intended may uncritically implement the program with fidelity because the system is treated as the best way to help BISOC.

DisCrit disrupts these ideas and provides new questions for us to ask when unlearning white superiority and deficit-based stories of BISOC. Teachers implementing Annamma's (2018) DisCrit pedagogy, including solidarity and pedagogy as they relate to classroom environment and teachers' behavior management, can transform harmful systems.

DisCrit Solidarity

Solidarity involves teacher–student relationships that are caring, trusting, and reciprocal. In solidarity, exclusion from the group for behavioral differences is not allowed. Most importantly, student needs are prioritized over the system's and teachers' need for efficiency, accountability, and control. Teachers in solidarity with BISOC maintain caring, reciprocal relationships of trust that encourage BISOC to express their thoughts and feelings. Behaviors previously called problematic or challenging within models like PBIS can be named as strengths and assets of BISOC. BISOC are encouraged to use strategies of resistance within a system that has traditionally pathologized and excluded them. DisCrit teachers collaborate with students to create classroom cultures that validate resistance.

Within this context, BISOC strategies of resistance are necessary and helpful rather than disruptive and disrespectful (Annamma, 2018): using humor, evading questions, using anger for protection, direct confrontation, or purposely leaving situations. BISOC may use strategies of distrusting the system, forgiving wrongs, adapting their language and message, and calculating benefits. Other strategies may be related to their sense of self: feeling a sense of control over life, determination to beat the odds, imagining possibilities, thinking positively, and identifying strengths and weaknesses. When DisCrit solidarity is the foundational framework for the culture of the classroom, traditional monitoring of disruptive behaviors or ODRs that permeates PBIS models is replaced with assets-based pedagogy.

DisCrit Pedagogy

DisCrit pedagogy is a form of praxis: a unified process of critical reflection and teaching practices leading to the transformation of inequities (Freire, 2018); this has direct implications for creating an inclusive classroom culture and interacting with students. DisCrit classrooms upend the asymmetrical power dynamics between teachers and students. DisCrit teachers do not unilaterally create rules and enforce them; they relate to students with care rather than through transactions that can be broken down into antecedent-behavior-consequence sequences. As warm demanders, DisCrit teachers nurture students by deliberately building relationships, respecting culture, expressing expectations for success, and persisting through challenges (Cosier, 2019).

When students "act up," teachers ask questions about context, feelings, and thoughts so they can recognize strategies of resistance. Students' counterstories of experiences with oppression and their resistance (Solórzano & Yosso, 2002) are incorporated into trusting relationships. Restorative practices for managing conflicts are ongoing and comprehensive; power is equalized, and adult interests are not prioritized over BISOC. Further, critical questioning and resistance to structural oppression is modeled for students; DisCrit teachers interrogate and disrupt the deficit messages of traditional discipline systems.

CONCLUSION

When we teach BISOC to "do school" using systems like PBIS without examining whiteness and white liberalism, BISOC suffer. Critical questions of the system may never be asked if white educators are lulled into comfort and complacency. Educators who make a personal commitment to endure discomfort can move toward being DisCrit teachers.

DisCrit provides a lens for critical questioning and viewing how current practice and policies serve whiteness. We can shift our efforts to learning how to do school in ways that honor the humanity of BISOC, replacing the work of teaching BISOC students how to "do school."

REFERENCES

Annamma, S. A. (2018). *The pedagogy of pathologization: Dis/abled girls of color in the school-prison nexus*. Routledge.

Applebaum, B. (2017). Comforting discomfort as complicity: White fragility and the pursuit of invulnerability. *Hypatia, 32*(4), 862–875. https://doi.org/10.1111/hypa.12352

Bal, A., Thorius, K. K., & Kozleski, E. (2012). *Culturally responsive positive behavioral support matters*. The Equity Alliance.

Bornstein, J. (2017). Entanglements of discipline, behavioral intervention, race, and disability. *Journal of Cases in Educational Leadership, 20*(2), 131–144. https://doi.org/10.1177/1555458917696810

Broderick, A. A., & Leonardo, Z. (2016). "What a good boy." In D. J. Connor, B. A. Ferri, & S. A. Annamma (Eds.), *DisCrit-disability studies and critical race theory in education* (pp. 55–67). Teachers College Press.

Connelly, J. (2021). Interrogating the special education identification process for Black Indigenous Students of Color. *Multiple Voices for Ethnically Diverse Exceptional Learners, 21*(1): 78–92.

Cosier, K. (2019). On whiteness and becoming warm demanders. *Journal of Cultural Research in Art Education, 36*(1), 56–72. https://jcrae.art.arizona.edu/index.php/jcrae/article/view/126/106

Freire, P. (2018). *Pedagogy of the oppressed*. Bloomsbury.

Gay, G. (2018). *Culturally responsive teaching: Theory, research, and practice*. Teachers College Press.

Horner, R. (2016, January 27). *A brief history of PBIS* [podcast].TASH.org. https://tash.org/news/a-brief-history-of-pbis-with-rob-horner

Leonardo. Z. (2002). The souls of white folk: Critical pedagogy, whiteness studies, and globalization discourse, *Race Ethnicity and Education, 5*(1), 29–50. https://doi.org/10.1080/13613320120117180

Leonardo, Z. (2013). *Race frameworks: A multidimensional theory of racism and education*. Teachers College Press.

Matias, C. E. (2016). *Feeling white: Whiteness, emotionality, and education*. Brill | Sense.

Oviedo-Torres, N. (2020). *White liberalism: Jordan Peele reads Harper Lee*. [Undergraduate Honors Thesis]. William and Mary Scholarworks. https://scholarworks.wm.edu/honorstheses/1550

Solórzano, D. G., & Yosso, T. J. (2002). A critical race counterstory of race, racism, and affirmative action. *Equity & Excellence in Education, 35*(2), 155–168. https://doi.org/10.1080/713845284

Notes

Introduction

1. To pay homage to the Black Lives Matter (BLM) movement, we recognize that BLM was founded by three Black women: Alicia Garza, Patrisse Cullors, and Opal Tometi. https://blacklivesmatter.com/herstory

2. To donate to the George Floyd Memorial Foundation, see www.georgefloydmemorialfoundation.org.

3. To donate, see www.gofundme.com/f/9v4q2-justice-for-breonna-taylor or www.standwithbre.com.

4. Report anti-Asian racism here: https://stopaapihate.org

5. In response to the murder of eight Asian American women in Georgia, donate here: www.asianamericanadvocacyfund.org

Chapter 8

1. We purposefully choose to not capitalize the racialized term "white" as a stylistic form of resistance to white racial hegemony. In the same vein, we do capitalize the racial terms "Black," "Brown," and "of Color."

Index

About the Editors and Contributors

Cheryl E. Matias is a full professor in the School of Leadership and Educational Sciences at the University of San Diego. Her research focuses on race and ethnic studies in education with a theoretical focus on critical race theory, critical whiteness studies, critical pedagogy, and feminism of Color. Specifically, she studies the emotionalities of whiteness in teacher education and how it impacts racial justice education.

Paul C. Gorski is the founder of the Equity Literacy Institute and a former teacher educator at several universities. He has spent nearly 25 years supporting schools and school districts committed to transformative equity efforts. He's also a new dad, a lover of cats, a published poet, and a gardening enthusiast.

Tracey A. Benson is the founder of the Antiracist Leadership Institute. He has served as a university professor, high school principal, middle school vice principal, and elementary school teacher. His book, *Unconscious Bias in Schools: A Developmental Approach to Exploring Race and Racism*, appeared in August 2019.

Alina Campana is an arts educator and administrator who has worked in mulitple community, school, and government settings.

Elisabeth Chan has over 15 years of experience as an English language educator. She holds a PhD in multilingual multicultural education and interdisciplinary perspectives and social policy. She has presented, researched, and published on issues of social justice in education through a critical lens, where she draws upon her lived experiences as a second/fourth-generation Chinese American from the U.S. South.

Lavette Coney brings a wealth of wisdom and skills to the topic of social justice in English language teaching. She has 8 years of experience living and teaching in Japan, 56 years of lived experience as a person of African descent, and over 30 years as a TESOL and social justice educator providing workshops, lectures and seminars.

Jeanne Connelly is an assistant professor of special education at Metropolitan State University-Denver. After working in elementary schools for over 25 years, she completed her doctorate in 2021, critically analyzing disability and race in schools. She is preparing future teachers to create asset-oriented inclusive communities for all children and families.

Jennifer C. Dauphinais is an assistant teaching professor of education and coordinator of the social emotional learning teacher development program at Quinnipiac University in Hamden, Connecticut. Jennifer's research traces the meaning-making of educational discourse communities and teacher identities, investigating how competing discourses of schooling position youth across various goals and subjectivities.

Addison Duane is an Innovations for Youth post-doctoral research fellow at UC Berkeley. She researches the nexus of psychological trauma, systemic racism, and the brilliance of elementary-aged children. In both research and practice, she partners with students and educators to join the ongoing investigation of education as liberation.

Heidi Faust has over 25 years of experience in education specializing in language, literacy, culture and social justice. She has worked nationally and internationally facilitating capacity building programs in K–12 public schools and in higher education in support of multilingual learners. She draws on her own experiences as a white educator to critically examine intersections of power, privilege, and race in education.

Betty Forrester taught for 43 years in southeast Los Angeles and spent 9 years as an elected officer in United Teachers Los Angeles (UTLA) before retiring. She is currently using the lessons from this book as a member of the LA County Board of Education, in union sisterhood, and as a white ally.

J.P.B. Gerald is a graduate of the EdD program in Instructional Leadership from CUNY–Hunter College. He currently works in professional development for a nonprofit, and his work on whiteness, language, and disability has appeared in a variety of publications. He lives on unceded Munsee Lenape and Canarsie territory (NYC) with his dog, wife, and toddler, and released his first book in September 2022.

Simona Goldin is a research associate professor at the University of North Carolina. She studies ways to transform the preparation of beginning teachers to teach in more racially just and equitable ways, and has elaborated teaching practices that bridge children's work in schools with their home- and community-based experiences.

Daisy Han is a nationally recognized antiracist educator, speaker, and activist. Daisy has combined her expertise in experiential curriculum design and adult learning with her experience as a teacher, principal, instructional coach, and organizational leader for positive social change. Daisy founded the nonprofit organization Embracing Equity with the belief that education is the single most powerful lever to achieve greater equity and to cultivate love and belonging.

Debi Khasnabis is a clinical professor of education and chair of elementary teacher education at the University of Michigan School of Education. She teaches courses focusing on multicultural and multilingual education and conducts research on pedagogies of teacher education that support culturally responsive teaching and understandings of inequality in schools.

Katie Kitchens is a queer, white educator who has worked in Montessori environments for the past decade as an instructional coach, teacher educator, and primary and elementary guide. Currently, Katie is pursuing a PhD in educational studies, researching racial identity development in young white children.

Amelia M. Kraehe is the inaugural associate vice president for equity in the arts and associate professor of art and visual culture education at the University of Arizona. She is a founding co-director of the Racial Justice Studio. Her latest book is *Race and Art Education* (2021).

Anna Kushner is a PhD student in education policy at Teachers College, Columbia University. Their research interests include the politics of race, diversity, and equity in K–12 education and the role of community and student voice in education decision making.

Lindsay Lyons is an educational justice coach who inspires educational innovation for racial and gender justice, helps design curricula grounded in student voice, and builds shared leadership capacity. Lindsay taught in NYC public schools, holds a PhD in Leadership and Change, and hosts the Time for Teachership podcast.

Andréa C. Minkoff is an assistant professor in the child and adolescent development Master's program in the LaFetra College of Education at the University of La Verne. Her research and teaching interests focus on children's developing understandings of race, intergroup relations in schools, and teacher education.

Theresa Montaño is a professor of Chicano/a Studies at CSU-Northridge. An active unionist, the former CTA vice president remains involved in the

California Faculty Association. She is a member of California's Ethnic Studies Model Curriculum Advisory Committee and consults on the implementation of ethnic studies programs. She has published several articles and edited books.

Jenna Kamrass Morvay is a visiting assistant professor at Miami University in Oxford, Ohio. Her research considers the possibilities of combining different theoretical frameworks to consider questions of whiteness, gender, curriculum, and the agency of nonhuman bodies in school settings.

Crystena Parker-Shandal is currently associate professor in social development studies at the University of Waterloo, Canada. As a restorative justice practitioner and researcher, she focuses on how dialogic pedagogies facilitate inclusive spaces where all students can participate and have their voices heard.

Cherie Bridges Patrick is a stress- and trauma-responsive psychotherapist, leadership coach, and consultant. She helps people develop and hold on to a healthy sense of self in the face of social trauma. Her research, analysis, and writing examine how subtle and nuanced racial dominance is reproduced by justice-seeking professionals.

Maria Gabriela Paz is an organizer from Alexandria, Virginia, with a focus on community engagement through visual design. She has a passion for issues facing migrant communities, education reform, and organizing based on community care.

Brianne Pitts is an assistant professor of education at Western Michigan University. Her research interests include teaching/learning K–12 Black history, whiteness in the workforce, critical literacies, and culturally responsive social studies instruction.

Chris Seeger is a social studies teacher, curriculum designer, and researcher. His research explores the interlocking themes of race, gender, and class oppression in the U.S. history standards. His curriculum projects focus on diverse perspectives and the disruption of historical master narratives.

Gregory Simmons is a former teacher and current PhD student in social studies education at the University at Buffalo. A fellow at the Center for K–12 Black History & Racial Literacy Education, his research interests include the teaching/learning of Black history, social studies education and pedagogy, and whiteness in education.

Daniel Tulino is an assistant professor of education at Stockton University. His research interests include culturally sustaining practices, curriculum and instruction, and K–12 teaching Black history.

Katherine Wood studied history and social justice at Occidental College in Los Angeles. Her honors thesis focused on racism and antisemitism throughout modern Scandinavian history. Her research interests include the development of race ideology throughout history, decolonial education, and collective memory studies.